THE WORD
WITHIN THE WORD I

BY
MICHAEL CLAY THOMPSON
THOMAS MILTON KEMNITZ

Royal Fireworks Press
Unionville, New York

April 2018

Royal Fireworks Press
41 First Avenue, P.O. Box 399
Unionville, NY 10988-0399
(845) 726-4444
fax: (845) 726-3824
email: mail@rfwp.com
website: rfwp.com

ISBN:
Student Book: 978-0-88092-604-1

Publisher: Dr. T.M. Kemnitz
Design and graphics: Michael Clay Thompson
Photos and captions: Dr. T.M. Kemnitz
Cover designer: Kerri Ann Ruhl
Editor: Jennifer Ault

Printed and bound in Unionville, New York, on acid-free paper
using vegetable-based inks at the Royal Fireworks facility.

20ap18 ps

Dedicated to Julie Long, Zoa Rockenstein, and Mary Murphy

About the cover: The front cover is a photograph of a portion of the Elgin Marbles as they are displayed in the British Museum in London. Photograph by Dr. Thomas Milton Kemnitz.

The back cover is a photograph of the caryatid porch of the Erechtheion on the Acropolis at Athens. Photograph by Dr. Thomas Milton Kemnitz.

INTRODUCTION

This new edition of *The Word Within the Word* is designed to raise your awareness of the Greek origins of English. *The Word Within the Word* remains the premier text for understanding English language vocabulary; the vocabulary sections, which have proven so valuable to several million students, have not been altered or diluted. New to the text is the discussion of Greece in the Classical Age. In this and the subsequent two volumes, we want to give you more insight into Greece and Rome, the two ancient cultures from which much academic English is derived. This is not material that will be on the test, or at least it should not be. Its function in this volume is to give you some idea of the Greek world, of the chronological, geographical, and other relationships of the actors to one another. History should not be a story to be memorized but rather an exploration of relationships, of how people in very specific contexts acted and reacted, solved problems, and endeavored to live in ways that they found satisfactory. I chose the subjects of the short essays in this volume to give you a sense of what occurred during the fewer than 200 years that proved so important for the history of the world and to us today.

As you read these essays, it is important to realize and remember that the fundamental structure of ancient Greece was competition. The Greeks were competitive about everything; it was how they approached one another and the world around them. It was individual against individual, family vying with family, city against city, league against league, and finally all of Greece against the Persian empire. The Greeks were the originators of the Olympic games, but the Olympic games were only one of several Panhellenic games that involved athletes, musicians, charioteers, sailors, and other contestants from all of Greece. The Greeks did not simply have concerts, they had competitions between singers and between musicians; they did not simply go to plays, they had competitions between playwrights. If this does not seem strange to you, it is because much of our world is organized on the same premise. We have competitions and give prizes on a level that rises to the ancient Greek standard and perhaps even surpasses it. And after a lapse of 1,600 years, we revived the Olympic games and play them every four years, just as the ancient Greeks did.

With competition, the Greeks developed a concept of individualism and freedom and a portrayal of individuals striving and fighting for their own liberty and for the freedom of their homeland from enslavement. They had fewer protections of their individual rights than we do, but individuals had far more protections in Athens than they did in Egypt or Persia or elsewhere in the ancient world. Their freedoms might have been circumscribed, but they were no less precious to them.

The Greeks gave us many of the underpinnings of our life. Besides organized competitive games, they developed democracy, the importance of the individual and the will of the people, philosophy, the theater, comedy and tragedy, mathematics, medicine, rhetoric, history, the epic poem, and the fable. The most glorious manifestation of Greek culture and achievement might be Athens in the fifth century, although others would argue it was the fourteen years of Alexander's leadership of the Macedonians, and still others have pointed to Sparta. It was an exciting and vibrant period in the history of the world, and in these short essays I have tried to open up some aspects of it to you.

As interesting and important as the history of classical Greece may be, it is well to remember that the purpose of this book is to help you learn English vocabulary, specifically the academic English of learned discourse. The essays and photographs about the Greek world are not an end in themselves but an aid to your comprehension of academic English.

Thomas Milton Kemnitz

ante	*(before)*	antedate, antecedent, antebellum, anterior, ante meridiem, antepenult	*Latin*
anti	*(against)*	antiaircraft, antibody, anticlimax, anticline, antitoxin, antithesis	*Greek*
bi	*(two)*	bilateral, bicycle, binary, bimonthly, biped, bipolar, binocular, bicuspid	*Latin*
circum	*(around)*	circumnavigate, circumspect, circumvent, circumlocution, circus	*Latin*
com	*(together)*	combination, comfort, commensurate, common, complete, combo	*Latin*
con	*(together)*	contract, confidence, confine, confederate, conjunction, contact	*Latin*
de	*(down)*	deposit, descent, despicable, denounce, deduct, demolish, decrepit, deplete	*Latin*
dis	*(away)*	distract, distort, dispute, dissonant, disperse, dismiss, dissuade, disprove	*Latin*
equi	*(equal)*	equitable, equilateral, equivocate, equinox, equation, equilibrium	*Latin*
extra	*(beyond)*	extraterrestrial, extraordinary, extravagant, extrovert, extramural	*Latin*
inter	*(between)*	international, interdepartmental, interstellar, interject, interlude	*Latin*
intra	*(within)*	intracellular, intravenous, intracranial, intrastate, intrauterine	*Latin*
intro	*(into)*	introduce, introspective, introvert, introject, introrse, intromission	*Latin*
mal	*(bad)*	malevolent, malcontent, malicious, malign, malady, malapropism, malonym	*Latin*
mis	*(bad)*	misfit, mistake, misfortune, misfire, misdeed, misguided	*Germanic*
non	*(not)*	nonstop, nonprofit, nonconformity, nonplussed, nonchalant	*Latin*
post	*(after)*	postgraduate, posthumous, postscript, posterity, posterior, postlude	*Latin*
pre	*(before)*	prelude, preposition, premonition, premature, predict, predecessor	*Latin*
semi	*(half)*	semitone, semiaquatic, semicircle, semiweekly, semiannual, semiformal	*Latin*
sub	*(under)*	subterranean, subtract, subordinate, submarine, subterfuge, substantial	*Latin*
super	*(over)*	supervise, superb, superior, superfluous, supercilious, supernatural	*Latin*
sym	*(together)*	sympathy, symbiosis, symbol, symmetry, symphony, symposium	*Greek*
syn	*(together)*	synthetic, synchronize, syndrome, synonym, synopsis, syntax	*Greek*
tri	*(three)*	tricycle, triangle, triceps, triad, trichotomy, triceratops, trivia, trialogue	*Greek*
un	*(not)*	unfit, unequal, undone, unequivocal, unearned, unconventional, untenable	*Old English*

de

down • away • from

The Latin stem **de**, which we define as meaning *down*, actually can have a wide variety of meanings and is a relative of the stem **dis**. Though **de** often means *down*, it can mean *away, off, from, entirely*, or even *undo*. Here are some of the interesting words that contain **de** in its various shades of meaning:

debacle: an overwhelming defeat. Alexander's attack was a debacle for Darius.

debark: to get off of a ship or airplane. They debarked immediately.

debauch: to lead astray morally. Dorian's life was increasingly debauched.

debris: rubble or fragments. The barbarians lived in the debris of Rome.

decamp: to depart suddenly or secretly. In the night, the enemy had decamped.

declivity: a downward slope. The horses stumbled down the declivity.

defalcate: to embezzle funds. He had defalcated the funds and vanished.

defeasible: able to be undone or voided. The provision proved to be defeasible.

defoliate: to strip of leaves. The chemical defoliated most of the jungle.

deliquesce: to melt down. In the movie, the villain's face deliquesced in the blast.

demure: modest or affectedly modest. Her demure pretensions fooled no one.

denizen: an inhabitant. The denizens of the forest could be heard in the night.

depravity: wickedness. The depravity of the criminal was beyond belief.

depredation: plundering. Ghengis Kahn's depredations terrified the villages.

deracinate: to pull up by the roots. He weeded with deracinating frenzy.

deride: to ridicule. He mercilessly derided the new student.

derogate: to detract. Why derogate another's reputation?

desecrate: to profane what is sacred. Vandals had desecrated the shrine.

desiccate: to dry completely. The desiccated apples fell out of the package.

desideratum: something considered essential. Our primary desideratum was cost.

desperado: an outlaw. The cove was a haven for desperadoes and escapees.

1. The Civil War **antedates** the Korean War by decades.

2. The **antiaircraft** fire shot down the enemy planes.

3. The two nations have a **bilateral** agreement.

4. The **circumspect** spy is difficult to catch.

5. The two together are an interesting **combination**.

6. He was **confined** to the asteroid's detention center.

7. The lunar lander **descended** through the atmosphere.

8. His attention was easily **distracted**.

9. She made an **equilateral** triangle with three straws.

10. It was an **extraordinary** achievement.

11. They were lost in **interstellar** space.

12. He received an **intravenous** solution through a tube in his arm.

13. The boy was a lonely **introvert** who kept to himself.

14. He looked fearfully at the glowing, **malevolent** demon.

15. He had the **misfortune** to forget his wallet.

16. The foundation is a **nonprofit** organization.

17. She added a **postscript** at the bottom of the letter.

18. Before Romeo left, Juliet had a frightening **premonition**.

19. The circle was divided into two equal **semicircles**.

20. The lieutenant gave a sharp order to her **subordinate**.

21. The talkative fool made several **superfluous** comments.

22. The **symbiotic** species could not survive without each other.

23. Please **synchronize** your watches at this time.

24. Rome was sometimes ruled by a **triumvirate**.

25. **Unearned** income must be reported to the Internal Revenue Service.

synthesis

1. Invent three words that each combine two or more of the stems in List #1. Write definitions for these words.

2. Write a paragraph about an **intracranial** operation, and use at least ten example words from List #1 in your paragraph.

divergence

1. List as many words as you can think of that contain the stem *pre*. Keep listing until you find unexpected, creative examples.

2. How many things can you think of that need to be **synchronized**?

analysis

1. What is the difference between **interstate** highways and **intrastate** highways? Explain by examining parts of the words.

2. If *nav* means ship, explain the origin of the word **circumnavigate**.

evaluation

1. Are politicians morally obligated to speak **unequivocally**, or do they have a practical right to be **equivocal** in order to be elected?

2. Is it wrong to be an **introvert**, or is it just a matter of style? Is it better to be sociable? Should you force yourself to socialize if you feel like being alone?

intuition

1. What images flash in your mind when you hear the following words: **preschool**, **misfortune**, **symbol**, **deposit**, **interstellar**, and **descent**?

2. If you could do something truly **extraordinary**, what would it be?

The typical Greek terrain with its mountains and narrow valleys is evident in this view of the amphitheater at Delphi. Delphi was thought by the Greeks to be the center of the Earth. It was here to the oracle in the sacred temple of Apollo that Greek people came—often journeying hundreds of miles—for advice and answers to pressing questions. It was the oracle who pronounced Socrates the wisest man in the world, who foretold that the Spartans would have a king killed in combat or their city would be destroyed, and who said that Athens would be destroyed and the Athenians should seek protection behind a wooden wall (which Themistocles interpreted as the navy). Alexander the Great visited the oracle before setting off to conquer Persia.

THE LATE BRONZE AGE: POLITIES AND HOMER

Dr. Thomas Milton Kemnitz

Greece is mountainous and its land rocky. Its climate is too dry in the summer, and its soil not rich enough for the lush crops of the Nile or the Tigris and Euphrates valleys. The inhabitants of Greece were about 2,000 years behind the occupants of those more fertile lands in the development of a literate culture. But with the husbanding of animals, the bounty of the sea, the produce of olive trees and grape arbors, and other assets, the Greeks managed to feed themselves and find the resources for trade throughout the eastern Mediterranean.

In the second millennium B.C., the inhabitants of Greece organized themselves into polities—city states— of some sophistication. This is known as the Mycenaean culture, after the location in Greece of the most complete ruin. They developed an alphabet and a system of writing, known as Linear B. Besides some buildings, most of what survived has been found in graves of royal personages, including many elaborately worked items of gold jewelry and death masks.

Though their cities were widely scattered through the Greek peninsula, the surrounding islands, and the shores of what is now Turkey, the Greeks developed a shared identity and a common culture. Toward the beginning of the twelfth century B.C., they made common cause in a war against the city of Troy and its allies. If we can believe the oral tradition that Homer and other sources recorded, the conflict involved the entire northeastern Mediterranean and lasted for a decade before it ended with the destruction of Troy.

Homer's story of the Trojan War, the *Iliad*, and of the return home from the war of Odysseus and his men, the *Odyssey*, are two of the greatest pieces of literature ever composed. The ancients themselves recognized the enormity of the achievement, and busts of Homer were common in the ancient world. All we know about Homer the man is that he was blind. The busts of him are probably idealized visages sculpted generations after his demise. For the ancient Greeks and Romans, Homer's works were great classics, a status they retain today. Scenes from the *Iliad* and the *Odyssey* were often used to decorate walls and vases in ancient Greece and Rome. The martial prowess of Achilles, the cunning of Odysseus, the wisdom of Nester, the prescience of Cassandra, and many of the other traits of the principal characters and the salient incidents of the war and voyage home resonated with the ancients and were part of the shared culture of Greece and Rome. Alexander the Great liked to portray himself as the successor to Achilles, and throughout his campaigns, he kept with him a copy of the *Iliad* which Aristotle had annotated for him; after the battle of Issus, he used a golden chest taken from the Persians to protect his *Iliad*.

To understand the colossal status of the *Iliad* and the *Odyssey*, imagine a book published today that is translated into every language, taught in every university, and read by every educated person in the year 4915!

For centuries after the Mycenaean culture was destroyed, Greece seemed to go through a dark age, until the ninth century when once again polities and culture began to flourish.

Mycenaean culture flourishes	Fall of Troy	Destruction of Mycenaean cities	Greek migration to the islands, Ionia	
1600–1100 B.C. Late Bronze Age	**c. 1184**	**c. 1150**	**1100–900 B.C.** Dark Age	**900–700 B.C.** Geometric Period

1. **ANTEBELLUM : BELLIGERENCY ::**
   a. antiaircraft : aircraft
   b. nonstop : continuous
   c. cause : effect
   d. morning : afternoon

2. **INTERSTELLAR : STELLAR ::**
   a. submarine : marine
   b. interstate : intrastate
   c. mortar : bricks
   d. intracellular : cell

3. **SUPERFLUOUS : INADEQUATE ::**
   a. excess : insufficiency
   b. malevolence : benevolence
   c. superior : mediocre
   d. euphony : cacophony

4. **SUPERCILIOUS : IDOLIZING ::**
   a. depression : euphoria
   b. condescension : admiration
   c. synthesis : antithesis
   d. zenith : nadir

5. **CIRCUMVENT : COMPLY ::**
   a. noncooperation : complaisance
   b. superior : subordinate
   c. preposition : position
   d. circumnavigate : navigate

6. **ANCESTRY : POSTERITY ::**
   a. eohippus : horse
   b. intracranial : cranial
   c. anteroom : gazebo
   d. syncline : anticline

7. **ANTECEDENT : PRECEDENT ::**
   a. grammar : law
   b. circumlocution : equivocation
   c. malaprop : malevolence
   d. inspection : introspection

8. **PRENATAL : POSTHUMOUS ::**
   a. bilateral : unilateral
   b. pathogen : syndrome
   c. intravenous : vein
   d. subterfuge : evasion

9. **BIPED : BICYCLE ::**
   a. quadruped : automobile
   b. rectangle : tetragon
   c. binary : unitary
   d. biceps : triceps

10. **CIRCUMSPECT : RECKLESS ::**
    a. circumlocution : equivocation
    b. conjunction : disjunction
    c. supercilious : despicable
    d. homophone : homonym

Achilles and Ajax are depicted playing a board game on a vase made in Athens about 520 B.C. The Trojan War was a common theme of Greek art and was used to emphasize a common Hellenic identity far more important than the rivalries and battles and wars that separated one polity from another. The Hellenic identity became even more important in the face of the threat of Persian invasion because it emphasized Greek unity against an enemy from the other side of the Hellespont. Note the pointed beards on the faces of the players on the Athenian vase; Achilles and Ajax are depicted in the fashion of fifth- and sixth-century Athenians. This vase was made at a time when Athenian potters and ceramic painters were eclipsing most of their rivals in the quality and sophistication of their output. Athenian potters used both the black-figure style on this page and about 530 B.C. developed the red-figure style seen on page 9.

1. The interior of a word often contains a striking image that only a person who knows the meaning of the stems will enjoy. In the case of **circumspect**, which means cautious, we see the cautious person looking (*spec*) around (*circum*) for signs of danger.

2. Many other *spec* words contain memorable images. The **introspective** person is not merely thoughtful but is looking inside himself. And we **respect** a person when something that person does causes us to look at him again in a new way.

3. Some words offer moments of humor. The person who **equivocates** is deliberately ambiguous, but we see in the word an image of someone having problems with his mouth as he attempts to give equal (*equi*) voice (*voc*) to both sides of an issue!

4. Depending upon how it is used, **introvert** contains an unsettling, sad image. The *intro* (into) *vert* (turn) is turned into himself—his back to the beautiful, unnoticed world.

5. Even familiar words take on new light at times. Why is a **preposition** called a preposition? Because of its position—it always (almost) comes at the beginning of a prepositional phrase. It occupies the *pre* position.

6. The word **posthumous**, as in posthumous award, contains a portrait of tragedy. A posthumous award is only granted after (*post*) its recipient has been buried in the ground (*humus*).

7. The foolishness of a too-talkative person's excessive questions and comments is wittily described by the word **superfluous**. The talker has provided all of the comments that can be contained, and now the comments begin to over (*super*) flow (*flu*).

8. Can a word help to sharpen one's senses? The beauty of a **symphony** arises largely from just what the word *symphony* emphasizes: the musicians play their instruments in unison so that the sounds (*phon*) rise together (*sym*).

9. **Spanish Cognates**: One of the most important observations to gain from the study of the etymology of English vocabulary is that English and Spanish share thousands of words that are cognates—related words—that have common origins. Often, the English and the Spanish words share not only a stem but even more than one stem, and often in the same order. As examples, here are some English words from this lesson and their Spanish cognates:

   semiannual : semianual
   introduce : introducir
   posterity : posteridad
   superior : superior
   superfluous : superfluo
   malicious : malicioso

This Athenian vase of about 520 B.C. shows the same scene of Achilles and Ajax playing a board game and was found in Italy. It reflects the spread of Greek culture through the Mediterranean in the middle of the first millennium B.C. The red-figure style was easier to work and was associated with a more natural representation, characterized here by the warriors having shed their helmets and armor, which are shown behind them.

In each case below, one of the choices was really the word used by the author in the sentence provided. All of the choices can be found in the example words on the first page of this lesson. Your challenge is to decide which word the author used. This is not a test; it is more like a game because more than one word choice may work perfectly well. See if you can use your sensitivity and intuition to guess correctly which word the author used. You may need a dictionary.

1. **From F. Scott Fitzgerald's *The Great Gatsby***

   The _____ assumption was that on Sunday afternoon I had nothing better to do.
   a. commensurate
   b. supercilious
   c. introverted
   d. symbiotic

2. **From Herman Melville's *Moby Dick***

   He was _____, evincing a confusion.
   a. equivocal
   b. circumspect
   c. equitable
   d. nonplussed

3. **From James Joyce's *A Portrait of the Artist as a Young Man***

   His life had grown to be a tissue of _____ and falsehood.
   a. subterfuge
   b. antithesis
   c. nonchalance
   d. introversion

4. **From Harper Lee's *To Kill a Mockingbird***

   Inside the house lived a _____ phantom.
   a. subordinate
   b. superfluous
   c. malevolent
   d. dissonant

5. **From Eudora Welty's *One Writer's Beginnings***

   I found my own _____ way into becoming part of it.
   a. introspective
   b. synthetic
   c. untenable
   d. posthumous

archy	*(government)*	monarchy, oligarchy, hierarchy, anarchy, matriarchal, patriarch	*Greek*
ard	*(always)*	drunkard, coward, braggart, laggard, dullard, sluggard, niggardly	*Germanic*
cide	*(kill)*	herbicide, homicide, matricide, suicide, regicide, genocide, fratricide	*Latin*
ician	*(specialist)*	technician, musician, beautician, physician, statistician, clinician	*Latin*
itis	*(inflammation)*	appendicitis, tonsillitis, bursitis, arthritis, gastroenteritis	*Greek*
aqua	*(water)*	aquarium, aquatic, aquaplane, aqueduct, aquifer, aqueous, semiaquatic	*Latin*
audi	*(hear)*	audiophile, audience, audition, auditory, audiometer, audit, audiology	*Latin*
bell	*(war)*	bellicose, belligerent, rebel, casus belli, counterrebellion	*Latin*
cap	*(take)*	capture, captive, captor, captious, captivate, captivity, caption, capsule	*Latin*
cise	*(cut)*	excise, incisors, incision, circumcise, incisive, precise, concise, decision	*Latin*
bio	*(life)*	biography, biology, biomorphic, biochemistry, exobiology, biogenesis	*Greek*
auto	*(self)*	autobiography, automobile, autograph, automatic, automaton, autocracy	*Greek*
port	*(carry)*	transport, import, report, porter, deport, important, portage, portly, comport	*Latin*
scrib	*(write)*	scribble, inscribe, scribe, describe, conscription, transcribe, ascribe	*Latin*
logy	*(science)*	biology, anthropology, geology, entomology, philology, mythology	*Greek*
dict	*(say)*	dictionary, predict, malediction, dictation, addict, interdict, contradict	*Latin*
cred	*(believe)*	credit, incredible, credible, incredulous, discredited, credibility, credo	*Latin*
cent	*(one hundred)*	century, bicentennial, centimeter, centipede, centurion	*Latin*
neo	*(new)*	neologism, neophyte, neon, neolithic, neoclassic, neoPlatonist, neonatal	*Greek*
ad	*(to)*	adhesive, adapt, addendum, addition, adherent, addict, advent, advocate	*Latin*
cede	*(go)*	recede, precede, antecedent, proceed, secede, concede, intercede, succeed	*Latin*
miss	*(send)*	dismiss, remiss, missile, admission, missionary, emission, promissory	*Latin*
centri	*(center)*	centrifugal, centripetal, centrist, concentric, decentralize, eccentric	*Latin*
biblio	*(book)*	bibliography, bibliophile, bibliolatry, bible, bibliomania, bibliophobia	*Greek*
anthropo	*(man)*	anthropology, anthropomorphic, anthropoid, lycanthrope, misanthrope	*Greek*

per
through • away

The Latin stem **per**, which we define as meaning *through*, actually can have a wide variety of meanings, including *through*, *throughout*, *away*, *thoroughly*, *completely*, and other related meanings. In most cases, the *through* idea seems to convey the meaning sensibly enough. Some of the English words that contain this Latin stem are provided below. Look up some of the most intriguing words, and note the way in which their definitions are functions of their etymologies.

peremptory:	dictatorial or imperious. Her peremptory command made him jump.
perambulate:	to walk through. They perambulated happily through the park.
perennial:	perpetual. The quartet was a perennial favorite among the Vienna crowd.
perdition:	damnation. Marlowe's Faustus is dragged away to perdition.
perfunctory:	done in superficial routine. He gave the table a perfunctory wipe.
perfidy:	treachery. In his perfidious act, he broke faith with his companions.
perfuse:	pour over. The objects in the room were perfused with the red liquid.
permeate:	penetrate and spread through. The ink permeated the cloth.
perpetrate:	to do evil. In the dark of the moonless night, he perpetrated his foul crimes.
pernicious:	destructive. The false rumor had a pernicious influence on the crowd.
peroration:	conclusion of a speech. At length Pericles came to his sublime peroration.
perseverate:	pathological persistence. He perseverated in his effort to speak to Moses.
persiflage:	flippant style. Their sarcasm and persiflage carried them through the crisis.
perspicacious:	insightful. Sappho's perspicacious poems have endured for millennia.
pertinacity:	obstinacy. With grim-mouthed pertinacity, he refused to let go.
perforce:	necessarily. After the debacle, he perforce went into hiding.
permutation:	radical rearrangement. She marveled at the weird permutations of his ideas.
perpend:	to ponder. "Perpend," said Polonius, as he held out Hamlet's letter.
perquisite:	a privilege or benefit of title. The position included attractive perquisites.
perturbation:	disturbance. Dracula detected the psychic perturbations in his victim's fear.
pervasive:	spread throughout. Aristotle's influence was pervasive in Medieval theology.

1. England is, or once was, ruled by a **monarchy**.

2. The **dullard** was always boring everyone to tears.

3. In killing his father, Oedipus was guilty of **patricide**.

4. Mustafa is an electronic **technician**.

5. The **dermatitis** on his skin was painful and unpleasant.

6. Balthazar, the scuba diver, collects **aquatic** species.

7. The deaf moose had an injured **auditory** nerve.

8. **Belligerent** nations gain nothing from their many wars.

9. The hostile island tribe **captured captives**.

10. The design was **incised** into the oaken door with a knife.

11. **Biomorphic** abstract sculpture resembles living shapes.

12. The general wrote a tedious **autobiography** about his exploits.

13. The **porter** will carry your bags to the train.

14. Please **inscribe** my yearbook.

15. Since he loved insects, he studied **entomology**.

16. The grand jury returned a robbery **indictment** against him.

17. A **credulous** person will believe anything.

18. Fortunately, the **centipede** wears no shoes.

19. Homer was a **neophyte** in the business world, but he learned quickly.

20. The **adhesive** allowed the poster to stick to the wall.

21. At last the flood waters began to **recede** from the land.

22. The unfortunate **missionary** was sent to the cannibal tribe.

23. The ripples on the pond spread out in **concentric** circles.

24. The quick-reading Hortense was a lifelong **bibliophile**.

25. The unsympathetic grouch was sometimes called a **misanthropist**.

For five days on the plain at Marathon, the belligerent armies eyed each other. The heavily-armored Greek soldiers fighting in phalanxes with overlapping metal shields and metal breastplates and helmets had a significant advantage over the Persians, who were equipped with shorter spears, wicker shields, and padded jackets designed to deflect arrows, but the Greeks could not match the Persian cavalry. On the sixth day, the Persians boarded their cavalry on horse transports and put to sea. One Greek general, Miltiades, insisted that the Athenians attack the remaining Persian foot soldiers immediately. He eventually convinced the other generals, and they formed up their hoplites (heavily armed foot soldiers). The invaders responded by forming their own battle line. The outnumbered Athenians had to reduce the depth of the middle of their line to two men instead of the usual eight to stretch their line the length of the Persian line. The Athenians charged the Persians at a run. The painter of this vase deprived the Persian of his spear and shield, but otherwise he illustrates the problem the enemy faced in being vulnerable long before he could bring his sword into play. Several thousand Persians died; the Athenians lost 192 men, whose memory would be honored for generations. The Athenians took the trophies of victory from the Persians to Delphi, where they displayed them along the south wall of their treasury. [See page 132.]

WAR WITH THE PERSIANS—THE FIRST INVASION

Dr. Thomas Milton Kemnitz

The great flowering of ancient Greek culture came in the fifth century B.C. when the Greeks faced a threat of invasion from the Persians, who fielded a formidable army organized by a forceful monarch deploying the resources of a rich and enormous empire.

The Greeks meanwhile continued to be divided into some 200 or so small city states. They—mostly the Athenians—had founded a series of cities along the coast of what is now Turkey. These were known as the Ionian cities, named after a people who had settled central Greece and then been driven out by the Dorians, taking refuge in Athens, the Aegean islands, and Asia Minor. In the 540s B.C. the Persian king Cyrus I conquered those cities in what is now Turkey and annexed them into his empire. The Ionians were never willing subjects, and the Persian kings found it convenient to rule them by means of local rulers, called tyrants. These tyrants were not popular—as the name might indicate—and the Ionian cities rebelled about 500 B.C. The Ionians were assisted by the polities of Athens and Eritrea in their revolt and were initially successful. But then the forces of the Persian king Darius I defeated them in a naval battle and reconquered their cities. Darius wanted to punish Athens and Eritrea for their part in assisting the Ionians and also to secure his western border and gain a foothold in Europe. So he set out to conquer Greece.

In 492 B.C., Darius sent an army west led by his son-in-law, Mardonius, who conquered Thrace and forced Macedonia to submit to his rule. Then the Persian fleet was wrecked off Mount Athos in a storm that sank 300 ships, drowned 20,000 men, and ended the expedition. In 491, Darius sent emissaries to the Greek cities to demand that they submit to his hegemony by offering earth and water as a symbol of total subjugation. Most of the polities did, but the two most powerful, Sparta and Athens, executed the emissaries. In Athens they were tried and then executed; in Sparta they were simply thrown down a well as the best place for them to find all the water and earth they could use.

In 490 B.C., Darius sent an amphibious force to attack the Cycladic Islands and then Greece itself. After successfully invading a number of islands, where the Persians took hostages and forced inhabitants into their army, they sailed to Eritrea, which they conquered, enslaving all the inhabitants they did not kill. Then they landed more than 20,000 men and a cavalry of 1,000 or more at Marathon, twenty-five miles north of Athens. The Athenians met the Persians with 9,000 of their own troops and an additional 1,000 allies to prevent the invaders from advancing beyond the plain at Marathon; despite the numbers, the Athenians decisively won the Battle of Marathon.

There is a myth that a messenger ran the more than twenty-five miles from Marathon to Athens and collapsed and died after delivering the news of the victory. The distance from Marathon to the Acropolis became the basis for the race we today call the marathon. In ancient myth the messenger—Pheidippides (his name was remembered by the Greeks for centuries)—first ran to Sparta to seek help—a distance of 153 miles, which we are told he made in a day and a half—came back to Marathon, and then apparently ran to Athens with news of the glorious victory, after which he collapsed and died. The Spartans arrived too late to take part in the battle. Pheidippides reported that on his initial run to Sparta, the god Pan fell in with him and asked him why the Athenians did not pay him more homage since he had done much for Athens and would in the future do more. After the battle, the Athenians gave Pan increased respect and honor. The modern marathon conveniently excises the first 306 miles of the run Pheidippides purportedly made.

Earliest known Olympic games		Establishment of democracy in Athens		Battle of Marathon
776 B.C.	700–600 B.C. Orientalizing Period	600–490 B.C. Archaic Period	508/507 B.C.	490–323 B.C. Classical Period	490 B.C.

emotion

1. What words in List #2 do you associate with feelings of anger?

2. When was the last time you were **incredulous**? What happened to make you feel that way?

aesthetics

1. If you could use **adhesive** to glue anything you wanted to your wall, what would you glue there?

2. If you could make a **biomorphic** abstract sculpture, would you make one that was swimmy, or flappy, or toothy, or full of eyes, or what?

synthesis

1. Write a paragraph about an **anthropologist** studying Neanderthal remains in a cave in France. Use at least ten example words from List #2.

2. Use various other stems to build as many words as you can around the stem *scrib* (or *script*). Feel free to make up words, even humorous ones.

divergence

1. Why are people **deported** from the United States? List as many reasons as you can think of. Then brainstorm reasons why people should not be deported.

2. How many things can you think of that are composed of or that resemble **concentric** circles?

analysis

1. Why is the noun that the pronoun takes the place of referred to as the **antecedent**? Explain why this combination of stems is a logical choice for the name of a pronoun's noun.

2. Explain how the pieces of the word **autobiography** total up into a logical meaning.

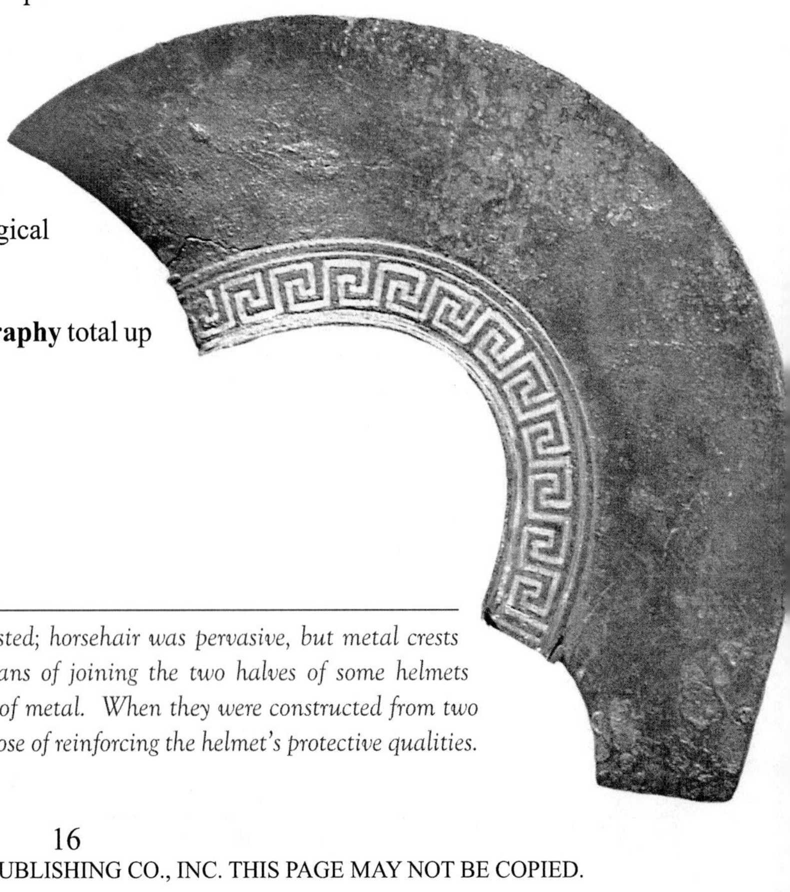

Helmets in the ancient world were generally crested; horsehair was pervasive, but metal crests like the one pictured here were useful as a means of joining the two halves of some helmets together. Many helmets were made of one piece of metal. When they were constructed from two pieces, a joining piece might serve the added purpose of reinforcing the helmet's protective qualities.

1. **AUTOBIOGRAPHY : BIOGRAPHY ::**
    a. malediction : benediction
    b. automobile : horse cart
    c. audiophile : audience
    d. murder : suicide

2. **BIBLIOPHILE : BIBLIOPHOBIA ::**
    a. philanthropist : misanthropy
    b. laggard : dullard
    c. monarchy : anarchy
    d. belligerence : treaty

3. **ANTHROPOLOGIST : ANTHROPOLOGY ::**
    a. science : scientist
    b. biology : biologist
    c. captain : ship
    d. artist : art

4. **SCRIBE : DICTATION ::**
    a. reporter : report
    b. geologist : rock
    c. anthropologist : anthropoid
    d. captor : captive

5. **ARTHRITIS : TONSILLITIS ::**
    a. arthropod : gastropod
    b. knuckle : throat
    c. disease : decay
    d. bibliophile : bibliolatry

6. **INCREDULOUS : CREDULOUS ::**
    a. disbelief : belief
    b. incredible : amazing
    c. faith : agnosticism
    d. homicide : herbicide

7. **PHILOLOGY : ANTHROPOLOGY ::**
    a. word : science
    b. word : man
    c. science : diction
    d. anthropology : eloquence

8. **NEOLITHIC : PALEOLITHIC ::**
    a. stone : ceramics
    b. artifact : neon
    c. rock : rock
    d. new : old

9. **ANTHROPOID : HUMAN ::**
    a. asteroid : star
    b. anthropologist : culture
    c. homicide : victim
    d. audition : audience

10. **NEOLOGISM : WORD ::**
    a. neophyte : plant
    b. neon : chemist
    c. neolithic : savage
    d. neoclassic : old classic

Hoplites were so named because of their shield, the hoplon, which was made of wood and covered with bronze or leather. The hoplon weighed twenty pounds or more and had a handle for the left hand and a strap that fit around the left forearm at the elbow. The Spartans decorated their shields with a capital Lamba for their Laconian homeland; many Athenian shields were decorated with a white owl, the bird associated with Athena. The now-absent spear in this hoplite's hand would have been painted. Viewed from the rear, he is leaning his weight into the hoplon.

1. What would it mean if a piece of abstract modern sculpture were described as **biomorphic**? It would mean that, while the sculpture is not representative of any particular life form, it draws its shapes and lines from those found among living things. It is a study of shapes (*morph*) found among living (*bio*) things.

2. A **Micropoem**: Sometimes words are metaphors. To say that an artist is a **neophyte** in the art world, meaning that the artist is a beginner, is to compare the artist to a tiny new (*neo*) plant (*phyte*) just emerging from the seed.

3. We say that someone is **remiss** in his duties if he is lax or negligent. But the stems tell the real story: if he is remiss, we have to send (*miss*) him back to do the job again (*re*)!

4. If something is **important**, then it is valuable enough to carry (*port*) in (*im*). We carry things into the building out of the rain, and we carry truths into the mind out of the world.

5. A supporter of a viewpoint or of a politician is known as an **adherent**, but in our mind's eye, we see the adherent stuck (*here*) to (*ad*) the side of the admired person or opinion!

6. Does a pronoun have an **antecedent**? An antecedent is simply the noun that goes (*cede*) before (*ante*) the pronoun. The pronoun refers backwards to the go-before noun.

7. Does the term **bibliography** intimidate you? It needn't. To make a bibliography, you merely write (*graph*) down a list of the books (*biblio*) you read for your report. The books should be listed in alphabetical order by the authors' last names.

8. **Spanish Cognates**: One of the most important observations to gain from the study of the etymology of English vocabulary is that English and Spanish share thousands of words that are cognates—related words—that have common origins. Often, the English and the Spanish words share not only a stem but even more than one stem, and often in the same order. As examples, here are some English words from this lesson and their Spanish cognates:

matriarchal : matriarcal
herbicide : herbicida
capture : capturar
automatic : automático
centurion : centurión
neologism : neologismo

This Athenian-made vase depicts a Greek archer and hoplite in combat with a mounted Persian warrior, whose horse has been impaled by the spear of the hoplite before the Persian could use his lance. In battle, cavalry presented a formidable challenge for foot soldiers. Cavalry generally was massed on the flanks and used to attack from the sides or the rear and often turned the tide of battle. Most casualties came after the battle line was broken when warriors began to flee and were cut down from behind, frequently by enemies on horseback. The representation of the hoplite is intended to be heroic rather than realistic, but that of the Persian is more accurate as to his clothes.

In each case below, one of the choices was really the word used by the author in the sentence provided. All of the choices can be found in the example words on the first page of this lesson. Your challenge is to decide which word the author used. This is not a test; it is more like a game because more than one word choice may work perfectly well. See if you can use your sensitivity and intuition to guess correctly which word the author used. You may need a dictionary.

1. **From James M. Barrie's *Peter Pan***

   The order came sharp and _____.
   a. incisive
   b. concise
   c. incredulous
   d. neolithic

2. **From Joseph Conrad's *Lord Jim***

   He lived solitary, but not _____, with his books and his collection.
   a. bellicose
   b. centripetal
   c. misanthropic
   d. patriarchal

3. **From John Hersey's *Hiroshima***

   He became a(n) _____, mechanically wiping, daubing, winding, wiping, daubing, winding.
   a. automaton
   b. antithesis
   c. nonchalance
   d. introversion

4. **From Rachel Carson's *Silent Spring***

   Honeybees become wildly agitated and _____ on contact with it.
   a. biomorphic
   b. eccentric
   c. matriarchal
   d. bellicose

5. **From Martin Luther King, Jr.'s *Why We Can't Wait***

   We were not _____ advocating lawlessness.
   a. anarchists
   b. belligerents
   c. centrists
   d. audiophiles

homo	*(same)*	homogenize, homonym, homophone, homologous, homozygous	*Greek*
spec	*(look)*	spectacles, specter, specious, spectrum, respect, inspect, prospectus	*Latin*
duct	*(lead)*	conduct, ductile, induct, product, reduction, deduction, reproduction	*Latin*
fer	*(carry)*	transfer, infer, refer, defer, conifer, Lucifer, aquifer, auriferous	*Latin*
pend	*(hang)*	pending, pendulum, pendant, impending, depend, pendulous, suspend	*Latin*
micro	*(small)*	micron, microscope, microwave, microphone, microcosm, microbiotic	*Greek*
hydro	*(water)*	hydroplane, hydroponics, dehydrate, hydrant, hydrogen, hydrophobia	*Greek*
photo	*(light)*	photograph, photometer, photon, photogenic, photosynthesis	*Greek*
pan	*(all)*	panorama, panoply, pandemic, pantheism, pantheon, Pan-American	*Greek*
penta	*(five)*	pentagram, pentagon, pentameter, pentathlon, pentarchy, pentahedron	*Greek*
tele	*(far)*	telescope, telephone, telekinesis, telepathy, teleology, telesthesia, telex	*Greek*
vid	*(look)*	video, invidious, Montevideo, evidence, provide, videogenic, vide, videlicet	*Latin*
omni	*(all)*	omnifarious, omnipotent, omnivorous, omniscient, omnibus, omnipresent	*Latin*
ex	*(out)*	exit, except, excise, exculpate, elucidate, exorbitant, eccentric, enumerate	*Latin*
poly	*(many)*	polyphony, polygyny, polygamy, allopolyploidy, polyvalent	*Greek*
re	*(again)*	return, review, retouch, reiterate, retail, revive, regenerate, regurgitate	*Latin*
hypo	*(under)*	hypodermic, hypocrite, hypotenuse, hypothermia, hypothesis	*Greek*
pseudo	*(false)*	pseudonym, pseudopod, pseudomorphic, pseudoscience, pseudoevent	*Greek*
neuro	*(nerve)*	neuron, neurosurgeon, neurosis, neurology, neuralgia, neurotomy	*Greek*
tomy	*(cut)*	tonsillectomy, appendectomy, neurotomy, dichotomy, anatomy, lobotomy	*Greek*
hema	*(blood)*	hematic, hematite, hematology, hematoma, hemal, hematogenesis	*Greek*
proto	*(first)*	protoplasm, prototype, protozoa, proton, protohuman, protomorphic	*Greek*
phon	*(sound)*	symphony, telephone, phonetic, phonograph, euphony, cacophony	*Greek*
mono	*(one)*	monotonous, monomania, monocular, monogamous, monolithic, monotone	*Greek*
viv	*(life)*	vivid, vivisection, vivacious, convivial, bon vivant, viva, viviparous, revive	*Latin*

apo

away • up • off

The Greek stem **apo**, which we define as meaning *away*, actually can have a wide variety of meanings and is sometimes shortened to **ap**. Though **apo** often means *away*, it can mean *detached*, *from off*, *from*, or even *back*. Here are some of the interesting words that contain **apo** in its various shades of meaning:

apodictic:	shown by argument. His argument developed an apodictic certainty.
apothecary:	a pharmacist. Romeo bought his fatal potion from an apothecary.
apogee:	farthest point. The moon reached its apogee from the earth.
aperture:	an opening. The lovers saw each other through the aperture in the wall.
aphorism:	a concise statement. Franklin delighted France with his witty aphorisms.
apocalypse:	a revelation. He was mesmerized by the ancient apocalyptic writings.
apogeotropism:	growing away from gravity. The apogeotropic plants grew high in the wind.
apocope:	dropping the end of a word. He used apocopes such as "my *bes'* friend."
aposiopesis:	a break in thought. "I wish—but you don't care," he said in aposiopesis.
apophasis:	saying that you won't mention. "I won't remind you," his apophasis began.
apoplexy:	a stroke. His former vigor was damaged by dissolution and apoplexy.
apotheosis:	deification. Odysseus refused apotheosis to return to his wife.
apostrophe:	addressing someone in speech. He began with an apostrophe to the Muse.
apostle:	one sent on a mission. The computer representative had an apostle's zeal.
apology:	a formal defense. Plato wrote about Socrates's *Apology* to the Athenians.
apostate:	a renegade. The cynical apostate had once led the opposition party.
aposematic:	warning. The insect's bright, aposematic colors warned frogs of its poison.
apophyge:	curve at the end of a column. They leaned on the apophyge of the column.
apopemptic:	valedictory. They used to call a lachrymose parting an apopemptic farewell.
apomixis:	nonsexual reproduction. The botanist studied apomixis in plants.
apologue:	a short allegory. The historian collected charming medieval apologues.

1. The English language contains many **homophones** like *two* and *too*.

2. It was a **specious** argument, but it sounded convincing.

3. The youth was **inducted** into the army.

4. The **transfer** was made in the darkness of a moonless night.

5. The patent is still **pending** on that product.

6. The two bacteria were only a **micron** apart.

7. The fire **hydrant** stood in front of the school.

8. An overexposure to the sun's **photons** gave her a sunburn.

9. The god Apollo was a member of the Greek **pantheon**.

10. He wore a **pentagram** on his sleeve, not a **pentagon**.

11. The strange boy could move distant objects by **telekinesis**.

12. The kids played **video** games for hours.

13. The all-consuming furry muncher had an **omnivorous** appetite.

14. The surgeon was able to **excise** the tissue with a scalpel.

15. Johann Sebastian Bach composed **polyphonic** music.

16. His new novel was carefully **reviewed** by the literary critic.

17. The crash victims suffered **hypothermia** on the frozen tundra.

18. The amoeba uses its **pseudopods** to move across the surface.

19. The brain is said to contain more than 100 billion **neurons**.

20. The clown received an emergency **appendectomy** in the medical tent.

21. Iron ore is called **hematite** because of its deep red color.

22. Single-celled animals are known as **protozoa**.

23. Musicians play together in a **symphony**.

24. The German prince peered through his gold-rimmed **monocular**.

25. Laws against **vivisection** prevent cruelty to animals.

evaluation

1. Why do you **respect** people? What is the difference between the people whom you do respect and the people whom you don't respect?

2. Do you think it would be better to write a short story from the author-**omniscient** point of view of from the point of view of only one of the characters?

intuition

1. If you were to be pursued by a ferocious, **carnivorous** critter, what critter would you least like to be pursued by?

2. Judging by the name, what do you think it looks like in **Montevideo**, Uruguay? Imagine everything you can about the city.

emotion

1. How would you feel if someone accused you of using **specious** reasoning, and did so in front of your friends? How long would your feelings last?

2. What emotions are associated with the word **convivial**?

aesthetics

1. Can you create a vivid mental image of a **spectrum**? Can you see the brilliance of each color? In what order are the colors? Which one is the most beautiful?

2. What colors would you like to use for an oil painting of a **protozoa**?

synthesis

1. How many words in List #3 could be considered to have anything at all to do with sound? After you find the words that are obvious, look for words that have a less obvious connection.

2. Pick out the words in List #3 that would be good to use in a ghost story.

On this vase painting of a fully-equipped hoplite, the elbow strap of the hoplon is evident. Note also the strap in his left hand. In his right hand he is pouring a libation of wine to the gods from a shallow bowl called a phiale.

The Persians came south by land with an army so large that Darius previously had erected supply depots for food along the route. They came north of Mount Athos and dug a canal large enough for their ships to pass two abreast because they did not want to chance the sea to its south. (In 492 a Persian invasion force under the command of Marodonius had been eradicated by a storm off that point.) Herodotus reported both the supply dumps and the canal, but he was disbelieved until recently when archaeologists found conclusive evidence of both. Most historians also disbelieve the figure Herodotus gives of 1,500,000 troops in Xerxes's army; the figures of combatants the ancients gave for battles generally seem inflated to modern historians. However, Herodotus lists all of the ships in Xerxes's fleet of 1,207 and gives their origins, and that figure is generally accepted.

WAR WITH THE PERSIANS—THE SECOND INVASION
Dr. Thomas Milton Kemnitz

Beaten at Marathon in 490, the Persians withdrew, but the Greeks knew that they would return. When the Persians invaded again in 480 B.C., both sides had made significant adjustments. Darius had died of old age, and his son Xerxes had become ruler. Xerxes amassed a huge army—perhaps 300,000 or more men—and a fleet of 1,207 warships. His plan was to bridge the Hellespont and march south through Greece, subduing any city that did not surrender. For three years the Persians stockpiled food along the route to feed this huge force. Xerxes's strategy was to demonstrate his might and ensure a compete victory with overwhelming numbers. He had with him as an advisor a deposed king of Sparta, Demaratus.

In about 485 the Spartans had received a shocking prophecy from the oracle at Delphi: either a Spartan king would die in battle (which apparently in the previous three centuries of warfare had never occurred), or Sparta itself would be destroyed. The Spartans were among the most pious of all the Greeks, and they took this prophecy seriously.

In Athens a brilliant and resourceful leader named Themistocles—one of the great figures of the ancient world—emerged with a strategy to make Athens a preeminent city. A rich vein of silver had been found in an Athenian mine in 483 B.C., and Themistocles convinced the people of the young democracy to use the money to build a fleet of warships rather than to give each citizen a moderate sum of silver coins. Within two years, his strategy turned Athens into the largest naval power in Greece and gave the Greeks a fighting chance at neutralizing the Persian fleet.

In 481 Persian intentions were evident, and representatives from seventy Greek polities met at Corinth to devise a strategy to meet the impending invasion. As early as 500 B.C., the Spartans had organized a Peloponnesian League with themselves as *hegemon*. Many of the city states of southern Greece belonged to it. Each member was allied to Sparta but not necessarily to one another. No tribute was expected from the members except in times of hostilities, and each city had an equal say in its council. However, Sparta was not obliged to follow the dictates of the council. The League was a defensive alliance that tended to foster oligarchies in the city states and oppose tyrannies and democracies. Its existence was fortuitous, for it formed the basis of the resistance to the second Persian invasion. As the foremost military power in Greece, Sparta was given the leadership of the resistance. Most of the Greek polities wanted to establish a line of defense at the Isthmus of Corinth and resist the Persian invaders there. This was not acceptable to Athens, which lay to the east of Isthmus and would not be defended from the barbarians (the Greeks made a sharp distinction between themselves and all others as barbarians). After some wrangling, it was decided to meet the Persians in narrow passes in the Vale of Tempe north of Thessaly, well north of central Greece.

The Persians crossed the Hellespont in April of 480 and came west and then south slowly, capturing everything in their path. The allies sent a force of about 10,000 to meet them, but they found that the Vale of Tempe was not defensible because the Persians could circumvent it via two other passes, and the allies withdrew. Themistocles devised an alternate bifurcated strategy to use the narrow terrain of Thermopylae Pass to negate the overwhelming numbers of the enormous invading army. Simultaneously they had to hold off the numerically superior Persian navy in the straits off the pass to prevent the Persians from simply putting to sea and landing farther south.

Battle of Marathon	Sparta receives a prophecy at Delphi	Silver find at Athenian mines; decision to build the navy	Greek polities meet to form defensive strategy	Persian invasions; Battles of Thermopylae, Salamis
490 B.C.	**485 B.C.**	**483 B.C.**	**481 B.C.**	**480 B.C.**

1. **EUPHONY : CACOPHONY ::**
    a. microcosm : microbiotic
    b. beautiful : ugly
    c. photon : photometer
    d. provident : future

2. **POLYPHONIC : POLYGAMY ::**
    a. pantheism : religion
    b. hydroponics : deduction
    c. homologous : monotone
    d. melody : marriage

3. **ECCENTRIC : CONVENTIONAL ::**
    a. pseudopod : pseudonym
    b. oligarchy : pentarchy
    c. deduction : reduction
    d. nonconformity : conformity

4. **PSEUDOSCIENCE : SCIENCE ::**
    a. revive : vivacious
    b. vivacious : revive
    c. anatomy : lobotomy
    d. pseudonym : name

5. **OMNIVOROUS : HERBIVOROUS ::**
    a. omnifarious : omnipotent
    b. Pan-American : river
    c. all : plant
    d. specious : authentic

6. **ELUCIDATE : EXPLAIN ::**
    a. reiterate : stolid
    b. reiterate : repeat
    c. symphony : cacophony
    d. eulogy : euphony

7. **TELEKINESIS : TELESTHESIA ::**
    a. moving : feeling
    b. telescope : microscope
    c. inspect : introspect
    d. eccentric : centrifugal

8. **DICHOTOMY : TRICHOTOMY ::**
    a. bicycle : tricycle
    b. viviparous : vivisection
    c. lobotomy : brain
    d. hydrant : hydrogen

9. **PENTAMETER : PENTARCHY ::**
    a. poetry : government
    b. government : poetry
    c. distance : five
    d. ruler : measure

10. **HYPOTHESIS : THESIS ::**
    a. guess : idea
    b. theory : supposition
    c. hypothecate : hypotenuse
    d. idea : image

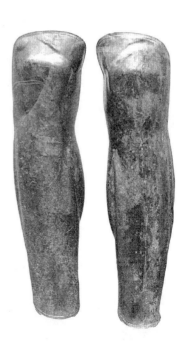

On the left is a hoplite's breastplate, known as a muscled cuirass. Made in two pieces, the sections were joined at the sides and top either by straps or by metal pins. This was a popular design that fit the Greek emphasis on physical development. On the right are greaves to protect the knees and shins from an attack beneath the hoplon. The warrior wore a sword on his left hip and carried his spear into battle in his right hand.

1. **Specious** reasoning is false reasoning, reasoning that may sound convincing at first but that upon further examination turns out to be false. The stems reveal the idea behind the word: a specious argument only looks good; it is full of (*ous*) look (*spec*), not truth.

2. What must one do in order to **provide** for the future? Providing for the future is a simple matter if one will only look (*vid*) forward (*pro*).

3. A **hypodermic** needle is appropriately named; it is a needle that goes under (*hypo*) the skin (*derm*).

4. A **Micropoem**: A parent with **dependent** children may find that the children are dependent in more ways than one. Imagine a parent who cannot move because of the children who are hanging (*pend*) down (*de*) on all sides!

5. **Invidious** comparisons are those that create jealousy, that excite envy. It would be invidious to choose one friend for special praise in front of other friends. An invidious action is one that admits one or more people and leaves the others on the outside looking (*vid*) in (*in*) enviously.

6. A biologist might note that a seal's flippers and a person's hands are **homologous** structures. This would mean that they serve a similar purpose, as their similar structure indicates. Flippers and hands share some of the same (*homo*) reasons (*log*) for being. (A note: The similarity of structure may reveal evidence of a long-ago common ancestor more than it does present-day similar purpose or usage. Homologous structures can be as different from one another as birds' wings and seals' flippers.)

7. **Spanish Cognates:** One of the most important observations to gain from the study of the etymology of English vocabulary is that English and Spanish share thousands of words that are cognates—related words—that have common origins. Often, the English and the Spanish words share not only a stem but even more than one stem, and often in the same order. As examples, here are some English words from this lesson and their Spanish cognates:

conduct : conducta
dehydrate : deshidratar
omnivorous : omnívoro
reiterate : reiterar
pseudonym : seudónimo
hematology : hematología

This vase painting of a fully-equipped hoplite shows the elbow and hand straps on the hoplon. The relationship of the height of the greaves and the bottom of the hoplon is clear in this painting. The scene suggests leave-taking. The woman on the right holds a phiale and a wine jug for an offering to the gods. This red-figure vase was made in Athens in the mid-fifth century.

In each case below, one of the choices was really the word used by the author in the sentence provided. All of the choices can be found in the example words on the first page of this lesson. Your challenge is to decide which word the author used. This is not a test; it is more like a game because more than one word choice may work perfectly well. See if you can use your sensitivity and intuition to guess correctly which word the author used. You may need a dictionary.

1. **From Emily Brontë's *Wuthering Heights***

   He might have had a _____ on the subject of his departed idol.
   a. cacophony
   b. prospectus
   c. telekinesis
   d. monomania

2. **From Rachel Carson's *Silent Spring***

   The present difficulties have been born of just such _____ reasoning.
   a. specious
   b. omniscient
   c. monolithic
   d. pendulous

3. **From Sir Walter Scott's *Ivanhoe***

   Gurth, knowing his master's irritable temper, attempted no _____.
   a. pantheon
   b. euphony
   c. vivisection
   d. exculpation

4. **From William Makepeace Thackeray's *Vanity Fair***

   He was lazy, peevish, and a _____.
   a. pentarchy
   b. pseudonym
   c. *bon vivant*
   d. protohuman

5. **From Joseph Heller's *Catch-22***

   Yossarian found himself listening intently to the fascinating _____ of details.
   a. polyphony
   b. elucidation
   c. exorbitance
   d. spectrum

morph	*(shape)*	amorphous, morphology, polymorphously, mesomorph, protomorphic	*Greek*
vest	*(clothes)*	vestry, vestment, vestibule, vest, investiture, divest, divestiture	*Latin*
bene	*(good)*	benefit, benevolent, beneficial, benediction, benefactor, benign	*Latin*
pond	*(weight)*	ponderous, ponder, preponderant, pound, imponderable, compound	*Latin*
corp	*(body)*	corpulent, corporation, corporeal, corporal, corpse, corpuscle	*Latin*
dorm	*(sleep)*	dormitory, dormant, dormer, dormancy, dormitive, dormient	*Latin*
pater	*(father)*	paternalistic, patronize, paternity, patriarch, expatriate, paterfamilias	*Latin*
nov	*(new)*	novel, nova, novice, novitiate, Nova Scotia, innovation, renovate	*Latin*
punct	*(point)*	punctuate, punctilious, puncture, punctual, acupuncture, contrapuntal	*Latin*
ject	*(throw)*	eject, reject, conjecture, dejected, inject, subject, projection, interject	*Latin*
tion	*(act or state)*	completion, reaction, devastation, production, creation, transition	*Latin*
loco	*(place)*	locomotive, location, local, locus, relocate, dislocate, localize, locomotor	*Latin*
dox	*(opinion)*	orthodox, heterodox, doxology, indoctrinate, paradox	*Greek*
amphi	*(both)*	amphibious, amphitheater, amphibian, amphigory, amphibolous	*Greek*
magn	*(great)*	Magna Carta, magnanimous, magnate, magnificent, magnum opus	*Latin*
eu	*(good)*	Eucharist, euphony, eulogy, euphemism, eugenics, euglena	*Greek*
endo	*(within)*	endoplasm, endocrine, endogamous, endoskeleton, endothermic	*Greek*
phobia	*(fear)*	claustrophobia, acrophobia, xenophobia, agoraphobia, hydrophobia	*Greek*
ortho	*(straight)*	orthopedics, orthodontist, orthodox, orthography, orthogonal	*Greek*
put	*(think)*	reputation, putative, impute, dispute, computer, disreputable	*Latin*
ver	*(true)*	verify, veracity, veritable, verdict, verisimilitude, aver, cinema verite	*Latin*
matri	*(mother)*	matricide, matron, matriarch, matrimony, matrilineal	*Latin*
mega	*(large)*	megalith, megaphone, megalomania, megalopolis, megahertz, megaton	*Greek*
pop	*(people)*	popular, populist, populate, population, popularize, populous	*Latin*
sangui	*(blood)*	sanguinary, sanguine, consanguinity, sangfroid, sangria	*Latin*

anti

against • opposite • counteract

The Greek stem **anti**, which we define as meaning *against*, actually can have a wide variety of meanings and is sometimes changed to **ant**. **Anti** can mean *against, prevent, opposite, reverse, hostile to, counteract,* or even *rivaling*. Here are some of the interesting words that contain **anti** in its various shades of meaning:

antibody:	protein that neutralizes an antigen. His antibodies helped fight the disease.
anticlimax:	a ludicrous conclusion. The ending of the play was a pathetic anticlimax.
anticline:	an upward bend in rock strata. The hill was actually based on a slate anticline.
anticoagulant:	drug that prevents clotting. He was given an anticoagulant to dissolve the clot.
antifebrile:	reducing fever. Aspirin has an antifebrile quality.
antihero:	an untraditional protagonist. The new cynicism produced film antiheroes.
antilogy:	a contradiction. The discussion was really a juxtaposition of antilogies.
antimatter:	opposite particles. For every proton, there may be an antiproton.
antinomian:	belief in faith alone. Antinomians demand more than obedience to moral law.
antipathy:	strong dislike. Achilles's antipathy for the Trojans seemed implacable.
antiseptic:	preventing infection. She used an antiseptic to prevent infection in the wound.
antivenin:	an antitoxin for venom. They had no antivenin for the rattlesnake bite.
antonym:	an opposite word. She thought synonyms were easier than antonyms.
antonomasia:	the use of epithets. Antonomasia was the custom in "His Honor's" court.
antidote:	a poison remedy. They administered the antidote in time to save his life.
antinovel:	a radical novel. In his antinovel, he violated the traditional forms of the genre.
antipode:	the exact opposite. Their views were antipodes of each other.
antimacassar:	a small cover for a chair back. She always kept antimacassars on the chairs.
antiscorbutic:	a remedy for scurvy. Some old fruit was the only antiscorbutic on the ship.
antilabor:	opposed to unions. The organization had a strong antilabor point of view.
antiballistic:	an antimissile missile. The antiballistic missiles saved the city from the attack.

1. The magic crystal dissolved into a lumpy, **amorphous** mass.

2. The silk **vestments** were hanging on pegs.

3. He never knew the name of his generous **benefactor**.

4. The **ponderous** burden was nearly impossible to lift.

5. His **corpulent** body was a result of his love of sweets.

6. The evil creature lay harmlessly **dormant** for centuries.

7. There was an annual birthday party for the family **patriarch**.

8. The recently invented laser toothbrush is a **novel** idea.

9. Her **punctilious** attention to small details was impressive.

10. He felt miserably **dejected** when the expedition left without him.

11. The **devastation** intensified our need for **creation**.

12. Self-motivated people have an internal **locus** of control.

13. The many-cultured United States is a **heterodox** nation.

14. The Martian **amphibians** emerging from the water had gray, impermeable skin.

15. His **magnanimous** victory speech was inspiring in its generosity.

16. The **euphony** of Mozart's beautiful music carried us away.

17. Human beings have **endoskeletons**, not exoskeletons like insects or crabs.

18. The trembling dog on the twenty-third floor has **acrophobia**.

19. The **orthodontist** straightened Count Dracula's fangs.

20. The **computer** hummed once and exploded.

21. We questioned the **veracity** of the doctor's strange and unbelievable story.

22. The town awoke to the details of the angry son's tragic **matricide**.

23. The massive granite **megalith** towered over the ancient ruins.

24. The **populist** candidate, a favorite of the voters, won the lunar colony primary.

25. The massed armies joined in **sanguinary** combat.

divergence

1.   What survival advantages can you think of that an organism, such as Homo sapiens, has as a result of its **endoskeleton**? What would be the advantages of an **exoskeleton**? Perhaps some light could be shed on this question by considering the lifestyles of creatures that have the two types of skeletons.

2.   Enumerate ways in which **innovation** could be beneficial to the future of the human race.

analysis

1.   Guess the meaning by analyzing the stems of **polymorphously**, **magnanimous**, **acrophobia**, **benediction**, and **matriarch**.

2.   What is the difference between a society known for its **heterodoxy** and a society known for its **orthodoxy**?

evaluation

1.   In our Keyboard Era, should we still attempt to teach **orthography**, or is handwriting becoming an **anachronism**?

2.   Which, if either, is more important: to be **punctual** or to be **punctilious**?

intuition

1.   A hero in a comic book saves a population from **devastation**. His performance is marked by **sangfroid** and self-discipline. What evil threatened the society?

2.   Locked in a darkened closet is an **amorphous** object. What is it?

aesthetics

1.   What are the most **euphonic** sounds, man-made or otherwise, on this planet?

2.   What are some creative ways to give aesthetic appeal to a metropolis or a **megalopolis**?

This helmet of the Laconian type was used by the Spartans. Made from a single sheet of bronze, the helmet gave good protection to the top of the head. Its shape is reminiscent of the woolen caps that hunters, mariners, and others wore.

1. **EUPHORIA : EUPHEMISM ::**
   a. joy : depression
   b. matrimony : marriage
   c. sanguine : sanguinary
   d. emotion : word

2. **MEGALITH : PONDEROUS ::**
   a. megahertz : preponderant
   b. verdict : popular
   c. megalopolis : populous
   d. creation : devastation

3. **MAGNANIMOUS : PUSILLANIMOUS ::**
   a. reputable : disreputable
   b. matrilineal : matriarchal
   c. megaton : megalomania
   d. magnate : magnet

4. **MICROBIOTIC : EUGLENA ::**
   a. immense : galaxy
   b. small : large
   c. life : inanimate
   d. corpuscle : blood

5. **CONTRAPUNTAL : POLYPHONY ::**
   a. contradictory : disruption
   b. paradox : orthodoxy
   c. metrical : poetry
   d. sangfroid : consanguinity

6. **PATRIARCH : MATRIARCH ::**
   a. patrilineal : children
   b. monarchy : plutocracy
   c. ruler : ruled
   d. father : mother

7. **ORTHODOX : HETERODOX ::**
   a. conformity : variety
   b. conglomerate : aggregate
   c. orthography : handwriting
   d. verify : aver

8. **XENOPHOBIA : AGORAPHOBIA ::**
   a. *magnum opus* : claustrophobia
   b. space : vacuum
   c. stranger : sangfroid
   d. stranger : open space

9. **INNOVATION : RENOVATE ::**
   a. invention : destruction
   b. idea : hypothesis
   c. invention : refurbish
   d. construction : hypothesis

10. **BENEFACTOR : MALEFACTOR ::**
    a. euphony : cacophony
    b. eulogy : euphemism
    c. benediction : contradiction
    d. imponderable : ponder

This is a helmet of the Corinthian type used by hoplites throughout Greece. Because the individual hoplites supplied their own equipment, they could pick the style they wanted, and their equipment might differ markedly from that of the other men in their phalanx. This style reduced the field of vision of the warrior and the amount he could hear.

This sculpture, known as the discobolus, was originally a bronze statue sculpted by Myron. The Greeks and Romans of later generations made numerous copies of it in marble. The original discobolus was probably made in Athens, perhaps in the 530s. Myron was widely admired for his ability to create bronze figures that seemed to pulsate with life.

The Olympics were held in Greece every four years beginning in at least 776 B.C., and all polities were punctilious in halting hostilities during the games. Only barbarians such as the Persians would force battle during the Olympic games. The Greek word for competitiveness was agonia, from which we get not only the word agony but also a clear sense of the intensity of the competition. Some of the ancient events, such as the pentathlon, are still held. Others, such as the four-horse chariot race and the race in full armor, were not continued when the modern games were revived in 1896 in Athens.

WAR WITH THE PERSIANS—THE SECOND INVASION
Dr. Thomas Milton Kemnitz

By the summer of 480, the Persians had reached central Greece. It was an Olympic year, and the Greeks did not fight when the Olympics were being held. Moreover, it was the time of the religious festival of the Carneia, when the Spartans certainly did not fight. However, the Persians were present, and the Spartans sent King Leonidas with a force of 300 men to lead the defense of Greece. Theirs was a suicide mission; the best outcome the Spartans could hope for was the death of their king, for only that would save Sparta itself from destruction, according to the prophecy at Delphi. The force of 300 who came with Leonidas were all men like him who had sons; their lines would all continue when they died in battle with their king. Because it was the time of the Olympics, the total Greek force numbered only 7,000 against a Persian army of 300,000.

Before they left Sparta, King Leonidas's wife, Gorgo—herself a truly extraordinary woman—asked him what she should do. His answer was not that from a man planning to return: "Marry a good man, and bear good children." When Xerxes's forces came to Thermopylae, they found that the Greeks had built a wall across the narrowest point of the pass, perhaps twenty feet wide from cliff face to the sea. Xerxes could not believe that so few men intended to stand against his mighty army. One reason to assemble so massive an army was to awe his opponents into immediate surrender. A mounted scout reported back to Xerxes that some of the Spartans were grooming their long hair, while others were engaged in athletics. Xerxes turned to Demaratus, the deposed king of Sparta, for an explanation, and Demaratus explained that the Spartans meant to fight to the death. Xerxes sent a messenger telling the Spartans to lay down their arms; Leonidas replied with two Greek words meaning "Come and take them." After four days—three of them stormy—of failing to overawe the Spartans with his superior numbers, Xerxes ordered an attack.

For two days the Persians attacked, only to be met by an unyielding line of Greek hoplites. Occasionally the Spartans would pretend to retreat, and the Persians broke ranks to chase them, only to have the Spartans turn in unison and easily kill the warriors who were not in a disciplined phalanx. Persian losses reached the thousands; few Greeks died; the Greek line held.

Meanwhile things were going well in the straits of Artemisium, where according to Herodotus about a third of the Persian fleet was wrecked by the storm before the first battle. Many of the Greeks had not wanted to risk their fleet in a battle at Artemisium, but the Euboeans gave Themistocles a bribe of thirty talents (a talent is roughly equivalent to a little less than a million dollars in today's American currency) to make the point of defense the north shore of their island. Themistocles's strategy had been to fight there in any case, but he used five talents to bribe the Spartan admiral and three to bribe the Corinthian admiral, and he pocketed the remaining twenty-two talents. On the first day of the land battle, the Persians detached a squadron of 200 ships to sail around the island and attack the Greeks from the rear. Late on that day, the Greeks sent out some of their ships, engaged some Persian triremes (warships), and captured or destroyed thirty of them. That night another storm wrecked the Persian ships trying to round Euboea. The second day of battle at Thermopylae saw the Persians remain in harbor, trying to repair the ships damaged in the storms. On the third day the Persians launched their entire surviving fleet, and the Greeks faced them. The result was a draw, with about the same number of ships on both sides disabled or sunk; this was an outcome that the Persians could afford more easily than the Greeks. However, this was the decisive day on shore at Thermopylae when things went badly for the Greeks.

Earliest known Olympic games	Battle of Marathon	Silver find at Athenian mines; decision to build the navy	Greek polities meet to form defensive strategy	Persian invasions; Battles of Thermopylae, Salamis
776 B.C.	490 B.C.	483 B.C.	481 B.C.	480 B.C.

1. What is the central characteristic of a **metropolis**? Perhaps it is that a metropolis is the mother (*metro*) city (*polis*) for the smaller towns and cities that grow up in the surrounding region. The *metro* in this word comes from the Greek *meter*, mother, and not from the Latin *matri*, which also means mother.

2. In a **dispute**, we disagree. But the word *dispute* offers a spatial metaphor for the contradicting ideas. The graphic image is that our ideas are away (*dis*) from each other. My thought (*put*) is here, and your thought is away (*dis*) over there!

3. A **Micropoem**: A **punctilious** person is full of (*ous*) attention to the details of conduct—to all of the fine points (*punct*). He is full of fine points!

4. How can you spot the **subjects** of the king? They are the ones who throw (*ject*) themselves down (*sub*) to the ground at his arrival. This graphic image contained in the stems offers a more profound understanding of the nature of subjection than a common definition could.

5. The jury's terrible burden is revealed in the name of the fateful decision it must return. In a **verdict**, the jury must speak (*dict*) the truth (*ver*).

6. Our modern concern for ecology has taught us to worry about **eutrophication**, which occurs when nitrogen fertilizer is washed into ponds and streams by rain, causing algae to grow so excessively that it clogs the water. The word **eutrophy**, however, is a surprisingly mild term for such an unfortunate process; it simply means good (*eu*) growth (*troph*). Too good!

7. **Sangfroid** is a vivid noun that is often used as the object of the preposition *with*. One must command a tense rescue operation with enormous sangfroid. Like **equanimity**, sangfroid refers to calmness or composure but in a more graphic way. Sangfroid literally means in cold (*froid*) blood (*sangui*).

8. Sometimes a word offers an interesting insight into the way we behave. A **reputation** is what you have when something you have done causes other people to think (*put*) about you again (*re*).

9. Are you in the wrong place? Try using a **locomotive** to move (*mot*) to the right place (*loco*).

10. **Spanish Cognates**: One of the most important observations to gain from the study of the etymology of English vocabulary is that English and Spanish share thousands of words that are cognates—related words—that have common origins. Often, the English and the Spanish words share not only a stem but even more than one stem, and often in the same order. As examples, here are some English words from this lesson and their Spanish cognates:

    expatriate : expatriado
    acupuncture : acupuntura
    heterodox : heterodoxo
    magnanimous : magnánimo
    reputation : reputación
    matrimony : matrimonio
    sanguinary : sanguinario

This helmet is of the Illyrian type; the ridges were used for affixing the plume. Like the Corinthian helmet, it protected the ears but evidently reduced auditory awareness considerably and also narrowed the field of vision.

In each case below, one of the choices was really the word used by the author in the sentence provided. All of the choices can be found in the example words on the first page of this lesson. Your challenge is to decide which word the author used. This is not a test; it is more like a game because more than one word choice may work perfectly well. See if you can use your sensitivity and intuition to guess correctly which word the author used. You may need a dictionary.

1. **From Henry James's *The American***

   He was not embarrassed, for his unconscious _____ was boundless.
   a. euphemism
   b. dejection
   c. sangfroid
   d. orthography

2. **From Charles Dickens's *David Copperfield***

   I had no peace of my life until he was _____.
   a. renovated
   b. expatriated
   c. relocated
   d. dejected

3. **From Harriet Beecher Stowe's *Uncle Tom's Cabin***

   She lingered, with needless _____, around the arrangements of the table.
   a. magnanimity
   b. xenophobia
   c. conjecture
   d. punctiliousness

4. **From Charlotte Brontë's *Jane Eyre***

   I should have appealed to your nobleness and _____ at first.
   a. magnanimity
   b. benediction
   c. ponderousness
   d. euphony

5. **From Frederick Douglass's *Narrative***

   I would allow myself to suffer under the greatest _____ which evil-minded men might suggest.
   a. indoctrinations
   b. euphemisms
   c. imputations
   d. interjections

vita	*(life)*	vitamin, vitality, vital, revitalize, viable, vitalism, devitalize	*Latin*
demo	*(people)*	democracy, demography, undemocratic, democratize	*Greek*
stereo	*(solid)*	stereoscope, stereophonic, stereotype, stereopticon, stereotropism	*Greek*
ism	*(doctrine)*	Marxism, capitalism, Imagism, Cubism, nihilism, pluralism, tribalism	*Greek*
cogn	*(know)*	recognize, cognizant, incognito, cognoscenti, cognomen, precognition	*Latin*
sur	*(over)*	surplus, surpass, surcharge, surface, surfeit, surmount, surname, surtax	*Latin*
alter	*(other)*	alternator, alteration, alter ego, alternative, altruism, altercation	*Latin*
astr	*(star)*	astronomy, astrology, asteroid, disaster, asterisk, astrophysics, astrolabe	*Greek*
dyna	*(power)*	dynamic, dynamo, dynamite, dynasty, dynamometer	*Greek*
chron	*(time)*	chronometer, chronological, synchronize, chronic, anachronism	*Greek*
hyper	*(over)*	hyperactive, hyperventilate, hyperbole, hyperacidity, hypertension	*Greek*
luna	*(moon)*	lunar, lunatic, lunate, luna moth, lunette, sublunar, lunular	*Latin*
octa	*(eight)*	octameter, octagenarian, octagon, octarchy, octave, octopus, octahedron	*Greek*
gyro	*(turn)*	gyration, gyroscope, gyre, gyrate, spirogyra, gyromagnetic, gyrocompass	*Greek*
contra	*(against)*	contradict, contrary, contrast, contrapuntal, contraband, contravene	*Latin*
geo	*(earth)*	geography, geothermal, geology, geophysics, geometry, geosynchronous	*Greek*
helio	*(sun)*	Helios, heliotropic, heliocentric, heliograph, perihelion, aphelion	*Greek*
thermo	*(heat)*	thermostat, thermos, thermotropic, thermonuclear, thermocouple	*Greek*
tetra	*(four)*	tetrameter, tetrahedron, tetroxide, tetragon, tetrachloride, tetracycline	*Greek*
meter	*(measure)*	thermometer, millimeter, octameter, hydrometer, odometer	*Greek*
scope	*(look)*	telescope, microscope, periscope, radarscope, horoscope, electroscope	*Greek*
son	*(sound)*	sonar, unison, sonorous, sonnet, dissonance, resonant, supersonic	*Latin*
dec	*(ten)*	decade, decaliter, decimal, decagon, decathlon, decimate, dodecahedron	*Greek*
stell	*(star)*	interstellar, stelliform, stellar, constellation, stellate, stellify	*Latin*
amat	*(love)*	amatory, amateur, amorous, amiable, amigo, amour-propre, amity	*Latin*

dia

across • through • apart

The Greek stem **dia**, which we define as meaning *across*, actually can have a wide variety of meanings. **Dia** can mean *across*, *through*, *throughout*, *apart*, or *between*. Here are some of the interesting words that contain **dia** in its various shades of meaning:

diachronic: of changes over time. The book was a study of many diachronic phenomena.

diadem: a crown. The diadem was placed carefully on her head.

diacritic: a mark to indicate that a letter is pronounced differently from the same letter unmarked. The macron is a diacritical mark.

dialect: local speech. He spoke a recognizable Northern Michigan dialect.

dialogue: conversation. Plato's philosophy is in the form of Socratic dialogues.

diagnosis: identifying disease. Her diagnosis determined that the patient had cancer.

diametrical: opposite. Their political views were diametrical opposites of each other.

diageotropism: growing along the earth surface. Diageotropic plants covered the ground.

dianoetic: logical rather then intuitive. She used a dianoetic process to decide.

diastema: a gap between teeth. The orthodontist was able to correct the boy's diastema.

diaphoretic: increasing perspiration. The medicine had a diaphoretic side-effect.

diapause: delay in growth. Some insects have periods of diapause in their life cycles.

diatonic: eight-note scale without intervals. The diatonic scale is widely used in rock n' roll.

diastole: dilation of the heart. With any luck, one's diastole will follow one's systole.

diarthrosis: a free-moving joint. The hip joint is an example of diarthrosis.

diathermic: letting heat pass through. The new glass had superior diathermic resistance.

diagenesis: change in sediments. Diagenesis occurs between deposition and consolidation.

diaphragm: the midriff. The pain came from somewhere in the diaphragm.

diathesis: a predisposition to a disease. Diathesis may call for certain precautions.

1. In the spring of 2215, the rebuilt New York was a **revitalized** city.

2. The theory of **democracy** was proven effective by the United States.

3. If there is **stereophonic** sound, can there be **stereo** smell?

4. Is **capitalism** the opposite of **Marxism**?

5. The Magnum Leader was traveling **incognito** to avoid **recognition**.

6. The overwhelming economic disasters could not be **surmounted**.

7. Our previously unchanged plans have suffered an **alteration**.

8. If the **asteroid** struck the earth, it would be a **disaster**.

9. Her **dynamic** personality made her an obvious choice for the powerful role.

10. Please **synchronize** your **chronometers**.

11. The **hyperactive** child began to **hyperventilate**.

12. Are **lunatics** really subject to **lunar** influences on their sanity?

13. The **octarchy** decided to invade Macedonia.

14. The dancers' spinning **gyrations** continued into the night.

15. Their **contradictory** remarks offered a sharp **contrast** of views.

16. Which earth study do you prefer: **geology**, **geography**, or **geophysics**?

17. Galileo thought that the solar system was **heliocentric**, not earth-centered.

18. The **thermotropic** plants were killed by the cold front.

19. Is a square a **tetragon** or a **tetrahedron**?

20. The **hydrometer** measured the flow of the trout stream.

21. Alien warships appeared on the **radarscope**.

22. The senator's **sonorous** voice was her best political weapon.

23. The Olympic **decathlon** winner was famous for a **decade**.

24. The **interstellar** spaceship launching was a **stellar** occasion.

25. The **amateur** astronomer was an **amiable** fellow who loved his hobby.

divergence

1. As the word **lunatic** indicates, we once believed that the moon sometimes had a direct effect on some people's sanity. Who are history's famous lunatics? Try to think of at least ten.

2. How many places can you think of where you would be forced to travel **incognito**?

analysis

1. Is the solar system **heliocentric** or **geocentric**? Explain how you can tell by analyzing the parts of the words.

2. Explain the composition of the word **constellation**.

evaluation

1. Do you think that perhaps a country ruled by an **octarchy** (Yes, I know—there aren't many octarchies around these days!) would make fewer serious mistakes in its foreign policy than one ruled by a **monarchy** or a presidency? What is the most logical form of government?

2. What is the difference between an old neighborhood that should be torn down and an old neighborhood that should be **revitalized**? If you were a city planner, what criteria would you use to make such a decision?

intuition

1. Think of a really creative use for a **thermos**. Think of a really creative use for a **thermostat**.

2. Think of an unpredictable **disaster** that might befall a mining colony on a large **asteroid**.

emotion

1. Which words in List #5 would only be used in very formal speech, such as a lecture?

2. Which words in List #5 might a coach use to fire up a team?

This scene shows a fully-armed warrior waiting while another hoplite puts on his greaves. Both are equipped with Corinthian-style helmets. This black-figure on white-ground art is on a vase used for holding oil.

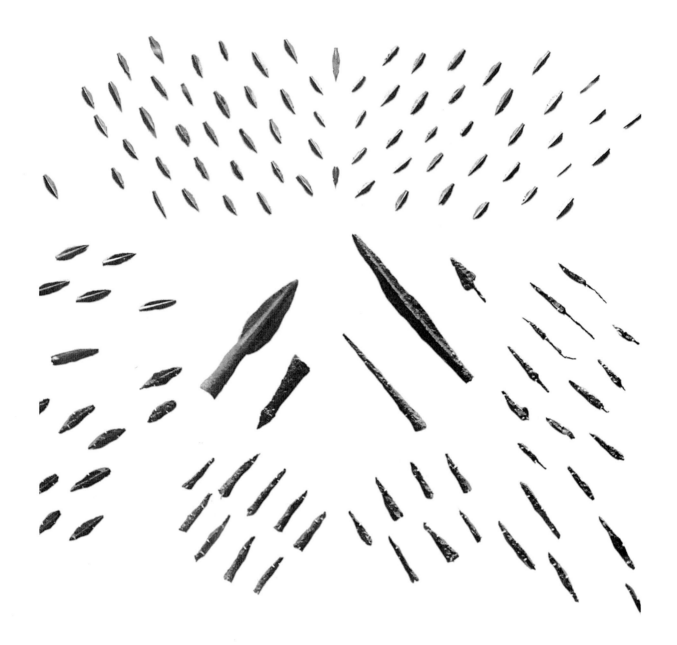

Herodotus reports the words of Dieneces, one of the Spartan 300, who was informed that the Persians had so many archers that their arrows would blot out the sun. Dieneces replied, "So much the better; we will fight in the shade." It was August in Greece, where temperatures might reach 100 degrees F. After each battle the Greeks awarded an honor—called an aristeia—to the warrior who had fought the best in the battle; Dieneces was given the award posthumously. An excavation in 1939 at Thermopylae (the name means hot gates), 2,419 years after the battle, turned up a rich trove of Persian arrowheads and lance and spear points where the Greeks had made their last stand; it enabled archaeologists to confirm Herodotus's account of the battle and locate the hill where the last Greeks died. King Leonidas had died earlier in the day; Herodotus tells of a battle for his corpse, which the Spartans successfully defended.

FROM THERMOPYLAE TO SALAMIS

Dr. Thomas Milton Kemnitz

After the second day of fighting at Thermopylae, a Greek traitor showed the Persians a path they could use to circumvent the pass. That night Xerxes dispatched his elite "Immortals" to surround the Greeks. The local warriors sent by Leonidas to defend the path failed to do so. The next morning the Greeks became cognizant that the Persians would soon engulf them. Most of the Greek warriors departed south to fight another day; the Spartans remained with 700 Thespians who stayed willingly and 400 Thebans whom Leonidas apparently detained against their will. The Persians attacked late in the morning. When the Greek lances were broken, they fought with their short swords. When those were broken, they fought with their hands and teeth. Eventually the few remaining regrouped on a hill; the surviving Thebans surrendered, and Xerxes ordered his archers to shoot until the rest of the Greeks were dead. Xerxes commanded that the Thebans who had surrendered be branded with his brand and Leonidas's body be decapitated and crucified. Xerxes lost two of his brothers in the fighting at Thermopylae, and he had clear indication that capturing Greece was not going to be as easy as his previous conquests.

After the Persians took Thermopylae, there was no longer any reason for the Greeks to defend the Straits of Artemisium. The Persians captured Athens and burned the city after killing all of its defenders. Themistocles had his sailors carve messages into the rocks at every possible landing point telling the Ionian Greeks with the Persian fleet that the best thing would be to defect to the Greek side, and second best would be not to fight hard against their Greek brethren. One ship left the Persians and came to the Greeks before the battle of Artemisium, and another before the next battle, but Herodotus reported that many of the Ionian Greeks did not fight hard at the next engagement at Salamis, where the Greek fleet put in after leaving Artemesium.

The Greeks had 380 ships at Salamis, the Persians probably more than 600. Many of the Greeks did not want to fight there, contending that they had lost that part of Greece anyway. But Themistocles did not want to let the Greeks sail away to their many home cities, believing that they would never re-assemble to fight the Persians, and he did not want to give up Salamis, where many of the Athenians had been evacuated. Themistocles knew that the Greeks had a better chance of winning against a numerically superior fleet if the battle were held in the narrow straits than if it were held in the open sea, where the Persians could bring all of their ships against the Greeks at once. Always a man to try any trick he could to win, Themistocles sent a messenger to Xerxes to tell him that he was secretly a friend to the Persian king, that out of friendship he was letting Xerxes know that the Greeks were intending to sail away, and that if Xerxes's fleet surrounded them, it would destroy them because the disunited Greeks were more likely to fight one another than the Persians. Xerxes took the bait and had his fleet put to sea just after dark, and the next morning the Greeks found themselves in a position of having to fight. In the event, Themistocles was correct; the Persians did not have enough water in the straits to arrange their entire fleet effectively, and they were exhausted from having spent the night at sea in cramped ships. The Greeks won an important victory in the confines of the straits. Xerxes watched the battle with growing consternation. At its conclusion the Phoenician captains complained that the Ionians had not fought hard enough for the great king's cause; Xerxes thought otherwise and had the Phoenicians executed. It was never prudent to irritate Xerxes.

Battle of Marathon	Sparta receives a prophecy at Delphi	Silver find at Athenian mines; decision to build the navy	Greek polities meet to form defensive strategy	Persian invasions; Battles of Thermopylae, Salamis
490 B.C.	485 B.C.	483 B.C.	481 B.C.	480 B.C.

1. **CUBISM : CAPITALISM ::**
   a. geometry : money
   b. art : economy
   c. doctrine : structure
   d. theory : philosophy

2. **HELIOCENTRIC : GEOCENTRIC ::**
   a. circle : square
   b. solar : lunar
   c. sun : center
   d. sun : earth

3. **PERIHELION : APHELION ::**
   a. solar : lunar
   b. perigee : apogee
   c. perimeter : circumference
   d. heliograph : telegraph

4. **DISSONANCE : RESONANCE ::**
   a. harsh : rich
   b. music : polyphony
   c. polyphony : instrument
   d. cacophony : pandemonium

5. **TETRAMETER : TETRAHEDRON ::**
   a. rhythm : pyramid
   b. music : musician
   c. four : angle
   d. number : figure

6. **PRECOGNITION : INCOGNITO ::**
   a. forecast : weather
   b. cognizant : ignorant
   c. foreknowledge : disguise
   d. prediction : verification

7. **CHRONIC : TRANSITORY ::**
   a. enduring : ephemeral
   b. subsonic : unison
   c. octave : octopus
   d. chronicle : transfix

8. **OCTAGON : OCTAHEDRON ::**
   a. plane : solid
   b. eight : octopus
   c. octave : sound
   d. antagonist : protagonist

9. **NIHILISM : HEDONISM ::**
   a. system : doctrine
   b. geothermal : thermotropic
   c. skepticism : pleasure-seeking
   d. Imagism : painting

10. **HYPERBOLE : UNDERSTATEMENT ::**
    a. democracy : demography
    b. decathlon : decathlete
    c. constellation : star
    d. surfeit : paucity

Athena celebrates a naval victory over the Persians.
Athena, patron goddess of Athens, holds in her left hand
the curved stern of a trireme with a head cap on it, almost
certainly representing a Persian. In her right hand, she holds
a spear. This red-figure amphora for transporting wine or olive
oil was made in Athens in the middle of the fifth century.

1. A **Micropoem**: Why were mathematical formulas invented for calculating areas and volumes of spatial objects? The answer is found in the name of that branch of mathematics. **Geometry** was devised so that ancient civilizations would be able to measure (*meter*) the earth's (*geo*) surface in order to accurately divide it for farming and other purposes. Geometry began as a method of earth-measuring.

2. You might expect the word **viable** to be based on the stem *via* (road, way). But it is actually a variation of *vita* (life). A fetus is viable when it is able to live.

3. Why is a musical **octave** called an octave? Because music is based on a system that recycles at the eighth (*octa*) note. The notes run A, B, C, D, E, F, G, and the next note is A again, but it is an octave higher than the previous A.

4. Are the voices of the chorus in **unison**? If they do not form one (*uni*) sound (*son*), then they are not.

5. What happens in my brain when I **recognize** you? To recognize you means that I know you now, and the next time I see you, I will know (*cogn*) you again (*re*).

6. The early astronomers' confusion about the nature of **asteroids** is apparent in the construction of the word. We know today that an asteroid is actually a big chunk of rock floating in space, but to the ancient astronomers, it had the appearance (*oid*) of a star (*aster*).

7. When an army is badly defeated, we say that it has been **decimated**. This once meant that one in every ten (*dec*) soldiers had been killed (*mat*).

8. Some words suggest sound effects. A **resonant** voice is a deep, echoing, far-carrying voice. It booms. It sounds (*son*) and sounds again (*re*).

9. A **Micropoem**: If you wanted to describe a terrible event that befell a person, you might call it a tragedy. But if you wished to describe an awesome, cosmic calamity, one that affected thousands or millions of people, then you might call it a **disaster**. The word *disaster* means unfavorable "aspect of a star"—the stars foretold good or bad fortune.

10. **Spanish Cognates:** One of the most important observations to gain from the study of the etymology of English vocabulary is that English and Spanish share thousands of words that are cognates—related words—that have common origins. Often, the English and the Spanish words share not only a stem but even more than one stem, and often in the same order. As examples, here are some English words from this lesson and their Spanish cognates:

   vitality : vitalidad
   incognito : incógnito
   altruism : altruismo
   anachronism : anacronismo
   geophysics : geofísica
   heliocentric : heliocéntrico
   amiable : amable
   constellation : constelación

This fragment of a pot shows a kneeling hoplite.

In each case below, one of the choices was really the word used by the author in the sentence provided. All of the choices can be found in the example words on the first page of this lesson. Your challenge is to decide which word the author used. This is not a test; it is more like a game because more than one word choice may work perfectly well. See if you can use your sensitivity and intuition to guess correctly which word the author used. You may need a dictionary.

1. **From Marjorie K. Rawlings's *The Yearling***

   The cubs made now and then a(n) _____ talking.
   a. undemocratic
   b. altruistic
   c. hyperbolic
   d. amiable

2. **From Charles Dickens's *David Copperfield***

   You have yet to learn the dignity of _____ and the responsibility of the human individual.
   a. vitality
   b. altruism
   c. anachronism
   d. nihilism

3. **From Maya Angelou's *I Know Why the Caged Bird Sings***

   I slept with Grandmother Baxter, who was afflicted with _____ bronchitis and smoked heavily.
   a. sonorous
   b. chronic
   c. cognizant
   d. viable

4. **From Martin Luther King, Jr.'s *Why We Can't Wait***

   I am _____ of the interrelatedness of all communities and states.
   a. dissonant
   b. incognito
   c. geosynchronous
   d. cognizant

5. **From Aldous Huxley's *Brave New World***

   The music of the radio was a labyrinth of _____ colors, a sliding, palpitating labyrinth.
   a. sonorous
   b. contraband
   c. stereophonic
   d. dissonant

germ	*(vital or related)*	germane, germinate, germicide, germinal, germ	*Latin*
greg	*(group)*	gregarious, egregious, gregariously, segregate, congregate, aggregate	*Latin*
mar	*(sea)*	marine, marina, ultramarine, maritime, mariner, marinate, submarine	*Latin*
prim	*(first)*	prime, primary, primate, primogeniture, primeval, prima donna, primo	*Latin*
pyro	*(fire)*	pyre, pyromania, pyrotechnic, pyrogenic, pyrophobia, pyrometer	*Greek*
clam	*(cry out)*	clamorous, exclamation, clamor, exclamatory, clamant, declaim	*Latin*
plu	*(more)*	plural, plurality, plus, pluralize, pluriaxial, pluralism, nonplussed	*Latin*
tang	*(touch)*	tangible, tangent, tangle, tangential, cotangent, intangible	*Latin*
string	*(bind)*	stringent, stringy, astringent, stringer	*Latin*
liber	*(free)*	liberate, liberty, liberal, libertine, deliberate, libertarian	*Latin*
junct	*(join)*	junction, conjunction, juncture, disjunct, injunction, adjunct	*Latin*
clud	*(close)*	exclude, include, preclude, exclusive, occlude, conclude, cloister	*Latin*
se	*(apart)*	secede, secret, sedition, seduce, segregate, select, separate	*Latin*
trib	*(pay)*	tribute, tributary, retribution, contribution, attribute, diatribe, distribute	*Latin*
dign	*(worthy)*	dignify, dignity, condign, dignitary, undignified, indignation	*Latin*
luc	*(light)*	lucid, translucent, lucidity, pellucid, Lucifer, elucidate, lucent, lucubrate	*Latin*
rupt	*(break)*	erupt, disrupt, rupture, corrupt, abrupt, incorruptible	*Latin*
grat	*(pleasing)*	gratifying, gratitude, ingrate, grateful, gratuitous, ingratiate	*Latin*
medi	*(middle)*	median, mediate, medium, mediocre, mediterranean, in medias res	*Latin*
soph	*(wisdom)*	sophomore, sophisticated, sophist, philosophy, pansophy, theosophy	*Greek*
curr	*(run)*	current, undercurrent, currently, recurrent, currency, incur	*Latin*
tempor	*(time)*	temporal, contemporary, temporize, temporarily, tempus fugit	*Latin*
migr	*(wander)*	migrate, transmigration, migrant, migratory, emigrant, immigrant	*Latin*
trans	*(across)*	transfer, translate, transmit, transfusion, translucent, transcend	*Latin*
gamy	*(marriage)*	monogamy, polygamy, bigamy, gamete, autogamous, exogamy	*Greek*

ob

against • upon • toward

The Latin stem **ob**, which we define as meaning *against*, actually can have a wide variety of meanings and is sometimes changed to **oc**, **op**, or even **o**. Though **ob** usually means *against*, it can mean *opposed to, toward, before, upon, over, completely*, or even *oppositely*. Here are some of the interesting words that contain **ob** in its various shades of meaning:

oblate:	flattened at the poles. The water balloon was oblate as it spun in the air.
obituary:	notice of death. The obituary page chronicled the spread of the virus.
oblivious:	forgetful. Grief had made them oblivious to life's ordinary concerns.
oblique:	evasive. She gave oblique answers to his direct questions.
obligate:	to bind. He felt obligated to fulfill his commitment.
obliterate:	to blot out. The boy soon obliterated all signs of the ant hill.
obnoxious:	very offensive. His ethnocentric language was obnoxious and repugnant.
obscurant:	one opposed to enlightenment. No proposal satisfied the obdurate obscurant.
obsecrate:	to beg. It was useless to obsecrate in such circumstances.
obsolete:	no longer in use. The practice of bleeding the patient is now obsolete.
obstinate:	stubborn. Listening carefully and being obstinate are inversely proportional.
obtuse:	slow to understand. He blinked at her, his countenance obtuse.
obvious:	evident. "We hold these truths to be obvious," he wrote perplexedly.
occult:	concealed or esoteric. Faustus followed an occult path to his own perdition.
opponent:	an adversary. On the basketball court the two friends became arch opponents.
oppress:	to tyrannize. The nation was oppressed under the power of the tyrant.
opportune:	fitting. It was an opportune moment to announce the appointment.
oppugnant:	antagonistic. He glowered up beneath his oppugnant eyebrows.
obbligato:	indispensable. The musical passage was marked *obbligato*, so he played it.
obovoid:	egg-shaped. The obovoid forms in the ground proved to be dinosaur eggs.
oblation:	a sacrifice. They discussed the necessary oblation to appease the god.

1. His irrelevant comments were not **germane** to the discussion.

2. The friendly alien proved to be well-mannered and **gregarious**.

3. The **mariner** steered through beautiful **ultramarine** waters.

4. The anthropologist was **primarily** interested in **primates**, especially gorillas.

5. The **pyromaniac** loved starting fires with **pyrogenic** materials.

6. The loudmouth's **clamorous exclamations** could be heard for blocks.

7. The candidate received a **plurality** but not a majority of votes.

8. The job has many **tangible** benefits, such as salary and a free car.

9. The regulations were too **stringent** for the footloose, creative artist.

10. Did the *Emancipation Proclamation* **liberate** the slaves?

11. There was a jungle near the **junction** of the Brazilian highways.

12. Would you rather be **excluded** from or **included** in our new group?

13. There was a **secret** decision to **secede** from the Union and to live apart.

14. The Amazon has many **tributaries** that pay their waters into the river.

15. Don't **dignify** his unworthy question with an answer.

16. Your **lucid** remarks greatly clarified the confusing issue.

17. The volcanic **eruption** of Vesuvius **disrupted** our celebration.

18. The **grateful** man was certainly no **ingrate**; he thanked us profusely.

19. It was a **mediocre** speech, neither excellent nor poor.

20. The **sophomore's** immature **philosophy** was **unsophisticated** and **sophomoric**.

21. His wandering remarks on current affairs were too **discursive** to endure.

22. Is human life **temporal** or eternal?

23. Do **migratory** species think about their distant destinations?

24. The **translucent** material allowed us to see the events on the other side.

25. Is the crime of **bigamy** a variation of **monogamy** or a form of **polygamy**?

aesthetics

1. Imagine that you are standing in an art gallery in front of an abstract modern painting called **"Pyromania."** What colors, textures, and shapes do you see?

2. There is a color called **ultramarine**. If you are not familiar with it, what do you think it looks like? Can you use *ultra* to make up a name for a color (ultratomato!)?

synthesis

1. How many of the words in List #6 would be good words to use in *National Geographic* articles about the cities, rivers, oceans, and forests of the earth? List the words that might be helpful.

2. What words in List #6 might be used by an engineer in her professional capacity?

divergence

1. Think of five times when it might be important to know how to analyze a word.

2. List as many careers as you can that require a strong vocabulary.

analysis

1. Why is an **exclamatory** sentence called an exclamatory sentence? Explain by examining the parts of the word.

2. Explain the composition of the word **conjunction**.

evaluation

1. Are **pyrotechnics** displays too dangerous? Should they be banned? Should there be public indignation if an injury occurs during a pyrotechnics display?

2. Is an **egregious** act of vandalism worse than the same act would be if committed in stealth and secrecy? Is it not as bad? Is it neither better nor worse?

This black-figure vase showing a warrior putting on his greaves was made in the vicinity of Athens about a decade before the first Persian invasion.

1. **GERMANE : IRRELEVANT ::**
   a. tangent : cotangent
   b. philosophy : theosophy
   c. sedulous : indolent
   d. lucid : pellucid

2. **GREGARIOUS : SOLITUDE ::**
   a. hermit : society
   b. sociable : society
   c. sociable : isolation
   d. aggregate : congregate

3. **SEGREGATED : CONGREGATED ::**
   a. secede : intercede
   b. selection : predilection
   c. temporary : contemporary
   d. divided : united

4. **PYROPHOBIA : PYROTECHNICS ::**
   a. agoraphobia : festival
   b. claustrophobia : fire
   c. pyromania : egomania
   d. gratitude : gratuitous

5. **MIGRATION : TRANSMIGRATION ::**
   a. transfusion : fusion
   b. animal : soul
   c. lucid : translucent
   d. migrant : emigrant

6. **EGREGIOUS : CONDIGN ::**
   a. gratuitous : indignation
   b. stringent : astringent
   c. diatribe : lucubrate
   d. blatant : fitting

7. **EMIGRANT : IMMIGRANT ::**
   a. exclusive : con
   b. segregate : congregate
   c. incur : recur
   d. exit : enter

8. **PRIMATE : PRIMEVAL ::**
   a. coelenterate : medieval
   b. deliberate : archival
   c. ingrate : credible
   d. migrate : primal

9. **JUNCTION : CONJUNCTION ::**
   a. injunction : conclusion
   b. interstate : interjection
   c. median : mediocre
   d. translate : transmit

10. **ULTRAMARINE : SUBMARINE ::**
    a. blue : ocean
    b. marina : dock
    c. mauve : pantechnicon
    d. surface : sailboat

This red-figure illustration painted on the bottom of a cylix shows a warrior about to pour a libation at an altar. The cylix was a shallow wine cup with two handles and a relatively flat bottom, often decorated. The Greek cylix became the Latin calix and then the English chalice.

Themistocles

Herodotus and his contemporaries called themselves Hellenes *(after an ancient and perhaps mythical King Hellen), and everyone who was not a Hellene was a barbarian—including most particularly the Persians. Graecos was said to be a descendant of King Hellen, but more likely the origins of the name for Greece lie in a tribe in northwestern Greece named the Graici or Graikoi. Colonists who settled in Italy were called Gracei by the Romans who encountered them in southern Italy, and from Latin the Hellenes became known as Greeks to most of the rest of the world. Even today the country name in Greek is Hellas. The identification of Hellenes as a people with a common language and heritage may have been fostered initially for reasons of forming defensive alliances, but clearly its basis in fact was demonstrated by a common culture and language that was part of the Mycenaean civilization of the second millennium B.C., that was behind the Greek force that fought the Trojan War, that survived the dark ages of the early part of the first millennium, and that was powerful enough to allow for the establishment of common institutions such as the Olympic games in 776 B.C. (or perhaps earlier).*

THEMISTOCLES AND METIS

Dr. Thomas Milton Kemnitz

After the Battle of Salamis, Xerxes began to worry that the Greeks might sail to the Hellespont, destroy the bridges, and trap him with his army in Greece. So he sent the Persian fleet to guard the bridges over the Hellespont. The Greek fleet gave chase for a day; Themistocles and the Athenians wanted to destroy the Persian fleet and the bridges and punish the Persians for their destruction of Athens. The allies, however, argued that it was better to let Xerxes leave Greece rather than run the risk that he might win if forced to fight. Themistocles secretly sent Xerxes another deceitful message, this time saying that out of friendship for the Persian king, he, Themistocles, was doing everything possible to ensure that the Greeks did not destroy the bridges over the Hellespont but that Xerxes should hurry to use them.

The Greeks placed a high value on what they called *metis*, a combination of cunning, problem solving, deceit of enemies, elan, wisdom, and pluck. In Greek myth, Odysseus was the great possessor of *metis*; his trick of the Trojan horse was the height of its use. Themistocles displayed *metis* continuously, and his part in the Greek success in 480 was widely recognized. After the battle of Salamis, no one was awarded the *aristeia*; the Greek admirals voted on whose contribution was most important to the outcome and whose was second most important. Each one voted for himself as most important, but all of them gave their second-place vote to Themistocles.

Xerxes returned to Asia with much of his army, but he left behind a large force under Maradonius. In 479 B.C., the Greek land forces won a decisive victory at Plataea, and the Spartans were able to penetrate the bodyguard of Maradonius and kill him. On the afternoon of the same day, according to Herodotus, the Greek fleet attacked the Persians at Mycale, where the Persian ships had been beached, destroying their triremes and capturing their camp. The Ionian Greeks with the Persian forces did not fight this time for the Persians; in fact, most of the Ionians turned on them. On this occasion the gambit Themistocles had initiated after Artemisium the year earlier bore fruit. The Persian invasion of Hellas ended, but the threat remained for many years.

We know as much as we do about the war between the Persians and the Greeks because Herodotus wrote about it and in doing so added history—in ancient Greek, *historia* meant inquiry—to human expression. Herodotus was born in an Ionian city in what is now Turkey in about 484 B.C. He traveled extensively and lived in Athens during the early stages of the Peloponnesian Wars. He took care to transmit what he had heard, but he went further and shaped his materials into the story of a clash between two civilizations. Herodotus presented the Persians as slaves to Xerxes and the Greeks as free men fighting to preserve their freedom. He gave prominence in his history to anecdotes that show the arbitrary behavior of Xerxes and his tendency to reduce the people around him to sycophants out of fear for their lives. Repeatedly he reports episodes of people executed on a whim by Xerxes. Herodotus evaluated some of the information he presented, but many of the stories he included seemed to later generations too incredible to believe. A few ancient authors referred to Herodotus as a "liar," but he was revered by the ancient Greeks and the Romans after them, and busts of him were to be found in many places in the ancient world. Archaeological evidence discovered in the past century has validated much that he recorded.

Earliest known Olympic games	Battle of Marathon	Silver find at Athenian mines; decision to build the navy	Persian invasions; Battles of Thermopylae, Salamis	Greek victories at Plataea, Mylcale
776 B.C.	490 B.C.	483 B.C.	480 B.C.	479 B.C.

1. An **egregious** act of vandalism is one that is flagrant, outrageous. Why? Because *egregious* combines the ideas of out (*ex*, shortened to *e*) and group (*greg*). An egregious act is committed out in front of the group, flagrantly.

2. One of the eight parts of speech is the **conjunction**. The term *conjunction*, like many others, is self-defining. A conjunction is a word that joins (*junct*) together (*con*) two words or two groups of words.

3. The word **abrupt** is used to indicate a change that is sudden and pronounced. But to feel the full descriptive force contained in the word, consider that *abrupt* describes the event that breaks (*rupt*) away (*ab*) from the present course. So *abrupt* implies both a suddenness and a violence. It is a breaking away.

4. Words sometimes make strange logic-mates. What do an ancient **mariner** and a **marinated** dish have in common? They are both pickled in brine!

5. What does an **exclamatory** sentence do? We typically answer with a definition such as that it shows strong emotion. But a breakdown of the word itself offers a more vivid, equally clear answer. An exclamatory sentence cries out (*clam*), way out (*ex*).

6. A **Micropoem**: Sometimes a word has an unexpected sharp edge. An **exclusive** club is not merely one that is fashionable and expensive; it is one that admits some people and closes (*clud*) out (*ex*) others. Politicians sometimes land in controversy over their membership in exclusive (out-closing) clubs.

7. It is possible for language to raise questions about the spirit. For example, is it consistent for a **congregation** (together/group) to practice **segregation** (apart/group)? Do these words express antithetical ideas? Are the ideas irreconcilable?

8. We say that clear glass is a **translucent** substance. Why? Because photons of light (*luc*) can cross (*trans*) through the glass without being turned back by the atoms in the glass. This light-crossing allows us to see what is on the other side of the glass.

9. **Spanish Cognates**: One of the most important observations to gain from the study of the etymology of English vocabulary is that English and Spanish share thousands of words that are cognates—related words—that have common origins. Often, the English and the Spanish words share not only a stem but even more than one stem, and often in the same order. As examples, here are some English words from this lesson and their Spanish cognates:

    germinal : germinal
    aggregate : agregar
    declaim : declamar
    conjunction : conjunción
    secret : secreto
    translucent : translúcido
    bigamy : bigamía
    mediterranean : mediterráneo

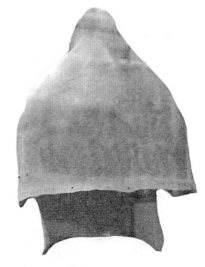

This is a bronze helmet made in the Thracian style and used by many Greek warriors.

In each case below, one of the choices was really the word used by the author in the sentence provided. All of the choices can be found in the example words on the first page of this lesson. Your challenge is to decide which word the author used. This is not a test; it is more like a game because more than one word choice may work perfectly well. See if you can use your sensitivity and intuition to guess correctly which word the author used. You may need a dictionary.

1. **From Henry David Thoreau's *Walden***

   Its water is green and _____ as ever.
   a. occluded
   b. gratuitous
   c. astringent
   d. pellucid

2. **From Martin Luther King, Jr.'s *Why We Can't Wait***

   The spread of unemployment had visible and _____ dimensions.
   a. egregious
   b. translucent
   c. tangible
   d. nonplussed

3. **From Aldous Huxley's *Brave New World***

   Primroses and landscapes...have one grave defect: they are _____.
   a. gratuitous
   b. intangible
   c. precluded
   d. primeval

4. **From Maya Angelou's *I Know Why the Caged Bird Sings***

   When I saw he was fairly _____ I went to the car.
   a. pyrophobic
   b. gregarious
   c. lucid
   d. deliberate

5. **From Marjorie Kennan Rawlings's *The Yearling***

   A loose sack was filled with agates and _____ stones.
   a. translucent
   b. primeval
   c. germane
   d. contemporary

Herodotus

"This is the presentation of the inquiry [historia] of Herodotus of Halicarnassos, to the end that neither the deeds of men may be forgotten by lapse of time, nor the works great and marvelous, which have been produced some by Hellenes and some by Barbarians, may lose their renown, and especially that the causes may be remembered for which these waged war with each other."

—Herodotus

numer	*(number)*	enumerate, numeral, numerous, supernumeraries, numerology	*Latin*
fort	*(strong)*	fortitude, fort, fortify, fortification, comfort, forte, fortissimo, pianoforte	*Latin*
osteo	*(bone)*	osteopath, osteology, osteopathy, osteoblast, osteocyte, osteotomy	*Greek*
ornith	*(bird)*	ornithology, ornithologist, ornithopter, ornithomancy, ornithosis	*Greek*
polis	*(city)*	metropolis, megalopolis, police, polite, policy, acropolis, necropolis	*Greek*
fus	*(pour)*	transfusion, infusion, refuse, fusillade, fusion, infuse, confusion	*Latin*
ego	*(I)*	egomaniac, egocentric, egotistical, egotist, egotize, egoism, alter ego	*Latin*
spir	*(breathe)*	inspire, respiration, perspiration, expire, spirit, aspire, conspire	*Latin*
dia	*(across)*	diagonal, diameter, dialogue, dialect, diatribe, diaphanous, dialectic	*Greek*
acr	*(sharp)*	acrimonious, acerbity, acrid, acridine, acrimony, acerate	*Latin*
acro	*(high, point or tip)*	acrobat, acronym, acropolis, acrophobia, acromegaly, acrocarpous	*Greek*
culp	*(blame)*	culprit, culpable, exculpate, inculpate, exculpatory	*Latin*
derm	*(skin)*	dermatologist, dermatitis, pachyderm, hypodermic, ectoderm, endoderm	*Greek*
zo	*(animal)*	zoo, protozoa, zoophilous, zooplankton, zoophagous, Mesozoic, zodiac	*Greek*
per	*(through)*	perception, perforation, percolate, perambulate, peregrination	*Latin*
pac	*(peace)*	pacify, pacific, pacifist, pacifier, pacifism, Pax Romana, pacification	*Latin*
brev	*(short)*	brevity, abbreviation, breve, breviary, brevirostrate, brief	*Latin*
necro	*(death)*	necropolis, necromancer, necrophobia, necrotic, necrobiosis	*Greek*
urb	*(city)*	urban, urbane, suburbs, urbanite, urbanologist, urbanism	*Latin*
pugn	*(fight)*	pugnacious, repugnant, pugilist, impugn, oppugn, inexpugnable	*Latin*
ecto	*(outer)*	ectoderm, ectozoa, ectomorph, ectothermic, ectoplasm, ectoparasite	*Greek*
plasto	*(molded)*	plastic, dermoplasty, rhinoplasty, plaster, plasticity, plastid	*Greek*
agog	*(leader)*	demagogue, pedagogue, synagogue, agogics, pedagogy, mystagogue	*Greek*
cle	*(small)*	molecule, corpuscle, follicle, minuscule, ventricle, particle, vesicle	*Latin*
il	*(not)*	illegal, illiterate, illicit, illogical, illegible, illiberal	*Latin*

ad

to • toward • nearness

The Latin stem **ad**, which we define as meaning *to*, can have a wide variety of meanings and is sometimes altered to **ac**, **af**, **an**, **al**, **ar**, or **ag**. Though **ad** often means *to*, it can mean *toward*, *addition to*, or *nearness to*. Here are some of the interesting words that contain **ad** in its various shades of meaning:

adapt:	to adjust. The species adapted for survival on the fourth planet.
ad infinitum:	to infinity. The tedious debate over rules dragged on and on, *ad infinitum*.
adjacent:	adjoining. Bobby Fischer heard Petrosian's phone ring in the adjacent room.
adduce:	cite as proof. She adduced three examples as proof of her position.
ad nauseam:	to a disgusting extreme. The star-struck host praised the celebrity *ad nauseam*.
affinity:	close relationship. They were related by affinity—not by consanguinity.
affluence:	rich abundance. Ellison's *Invisible Man* was not about an affluent protagonist.
agglutinate:	stick together. The sesquipedalian word was an agglutination of small words.
allege:	to claim without proof. He was innocent of the crimes alleged against him.
alleviate:	to lighten. Dr. Frankenstein refused to alleviate the monster's loneliness.
annul:	to invalidate. He immediately annulled the decrees of the former emperor.
annex:	to incorporate. The dictator intended to annex all adjacent nations.
arriviste:	an upstart parvenu. The old-money families scorned the pretentious arriviste.
arrogate:	to claim unrightfully. He arrogated to himself the benefits due to others.
accession:	attaining. Macbeth's accession to the throne was an evil accomplishment.
adjure:	to entreat solemnly. Hamlet's mother adjured him to remain in Denmark.
adscititious:	added externally. Adscititious data contradicted the initial internal findings.
advertent:	attentive. The students listened, intent and advertent, to the poet's every word.
adverse:	opposed. The national mood was adverse to her program for rigorous schools.
adjunct:	a secondary addition. She viewed vice-president as a fawning adjunct.
ad hoc:	for a special purpose. She appointed an *ad hoc* committee to investigate.

1. Please **enumerate** your reasons.

2. Her character is one of great personal **fortitude**.

3. The **osteologist** was called in for consultation on his bone condition.

4. **Ornithology** is a science for the bird lovers of the world.

5. **Metropolitan policy** called for the **police** to be **polite**.

6. The stubborn old man **refused** to have the blood **transfusion**.

7. Vic is not just **egocentric**; he is an **egomaniac**.

8. The ancient poet was **inspired** by the Muse of poetry.

9. Ralph expected a pleasant **dialogue** but received a scathing **diatribe**.

10. The **acrimonious** dispute was disturbing to everyone.

11. The unfortunate **acrobat** suffered from **acrophobia**.

12. Unfortunately, the **culprit** was **exculpated** and escaped punishment.

13. A **pachyderm** rarely suffers from dermatitis on its trunk.

14. Does the **zoo** have a **protozoan** exhibit with microscopes to look through?

15. The **perforations** let water **percolate** through the membrane.

16. The angry **pacifists** were not **pacified** by the president's militaristic speech.

17. A long discursive speech lacks **brevity**.

18. If you have **necrophobia**, avoid the **necropolis**.

19. The wealthy **urbanite** in Chicago had **urbane** manners.

20. His **pugnacious** attitude was **repugnant** to his peace-loving friends.

21. **Ectothermic** species enjoy the summer warmth.

22. A plastic surgery question: "Is **rhinoplasty** a form of **dermoplasty**?"

23. Is a corrupt politician a **demagogue** or a **pedagogue**?

24. Is a blood **corpuscle** larger than a **molecule**?

25. Your corrupt suggestion is both **illegal** and **illogical**.

intuition

1. What would be a good way to give a **metropolis**, or even a **megalopolis**, a more personal, more human feel? Could there be a practical, inexpensive way that no one has thought of?

2. What associations do you have with the word **plastic**? What rises in your mind when you think of that word?

emotion

1. Explain the emotions described by the word **acrimonious**.

2. Does the word **illiterate** have any emotional connotations?

aesthetics

1. What do you regard as the most beautiful bird? If you were an **ornithologist**, what bird would you most like to study? Have you seen John James Audubon's paintings of the birds of North America?

2. Think about movement. What adjectives describe the way a **pachyderm** moves? What adjectives would describe the movement of a single-celled **protozoa**? What adjectives would describe the movement of an **ornithopter**? Of a **pugilist**?

synthesis

1. One of the words in List #7 is **acropolis**. How many different ways of thinking can you combine in an attempt to know as much as possible about the acropolis? You could analyze the word itself; you could think historically; you could think like an architect; like an artist; like a poet; you could consider the religious function the acropolis once served; you could think like a scientist considering the effects of environmental pollution on ancient buildings; you could think like an engineer; like….

2. Use at least five words from List #7 to describe good principles of **pedagogy**.

divergence

1. **Enumerate** the harms that can come to a person who is **egocentric**.

2. What survival advantages can you think of that a **pachyderm** has as a result of its thick skin? List as many as possible. List some that are only possible advantages you aren't sure of. List some that are merely humorous.

This marble omphalos *(navel) is an ancient copy of the original used to mark the center of the Earth at Delphi: literally the navel of the world. It was erected at the purported meeting point of two eagles released by Zeus from opposite ends of the world. The original* omphalos *was wrapped in a woolen net; on this copy the net is represented in stone.*

THE PELOPONNESIAN AND DELIAN LEAGUES

Dr. Thomas Milton Kemnitz

The day after the victory at Mycale, the Spartans and the Athenians disagreed about strategy. The Spartans were more insular and defensive; they were content to drive the Persians across the Hellespont. They thought the Ionian cities that had given rise to the trouble with Persia were indefensible militarily and that the inhabitants should be relocated to Europe. The Athenians denounced the idea of abandoning the cities in Asia Minor; they wanted to pursue the Persians and punish them for the invasion of Greece. Viewing the Persian threat as extinguished, Themistocles now regarded the Spartans as the major rival and threat to Athens, but always concerned about the interests of Athens against every other city, he floated the idea of immediately destroying the fleets of the other Greek polities (yesterday's allies against the Persians) so Athens would have unchallenged control of the seas.

Many Greeks feared Persian reconquest of the Ionian cities and Cycladic Islands, and the Athenians used that to organize the Delian League, named after the island of Delos where it met and its treasury was housed. The Delian League was a nautically-oriented defensive alliance comprising the Ionian cities, the Greek islands, and various polities of Greece. All of the members were expected to provide either ships and crews or money to the League; most paid for protection; the Athenians provided the preponderance of naval power.

During the ensuing twenty-five years, many members found the Delian levy onerous, and some rebelled; the Athenians attacked them and forced them to submit, tear down their city walls, relinquish their triremes, and continue to pay the tax. The offending members lost their votes in the Delian League, and Athens continued to use the income to build and maintain its fleet. By degrees, Athens became the ruler of a large empire, with tribute flowing in to maintain its forceful control over client states. In 454 the Athenians moved the treasury from Delos to Athens and began to use the revenues for whatever they pleased. By degrees Athens became not only a preeminent naval power but also a *polis* that subjugated other Greek states.

A navy was very expensive. The Greek warship, the trireme, was named for its three banks of oars, which were its principal means of propulsion. The wooden ships were expensive to build and difficult to maintain. About 200 men were on each trireme, including 170 oarsmen who had to be skilled, disciplined, and fit. The trireme was long, relatively narrow, and sleek; the rowers could maintain about six miles an hour for an entire day. Triremes carried masts and sails that might be used on long journeys but were left ashore if a battle was imminent. The trireme had a bronze-covered ram at its bow just below the water line, and ramming another trireme was the most effective means of crippling an enemy ship. Grappling hooks and boarding parties also were used in naval warfare. Only skilled oarsmen made the trireme an effective warship because crippling an enemy trireme depended upon speedy maneuvering to get into position. It took long hours of practice to develop a crew capable of the maneuvers necessary to engage the enemy successfully. Crews had to be paid. In committing itself to a navy, Athens was committing itself to maintaining a professional military service composed of paid volunteers. Previously, the Spartans had been the only Greek polity supporting a military of full-time professionals. It was inevitable that Athens and Sparta should come to regard the other as rivals; no other Greek city matched their military power.

Greek victories at Plataea, Mylcale	Delian League formed	Themistocles ostracized	Cimon ostracized	Delian treasury moved to Athens
479 B.C.	478/477 B.C.	472/471 B.C.	461 B.C.	454 B.C.

1. **METROPOLIS : NECROPOLIS ::**
   a. condominium : cemetery
   b. acropolis : acrophobia
   c. acronym : pseudonym
   d. megalopolis : necrotic

2. **EXCULPATE : CULPRIT ::**
   a. illiterate : liberal
   b. enumerate : acrid
   c. abbreviate : ornithopter
   d. liberate : oppressed

3. **PUGILIST : PUGNACIOUS ::**
   a. mystagogue : religious
   b. dermatologist : dermatitis
   c. police : police
   d. pedagogue : pedant

4. **ECTOTHERMIC : ENDOTHERMIC ::**
   a. dermoplasty : rhinoplasty
   b. heterotrophic : autotrophic
   c. acrimonious : acerbic
   d. infuse : refuse

5. **OSTEOPATH : OSTEOTOMY ::**
   a. surgeon : surgery
   b. pedagogue : chalk
   c. ectozoa : ectoplasm
   d. demagogue : election

6. **BIRD : ORNITHOLOGY ::**
   a. ichthyologist : fish
   b. fish : ichthyologist
   c. fish : ichthyology
   d. necrotic fish : bird

7. **PACHYDERM : HYPODERMIC ::**
   a. dermatologist : ectoderm
   b. giraffe : telescope
   c. pedagogue : demagogue
   d. synagogue : mystagogue

8. **URBAN : URBANE ::**
   a. metropolitan : suave
   b. illiterate : illicit
   c. egotistical : egocentric
   d. fortify : fortitude

9. **ACROBAT : ACROPHOBIA ::**
   a. acronym : pseudonym
   b. acropolis : bibliophile
   c. merchant : agoraphobia
   d. demagogue : claustrophobia

10. **PROTOZOA : PACHYDERM ::**
    a. zooplankton : sequoia
    b. pacific : Pax Romana
    c. plastic : dermoplasty
    d. ectozoa : minuscule

These Greek bronze arrowheads have fins and barbs to make them devastating weapons capable of causing massive trauma to any part of the body they penetrated. If the initial hit or the act of removing one of these arrowheads did not prove quickly fatal, the unlucky warrior still faced the likelihood that infection would follow, and a lingering death from gangrene would result.

1. A **Micropoem**: We know that to be an **inspired** artist is to be moved by a profound need and ability to create. But there is an image of great beauty contained in the word **inspiration**. The ancients, like many creative people today, felt that their creative powers were not purely their own but that somehow they were able to receive their visions from forces beyond themselves. They believed in the Muses, beautiful goddesses of art, poetry, and music who provided the human artist with inspiration as a gift. Imagine the solitary poet, working late into the night, straining to find the word, sound, or image that will raise his poem to a state of beauty. He doesn't hear the Muse come into the room behind him; he doesn't feel a thing as she breathes (*spir*) the creative spirit into (*in*) him. But he has become in-spired, and as his poem comes to life, he realizes what has happened.

2. Sometimes words that we regard as dignified academic or scientific terms actually have an almost laughable worldliness. The highly specialized cardiologist examining the patient's heart finds himself listening to the right **ventricle**, literally the little (*cle*) belly (*ventri*)! And what does a **muscle** look like? It looks like a little (*cle*) mouse (*mus*) running under the skin!

3. **Egocentric** is an enjoyable adjective. It pictures the overly self-impressed person as the center of a sort of ego-system, with everything and everyone else in orbit around him in concentric circles. I (*ego*), this adjective claims, am the center (*centri*) of the universe. Sorry, Copernicus.

4. When we give a baby a **pacifier**, we are trying to make (*fy*) peace (*pac*) with the little guy, who is in a state of war.

5. **Expire** is a vivid and poignant verb. It describes the breathing (*spir*) out (*ex*) of one's last breath.

6. Words sometimes contain instructions for doing things. In order to find a **diameter**, we simply measure (*meter*) across (*dia*).

7. Burial customs vary with climate and terrain. In moist, cool climates with soft earth, burial underground is common. But in some desert areas, where the sun is blazing and the near-zero humidity dries everything quickly, a traveler might come upon a **necropolis**. This is a city (*polis*) of the dead (*necro*) where people have constructed rooms above ground to contain human remains. As the years pass and the number of rooms rises, the necropolis begins to resemble a true city.

8. Some words are based on historical attitudes that may even be prejudicial. A **polite** person, the word implies, is one with city (*polis*) manners, not country manners.

9. **Spanish Cognates**: One of the most important observations to gain from the study of the etymology of English vocabulary is that English and Spanish share thousands of words that are cognates—related words—that have common origins. Often, the English and the Spanish words share not only a stem but even more than one stem, and often in the same order. As examples, here are some English words from this lesson and their Spanish cognates:

fortification : fortificación
egocentric : egocéntrico
culpable : culpable
peregrination : peregrinación
urbane : urbano
repugnant : repugnante
demagogue : demagogo
follicle : folículo
minuscule : minúsculo

The larger arrowhead is Persian and was found at the site of the Battle of Marathon, as were the smaller arrowheads that came from the arrows of Scythian mounted archers. The Scythians were Persian allies from north of the Black Sea.

In each case below, one of the choices was really the word used by the author in the sentence provided. All of the choices can be found in the example words on the first page of this lesson. Your challenge is to decide which word the author used. This is not a test; it is more like a game because more than one word choice may work perfectly well. See if you can use your sensitivity and intuition to guess correctly which word the author used. You may need a dictionary.

1. **From T.S. Eliot's *Murder in the Cathedral***

   Here I have come, forgetting all _____.
   a. egotism
   b. perambulation
   c. acrimony
   d. pugnacity

2. **From Nathaniel Hawthorne's *The Scarlet Letter***

   Roger Chillingworth possessed all, or most, of the attributes above _____.
   a. inculpated
   b. enumerated
   c. respirated
   d. peregrinated

3. **From Upton Sinclair's *The Jungle***

   The _____ bartender was one of the most trusted henchmen of the Democratic leader.
   a. pacifist
   b. pedagogue
   c. pugilist
   d. diaphanous

4. **From Washington Irving's *The Legend of Sleepy Hollow***

   The hair of the affrighted _____ rose upon his head with terror.
   a. pedagogue
   b. urbanite
   c. osteopath
   d. necromancer

5. **From John F. Kennedy's *Profiles in Courage***

   Thomas Hart Benton was an unyielding and pompous _____.
   a. pacifier
   b. egocentric
   c. supernumerary
   d. demagogue

A very small representation of a long-haired Spartan warrior

sed	*(sit)*	sedentary, sediment, sedan, sedative, sedate, supersede, assiduous, insidious	*Latin*
leg	*(read)*	legible, legend, illegible, legendary, legibility, alleged	*Latin*
anim	*(mind)*	equanimity, animal, animated, animosity, magnanimous, animadversion	*Latin*
tort	*(twist)*	contorted, torture, tortuous, retort, distort, torturous, tort	*Latin*
nym	*(name)*	homonym, acronym, pseudonym, anonymous, patronymic, eponym	*Greek*
sanct	*(holy)*	sanctity, sanctimonious, sacrosanct, sanctuary, unsanctioned, sanctify	*Latin*
meta	*(change)*	metamorphosis, metaphor, metaphysics, metastasize, metabolism	*Greek*
petr	*(rock)*	petrify, petroleum, petrology, petroglyph, petrophilous, petrochemical	*Latin*
mir	*(wonder)*	miracle, mirage, mirror, mirabile dictu, admire, mirabilia, miracle play	*Latin*
man	*(hand)*	manual, manicure, manipulate, manacles, amanuensis, legerdemain	*Latin*
rect	*(right)*	correct, rectitude, direct, rectilinear, rectangle, rectify, rector, erect	*Latin*
volv	*(roll)*	revolve, involved, devolve, convoluted, volvox, revolution, volvulus	*Latin*
demi	*(half)*	demigod, demitasse, demisemiquaver, demimonde, demirep	*Latin*
retro	*(backward)*	retroactive, retrofire, retrogress, retrospection, retrofit, retrorse	*Latin*
sens	*(feel)*	sense, sensitive, sensation, sensory, extrasensory, insensate	*Latin*
fy	*(make)*	fortify, rectify, horrify, solidify, reify, transmogrify, sanctify, pacify	*Latin*
ocul	*(eye)*	binocular, monocular, ocular, oculist, oculomotor nerve, oculometer	*Latin*
cur	*(care for)*	cure, curator, curative, cure-all, sinecure, secure, curate	*Latin*
ultra	*(beyond)*	ultramarine, ultraconservative, ultraviolet, ultramundane	*Latin*
oid	*(appearance)*	android (droid!), anthropoid, asteroid, adenoid, xyloid, haploid	*Greek*
gest	*(carry)*	gestation, digest, ingest, congestion, gesticulate, gesture	*Latin*
apt	*(fit)*	adapt, aptitude, maladapted, adaptation, aptly, aptness	*Latin*
tact	*(touch)*	tactile, contact, tactful, intact, tactility, taction	*Latin*
voc	*(voice)*	vociferously, vocal, sotto voce, invocation, vocabulary, convocation	*Latin*
rid	*(laugh)*	ridicule, deride, derision, risibility, ridiculous	*Latin*

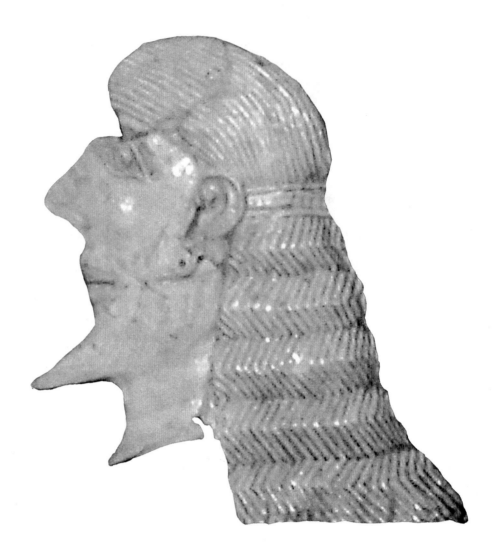

Spartan men grew their beards, shaped them to a point, and shaved their upper lips, a custom not generally followed elsewhere. It is possible that the Spartans distinguished themselves by shaving precisely because it hurt to do so, and they were showing their disdain for pain. After marriage, Spartan men grew their hair very long, as this small carving shows. Xerxes's scout reported that the Spartans were caring for their hair before the Battle of Thermopylae; they clearly had plenty to keep them busy. The fashion seems to have been to wear their hair down to the middle of their backs, to hold it in place with a variety of headbands and hair clips, and often to braid it.

Sparta was situated in the agriculturally richest valley in Greece along the Eurotas River; the area was known as Laconia, and the Spartans were also known as Lacedaemonians. The Spartans had invaded the Messina valley to their west, conquered and enslaved the inhabitants, and turned the produce of the land to Spartan enrichment. Sparta controlled much more land and much more fertile land than any other Greek polity, and that was key to making its way of life possible. Kalamata olives come from the Messina valley and from Laconia. They are twice the size of other Greek olives, but the trees are susceptible to cold and do not thrive in the rest of Greece.

SPARTA AND THE EDUCATION OF BOYS
Dr. Thomas Milton Kemnitz

Sparta was the preeminent land power among the Greeks for nearly three centuries beginning about 650 B.C. It was never a great city, but it had an effective war culture. Herodotus commented, "Their city is not built continuously and has no splendid temples or other edifices; it rather resembles a group of villages, like the ancient towns of Hellas." Sparta lies in an almost impenetrable valley where the need for defensive walls was eliminated, and hence the people were free to live in dispersed communities. In ancient myth, the unique organization of Sparta was said to be the work of Lycurgus, whose reputation as a lawgiver is enduring. It appears that the Spartan way of life came after a series of civil disturbances in the ninth and eighth centuries B.C. convinced people that a change was necessary. Lycurgus was credited with developing a planned society radically different from every other Greek city. The success of Sparta was greatly admired in the Greek and in the wider ancient world.

Lycurgus was said to value three virtues: military fitness, equality among citizens, and austerity. Sparta was organized as a communal society to foster these virtues. The land was divided into 9,000 lots, and each family was given one. Austerity and equality were made to go hand in hand with prohibitions on ostentatious display. Lycurgus banned gold and silversmiths, as well as craftsmen who created decorations, such as painters of pots or walls. Gold and silver coins were not allowed in Sparta. Regulations about how doors and ceilings were made precluded the possibility of elaborately decorated homes. Meals were served in mess halls, which were the prime units for Spartans, not their homes.

Spartan life was aimed at the success of the community as a whole. At birth, babies were examined to determine if they were healthy enough to be allowed to survive; the weak or deformed were left to die in a mountain pass. Spartan education for boys—called the *Agoge*—was harsh and designed to fortify character and toughness. At age seven, boys went to live in barracks where in primitive conditions they learned discipline, athletics, survival skills, hunting, weapons use, and endurance. The boys slept on mats made of rough reeds that they gathered themselves. They had little in the way of blankets. They were given one cloak for the year; they did not get shoes. Spartans went barefoot. They bathed in the Eurotas River winter or summer; no Spartan heated water for baths. They were expected to endure pain, cold, heat, hunger, and other hardships without complaint. Their rations were sparse; they were expected to supplement by stealing. If they were caught, punishment was severe. The story of the Spartan youth with the fox cub hidden under his cloak who endured the pain of being eaten alive by the fox rather than cry out was legend even in ancient times. Some fighting between the boys was encouraged; the elders watched them closely to see who would emerge as leaders. Punishment included flogging; crying out in pain would increase the punishment.

At the age of twenty the elite among them were sent out with a knife and expected to live off the land. If they could afford to, they were invited to join a mess and become full Spartan citizens, meaning that they became soldiers; they would eat their evening meal in the mess until at age sixty they were excused from further military duty. The soldiers ate, slept, and trained with their fellows. A man in good standing at thirty years of age was allowed to live with his wife and children.

	Battle of Marathon	Sparta receives a prophecy at Delphi	Silver find at Athenian mines; decision to build the navy	Greek victories at Plataea, Mylcale
600–490 B.C. Archaic Period	490 B.C.	485 B.C.	483 B.C.	479 B.C.

re

again • back • anew

The Latin stem **re**, which we usually define as meaning *again*, can also mean *back* or *anew*. It is one of the most common prefixes in English, which is not surprising since, as human beings, we exist in a continuum of time and memory that makes us aware of the againness of our experiences. The list of words beginning with **re** stretches for pages in any college dictionary. Here are some of the interesting words that contain **re** in its various shades of meaning:

rebate:	to give back. The company rebated ten percent of the purchase price.
rebut:	to refute. His mendacious testimony was rebutted by three witnesses.
recalcitrant:	defiant of authority. Athena's recalcitrant nature incurred Jove's anger.
recluse:	solitary person. The great poet Emily Dickinson lived as a recluse.
recoup:	to get back. She recouped her investment when the profits rose.
recreant:	a cowardly traitor. The unctuous recreant pretended loyalty to King Lear.
redoubt:	a stronghold. The Hobbit watched as the goblins stormed the redoubt.
redux:	restored. The diffident protagonist, redux, had survived his adventures.
refection:	refreshment. Light refections were served after the ceremony.
refurbish:	to renovate. Jane gradually refurbished Rochester's mansion.
rejoinder:	an answer. They were unprepared for Churchill's swift rejoinder.
relapse:	to fall back. After the seeming improvement, he suffered a serious relapse.
relucent:	bright. The beach shimmered with relucent reflections.
remand:	to send back. He was remanded into custody to await trial.
replicate:	a reproduction. They were unable to accurately replicate the reported effect.
repatriate:	send to country of birth. Eventually, most expatriates repatriate.
repugnant:	offensive. The skinhead's ethnocentric views were repugnant to decent citizens.
reprehend:	to reprimand. He was sternly reprehended for his reprehensible deeds.
retinue:	assistants. The naive king never suspected traitors among his retinue.
retentive:	having good memory. Her retentive powers were legendary.
revivify:	put new life into. His commitment was revivified by the victory.

1. His **sedentary** job left him weak and out of shape.

2. The college student's handwriting was **illegible**.

3. The bitter **animosity** made him lose his **equanimity**.

4. The **tortuous** highway was **torture** to drive.

5. NATO, RADAR, SCUBA, and OPEC are **acronyms** made of initials.

6. For many Americans, the principles of democracy are **sacrosanct**.

7. The werewolf is famous for his **metamorphosis** from man-shape to wolf-shape.

8. Is the **Petrified** Forest a desert?

9. After the surgery, it was a **miracle** to look in the **mirror**.

10. After the **manual** labor, she needs a **manicure** to restore her hands.

11. Follow the **directions** if you want the correct answers.

12. The wheels of the Volvo slowly **revolved**.

13. The beautiful near-human **demigod** drank from a dainty **demitasse** cup.

14. The class reunion left me in a sentimental, **retrospective** mood.

15. The explorer could **sense** the presence of the beast.

16. It is time to **solidify** the gains we have made before they evaporate.

17. Primates are known for **binocular** vision, which helps them judge distances.

18. The **curator** of the Pacific Museum cared for the Polynesian artwork.

19. Which color do you prefer: **ultramarine** or **ultraviolet**?

20. If an **asteroid** resembles a star, what does an **android** resemble?

21. **Congestion** is an unpleasant symptom of a cold.

22. It can be difficult to **adapt** to a new environment.

23. The electrodes sparked at the point of **contact**.

24. The noisy crowd made **vociferous** objections to the announcement.

25. When she was **derided** by her friends, she responded with **ridicule**.

analysis

1.   If the British refer to an eighth note in music as a quaver, what do they mean by a **demisemiquaver**?

2.   Why is it logical that **supersede** is spelled with *s-e-d-e* instead of *c-e-d-e*?

evaluation

1.   Do you think that some people's lives give them the right to be **sanctimonious**, or is a sanctimonious posture always unmerited?

2.   Which is worse: to be **pusillanimous**, or to be insincerely **magnanimous** in order to impress people? Or do you think that "insincerely magnanimous" is a self-contradiction?

intuition

1.   If you had the magic power to **metamorphose** into the shape of any living creature, what three creatures would you like to become first?

2.   If you could afford an **android**, what would you like it to do for you?

emotion

1.   What emotions do you associate with these words: **ridicule**, **manipulate**, **torture**, **sacrosanct**, **petrify**, **extrasensory**, **vociferous**, and **anonymous**?

2.   When you are in a **retrospective** mood, what do you usually think about? What feelings does that bring out in you?

aesthetics

1.   Which words in List #8 have pretty sounds? Which words sound scratchy or hard?

2.   Which words in List #8 sound cool? Which words sound hot? List at least five of each, and place them side by side. Could you make a poem out of these words?

The four-horse chariot was the ultimate in Greek sophistication. The horses always are depicted as harnessed side by side rather than as pairs in tandem. On this vase Nike is the charioteer. It seemed fitting that the gods should drive such a conveyance.

1. **PSEUDONYMOUS : ANONYMOUS ::**
   a. magnanimous : equanimity
   b. famous : infamous
   c. false : unknown
   d. homonym : acronym

2. **ANDROID : ANTHROPOID ::**
   a. animal : pachyderm
   b. sedative : sedentary
   c. robot : ape
   d. ridicule : deride

3. **VOCIFEROUS : SOTTO VOCE ::**
   a. manicure : manacle
   b. torturous : tortuous
   c. gesture : gesticulate
   d. loud : soft

4. **SUPERSEDE : REPLACE ::**
   a. sanction : authorize
   b. tactics : contact
   c. oculist : ocular
   d. sensory : extrasensory

5. **SENSITIVE : INSENSATE ::**
   a. legible : illegible
   b. asteroid : star
   c. xyloid : haploid
   d. horrify : reify

6. **AMANUENSIS : MANACLE ::**
   a. contact : tactic
   b. equanimity : animal
   c. anomaly : anonymous
   d. rector : binocular

7. **CURATOR : CURATE ::**
   a. museum : congregation
   b. sinecure : manicure
   c. anomaly : curiosity
   d. ultraviolet : ultramarine

8. **SACROSANCT : RIDICULOUS ::**
   a. holy : risible
   b. gestation : congestions
   c. metamorphic : amorphous
   d. sedate : stolid

9. **RETROGRESS : PROCEED ::**
   a. *sotto voce* : vociferous
   b. rectitude : rectilinear
   c. android : anthropoid
   d. anomaly : abnormality

10. **MAGNANIMOUS : PUSILLANIMOUS ::**
    a. maladapted : adapted
    b. sacrosanct : ridiculous
    c. insensate : extrasensory
    d. sedate : sedentary

The premier event at the Olympics was the four-horse chariot race. As far as we know in the entire Olympic history of nearly a thousand years of games in the ancient world, only one event was won by a woman, and she was a Spartan named Cynisca who entered her own team in the chariot race and won in 396 and 392. She erected a monument to mark her achievement. The owner of the horses and chariot was awarded the victory, not the charioteer.

71

1. The stem *meta* is a difficult stem to explain in a simple way. Sometimes it means change, sometimes afterwards, and sometimes beyond. Be flexible in your interpretation.

2. When a job provides a comfortable income but contains few responsibilities, we call the job a **sinecure**. Even though the word originally had an ecclesiastical meaning concerning the curing of souls, it is still true that a sinecure in the modern sense is a job without (*sine*) a care (*cur*).

3. Are you a **secure** person? Then you are also without (*se*) unnecessary cares (*cur*).

4. There are echoes of the past in many words. A **mirror** is a common object today, one that shows a reflection of a person's face. But there was a time when a good mirror was a new invention, when people had never seen their own faces as well as they had seen the faces of others, and in those days a mirror still had the power to strike a person with wonder (*mir*). We still use the term **admire** (wonder at) to describe how one regards oneself in the mirror. In modern times mirrors have sometimes been shown to primitive tribes who had no experience of them, and this event caused a great sensation among the tribespeople.

5. In mathematics we use exponents to raise numbers to higher powers. We occasionally do something similar inside a word. To **sanctify** something is to make it holy, and a **sacred** place is a holy place. To regard something as **sacrosanct**, therefore, is to consider it doubly holy, or holy^2. We achieve this point by bolting together two stems that both mean the same thing: holiness. **Cascade** is a similarly constructed word; it literally means fall (*cas*) fall (*cad*).

6. Don't confuse the words **tortuous** and **torturous**. They both contain the stems *tort* (twist) and *ous* (full of), but tortuous means full of twists (a tortuous highway), and torturous means full of torture (a torturous journey).

7. You might think that **supersede** means go (*cede*) over (*super*) and that the *c* in *cede* has been changed to an *s*. But actually, the word is based not on *cede* but on *sed*, meaning sit. Something that supersedes over-sits, or replaces, what has come before.

8. **Spanish Cognates:** One of the most important observations to gain from the study of the etymology of English vocabulary is that English and Spanish share thousands of words that are cognates—related words—that have common origins. Often, the English and the Spanish words share not only a stem but even more than one stem, and often in the same order. As examples, here are some English words from this lesson and their Spanish cognates:

assiduous : asiduo
equanimity : ecuanimidad
sanctimony : santimonio
sacrosanct : sacrosanto
sanctuary : santuario
metamorphosis : metamorfosis
rectify : rectificar
ultramarine : ultramarino
vociferous : vociferante

This amphora shows a stylized black-figure scene of a boxing match.

In each case below, one of the choices was really the word used by the author in the sentence provided. All of the choices can be found in the example words on the first page of this lesson. Your challenge is to decide which word the author used. This is not a test; it is more like a game because more than one word choice may work perfectly well. See if you can use your sensitivity and intuition to guess correctly which word the author used. You may need a dictionary.

1. **From James Hilton's *Lost Horizon***

   It was his fate in life to have his _____ always mistaken for pluck.
   a. sanctimony
   b. assiduity
   c. derision
   d. equanimity

2. **From George Orwell's *1984***

   His froglike face grew calmer, and even took on a slightly _____ expression.
   a. anomalous
   b. sanctimonious
   c. vociferous
   d. sacrosanct

3. **From H.G. Wells's *The Invisible Man***

   "What am I to do?" asked Marvel, _____.
   a. metaphorically
   b. insidiously
   c. *sotto voce*
   d. maladapted

4. **From Jane Austen's *Pride and Prejudice***

   She threw a _____ glance over the whole of their acquaintance, so full of contradictions.
   a. contorted
   b. retrospective
   c. maladapted
   d. risible

5. **From John Knowles's *A Separate Peace***

   It was the opposite of a(n) _____; it was all work and no advantages.
   a. sinecure
   b. convocation
   c. amanuensis
   d. curator

path	*(feeling)*	sympathy, pathetic, pathos, telepathy, empathy, apathy, idiopathy	***Greek***
a-	*(not)*	amoral, amorphous, atheist, apathy, agraphia, apolitical, aphasia, achromatic	***Greek***
nomy	*(law)*	astronomy, economy, Deuteronomy, taxonomy, heteronomy, nomothetic	***Greek***
fid	*(faith)*	infidel, fidelity, confidence, diffident, bona fide, fiduciary, perfidy	***Latin***
caco	*(bad)*	cacophony, cacography, cacodemon, cacoëthes, cacodyl, cacology	***Greek***
hetero	*(different)*	heterodox, heteromorphic, heterogeneous, heterosexual, heteronym	***Greek***
sci	*(know)*	science, conscience, prescience, omniscience, scientism, sciolist	***Latin***
graph	*(write)*	bibliography, photograph, autograph, polygraph, stenography	***Greek***
lat	*(side)*	bilateral, unilateral, lateral fin, multilateral, collateral, latitude	***Latin***
lith	*(rock)*	neolithic, paleolithic, lithograph, megalith, monolith, lithium, laccolith	***Greek***
tract	*(pull)*	tractor, detract, retraction, attractive, protractor, contract, traction	***Latin***
in	*(in or not)*	inscribe, insane, infidel, indefinite, incorrigible, insomnia	***Latin***
co	*(together)*	cooperate, coordinating, coterminous, colloquy, coauthor, cotangent	***Latin***
phile	*(love)*	philosopher, audiophile, bibliophile, philologist, philanthropy	***Greek***
ine	*(nature of)*	porcine, crystalline, saturnine, canine, ursine, vulpine, bovine	***Greek***
-ar	*(relating to)*	pulsar, stellar, lunar, solar, secular, columnar, linear, circular	***Latin***
hexa	*(six)*	hexagram, hexagon, hexapod, hexameter, hexahedron, hexarchy	***Greek***
fract	*(break)*	fracture, infraction, fraction, refraction, refractory, fractious	***Latin***
platy	*(flat)*	plateau, platyhelminthes, platypus, plate, platitude, platyrrhine	***Greek***
theo	*(god)*	theology, pantheism, atheism, monotheism, apotheosis, henotheism	***Greek***
fin	*(end)*	final, define, infinite, finial, finis, Finisterre, infinitive, fin de siecle	***Latin***
hedron	*(sided object)*	polyhedron, tetrahedron, heptahedron, octahedron, icosahedron	***Greek***
ambul	*(walk)*	ambulatory, somnambulism, funambulist, ambulance, perambulate	***Latin***
ous	*(full of)*	luminous, glorious, loquacious, vivacious, garrulous, anomalous, zealous	***Latin***
topo	*(place)*	topographical, topology, topic, topiary, toponym, topognosia	***Greek***

pro

forward • before • for

The Latin stem **pro**, which we usually define as meaning *forward*, actually can mean *before* or *for*. Furthermore, there is also a Greek stem **pro** that means *before*. Here are some of the interesting words that contain **pro** in its various shades of meaning:

procumbent:	lying face-down. They took a procumbent position in the tall grass.
progeny:	offspring. The father's physiognomy was written on the faces of his progeny.
profuse:	generous. There was something suspicious about his profuse apology.
prognathous:	projecting in the jaw. The prognathous jaw gave him a vaguely equine visage.
prolepsis:	anticipating. In brilliant prolepsis, she refuted his case before he even made it.
prolocutor:	a spokesperson. A green prolocutor stepped forth from the alien craft.
propitiate:	to appease. Achilles sacrificed an ox to propitiate the sensitive gods.
propagate:	to breed. Many species were unable to propagate in the deforested area.
pro rata:	proportionate. The spoils were divided on a *pro rata* basis.
propound:	to propose. Frederick Douglass propounded a series of antislavery policies.
proselyte:	a convert. The cult's proselytes were oblivious to the ominous implications.
protuberant:	bulging. The children's protuberant stomachs revealed the pain of the famine.
provident:	showing foresight. Their provident labor gave them ample food for the winter.
prospect:	a vista. From the hilltop, Hannibal had a prospect of the Roman army.
pronominal:	of a pronoun. Demonstrative adjectives have a pronominal function.
propaedeutic:	elementary instruction. The table of basic facts had propaedeutic value only.
pro patria:	for one's country. He regarded his career as a *pro patria* obligation.
prologue:	introductory remarks. The play begins with a prologue by the protagonist.
procryptic:	having protective coloration. The moth's bark-shade was a procryptic effect.
proboscis:	a trunk. Cyrano's proboscis reminded Christian of an elephant's trunk.
prodigy:	a genius. The young chess prodigy's combinations crushed the grandmaster.

1. The **pathetic** child received **sympathy**.

2. The unexpected **anomaly** was **amorphous** in shape and **atypical** in structure.

3. What is the difference between **astronomy** and **agronomy**?

4. Does a **diffident** person have self-**confidence**?

5. If **cacophony** hurts the ear, what sense organ does **cacography** hurt?

6. The **heterogeneous** mixture of odd substances had a noisome odor.

7. If **science** could give us **prescience**, would it be a good idea to know the future?

8. Would you like a **photograph** of my **autograph**?

9. Is this treaty **bilateral** or **multilateral**?

10. Did the **Neolithic** age come before the **Paleolithic** age?

11. The shiny red **tractor attracted** many buyers.

12. Please **inscribe** something **insane** in my yearbook.

13. He refused to **cooperate** with the **copilot**.

14. My friend, the **audiophile**, has a wonderful collection of recordings.

15. The **crystalline** substance began to evaporate.

16. The **lunar** surface is bombarded by **solar** rays.

17. What is the difference between a **hexagram** and a **hexagon**?

18. It's an **infraction** of the rules to **fracture** someone's nose.

19. The **platypus** has a **plate**-like bill.

20. The Greek **pantheon** of gods was not a **monotheistic** religious system.

21. Is outer space **infinite** or **finite**?

22. Is a **tetrahedron** a cube or a pyramid?

23. Can an **ambulatory** hospital patient **somnambulate** without waking up?

24. The **luminous** moonlight was **glorious** to behold.

25. The **topography** of the region was a fascinating **topic**.

synthesis

1. Can you find two example words in List #9 that have the same or closely related meanings? See if you can find five pairs of related terms.

2. Can you find five adjectives in List #9 that could be used to describe the same person, place, or thing? List the adjectives, and tell what they describe.

divergence

1. How many gods can you name from the Greek **pantheon**? Can you recall what each god was known for? Now, what powers can you think of that none of the gods in the pantheon had? List as many missing powers as possible.

2. Can you think of ten humorous causes of **insomnia**? More than ten?

analysis

1. Think about the word **topognosia**, and try to guess its meaning. Then look it up in an unabridged dictionary, and see how close your guess is.

2. What is the difference between a **lithograph** and a **petroglyph**? You may need a dictionary to solve this one.

evaluation

1. Which person has a richer, more fulfilling life: a **bibliophile** or an **audiophile**? Even though there can be no absolute answer to such a question, can you give an answer that seems probable to you? How would you even begin to think about such a question?

2. Do you think it is moral, **amoral**, or immoral for a corporation to require its employees to take a **polygraph** test?

intuition

1. Where would you choose to **amble** or **perambulate** if you could be instantly transported to the location of your choice?

2. What would be a creative way to cure **insomnia**?

These are the remains of the stadium at Delphi, where the Pythian games were held every four years.

This small statuette of a girl involved in athletics is quintessentially Spartan. Physical fitness was emphasized in Sparta for girls and young women. Spartan women had the reputation of being the most beautiful in all of Greece and also of being the most independent in their actions and affections. Helen of Troy was a Spartan woman, and her example and legacy were not lost on later Spartan women.

In the seventh and sixth centuries B.C., the Spartans made many statues and a good deal of pottery. This was the work of the Periocei, the free people who lived in Spartan territory but who were not full Spartan citizens. These statues would not have been made if the Spartans had not wanted them to be. While some statuary exists from the early fifth century, little was made after the middle of the century.

SPARTAN LIFE
Dr. Thomas Milton Kemnitz

It is possible to focus on the physical hardships of Spartan education to the exclusion of other areas. Apparently poetry, dance, music, song, and philosophy were an integral and abundant part of it. Spartan children were taught to express themselves tersely and thoughtfully. They were trained to think of the common good. Girls were educated also; their curricula included physical fitness as well as literature and the arts. There were games and athletic contests for girls, just as there were for young men. Women were considered an important part of Sparta, and they had more freedom and were better educated than women anywhere else in Greece.

The governance of Sparta gave each man a sense that he had a voice in the community. All Spartan men older than thirty had a vote in the Assembly. The Assembly chose a senate whose members were at least sixty years old and who were elected for life. The senate put forward laws for the Assembly to pass or reject. Each year the Assembly elected five *ephors* (overseers) who presided over the senate and Assembly and put forward legislation about education and moral conduct. A Spartan became an *ephor* only for a year and only once in his life; relatively young men could be elected as *ephors*. Sparta had two kings who ruled simultaneously; the kings of Sparta were primarily military leaders; policy was largely decided by the senate and *ephors*.

Only citizens became soldiers, and only they were able to vote in the Assembly; they were the ones who could trace their families back to the original Spartans. Below them were a class of freemen called *Periocei* who were not citizens but who functioned as merchants and who organized commercial life. Below them were the *Helots*, the serfs, most of whom were Greeks who were the descendants of people who lived in the Messina valley to the west of Sparta and who had been enslaved when the Spartans took their territory.

There were many more Helots than citizens in the Spartan state. The problem for the Spartans was keeping the Helots from revolting. In 464 B.C. a major earthquake provided the opportunity for a Helot revolt. Sparta had to seek assistance from other Greek cities to put it down. Each autumn the *ephors* declared war on the Helots, a legal shield to allow for the killing of them by *cryptes*, an elite group of boys who had reached eighteen years of age. The *cryptes* were given a knife and sent out into the countryside with instructions to steal the food they needed, to spy on the Helot population, and to kill any Helot out after dark or who seemed likely to rebel.

The Spartans were reluctant to go to war for long for fear of a Helot uprising, and they devised various strategies for eliminating potential Helot leaders. Thucydides tells of an event in 425 B.C. when the Helots were invited by a proclamation to select those of their number who had most distinguished themselves so that they might receive their freedom, the object being to identify the first to claim their freedom because the Spartans believed they would be the most likely to rebel. About 2,000 Helots were selected, allowed to rejoice in their new freedom, and then disappeared without any explanation. When they were not outright killing the Helots, the Spartans found many ways to humiliate them. One practice noted by ancient writers was to make a Helot drink unwatered wine (the Greeks added water to their wine so as not to get drunk) until he was drunk and then bring him to the mess halls to sing songs that were described as "low." This was a means the Spartans used to engender in their youth an abhorrence of drunkenness, as well as a way of demeaning the Helots.

Delian League formed	Themistocles ostracized	Battle of Eurymedon	Earthquake at Sparta; Helot revolt begins	Cimon ostracized
478/477 B.C.	472/471 B.C.	469 or 466 B.C.	464 B.C.	461 B.C.

1. **PERFIDY : FIDELITY ::**
    a. luminous : luminary
    b. loquacious : garrulous
    c. cacophony : euphony
    d. funambulist : somnambulist

2. **HEXAHEDRON : HEXAGON ::**
    a. triangle : pyramid
    b. polyhedron : cube
    c. topology : topognosia
    d. cube : square

3. **VULPINE : PORCINE ::**
    a. clever : gluttonous
    b. fox : grapes
    c. telegraph : photograph
    d. ignominious : glorious

4. **SATURNINE : VIVACIOUS ::**
    a. calligraphy : cacography
    b. apathy : empathy
    c. bibliophile : audiophile
    d. pantheism : henotheism

5. **OMNISCIENCE : PRESCIENCE ::**
    a. pantheism : monotheism
    b. multilateral : prelude
    c. omnivorous : anteroom
    d. all-knowing : foreknowledge

6. **CRYSTALLINE : AMORPHOUS ::**
    a. octahedron : tetrahedron
    b. topology : topiarist
    c. polyhedron : polygon
    d. glorious : ignominious

7. **INFIDEL : MONOTHEIST ::**
    a. diffident : confident
    b. telepathy : empathy
    c. multilateral : unilateral
    d. detract : retract

8. **PLATYHELMINTH : PLATYPUS ::**
    a. plateau : platitude
    b. worm : marsupial
    c. mammal : science
    d. crystalline : canine

9. **COLLOQUY : LOQUACIOUS ::**
    a. somnambulism : ambulatory
    b. plateau : flat
    c. octahedron : eight
    d. toponym : noun

10. **HETERODOX : ORTHODOX ::**
    a. vivacious : zealous
    b. divergence : adherence
    c. infraction : refractory
    d. conscience : omniscience

These are jumping weights, which Greek athletes used in the long jump. Unlike the running start in the current event, the Greeks must have jumped from a standing start. The weights were used to give the jumper added momentum. There is some speculation that the athletes made a series of jumps—perhaps five—to see who got the farthest. If that is the case, the weights would have provided not only momentum but also an aid to balance. Many sets of the weights have been found, varying between three and five pounds. The weights were made differently for the left and right hands.

1. We sometimes say that terms like *a lot* are **colloquial**, meaning that they are conversational—too informal to be used in a formal research paper. What does *colloquial* literally mean? It refers to the sort of language you use when you talk (*loqu*) together (*co*).

2. A **Micropoem**: If a **platypus** is a flat-billed critter, what is a **platitude**? It is a flat remark, one that is stale and uninteresting, trite. A platitude is a FLATitude! The ironic point about platitudes is that they are usually uttered as though they were novel and witty. Ho hum.

3. Everyone knows that **polygraph** is the scientific name of the lie detector test. But why is the lie detector test known as the polygraph, since *poly* means many and *graph* means write or record? The answer is that the polygraph is an instrument that makes a record of many different things simultaneously as the subject answers questions. The polygraph records changes in blood pressure, pulse rate, respiration, and other factors.

4. A person who is **saturnine** is a person with a personality in the nature of (*ine*) the planet Saturn. Saturn is distant, cold, dark, and cloudy. You wouldn't like it there, and a saturn-like person is not much fun to be around either.

5. Like animal crackers, animal adjectives are small but tasty. With animal adjectives you can describe a huge man as **ursine** (bearlike), a gobbling eater as **canine** (doglike), a messy slob as **porcine** (piglike), or a person with long, protruding jaws as **equine** (horselike). A crafty person could be **vulpine** (foxlike), and a predatory person might be **lupine** (wolflike). Although these adjectives have wonderful impact, they can be cruel, so it is best to use them with care.

6. **Spanish Cognates**: One of the most important observations to gain from the study of the etymology of English vocabulary is that English and Spanish share thousands of words that are cognates—related words—that have common origins. Often, the English and the Spanish words share not only a stem but even more than one stem, and often in the same order. As examples, here are some English words from this lesson and their Spanish cognates:

    apathy : apatía
    perfidy : perfidia
    cacophony : cacofonía
    omniscient : omnisciente
    incorrigible : incorregible
    fracture : fractura
    monotheism : monoteísmo
    somnambulism : sonambulismo
    topographical : topográfico

Boxing was a Greek sport often depicted on vases. Prowess in boxing was valued for its relationship to hand-to-hand combat, as well as for the ability of the individual victor in the agonia. The Greeks used strips of leather to make boxing gloves. This black-figure amphora made in Athens about 550 B.C. shows a match in progress; the boxer on the left is bleeding from his nose.

In each case below, one of the choices was really the word used by the author in the sentence provided. All of the choices can be found in the example words on the first page of this lesson. Your challenge is to decide which word the author used. This is not a test; it is more like a game because more than one word choice may work perfectly well. See if you can use your sensitivity and intuition to guess correctly which word the author used. You may need a dictionary.

1. **From Rachel Carson's *Silent Spring***

    The budworm populations, instead of dwindling as expected, have proved _____.
    a. refractory
    b. incorrigible
    c. vulpine
    d. saturnine

2. **From Bram Stoker's *Dracula***

    It was that his cast of face made his smile look malignant and _____.
    a. loquacious
    b. garrulous
    c. saturnine
    d. diffident

3. **From E.L. Doctorow's *Ragtime***

    He had the _____ of the amateur before the professional.
    a. omniscience
    b. diffidence
    c. insomnia
    d. somnambulism

4. **From Jack London's *White Fang***

    In San Quentin prison he had proved _____.
    a. anomalous
    b. vivacious
    c. multilateral
    d. incorrigible

5. **From Toni Morrison's *Song of Solomon***

    She was as tranquil as he was agitated, as monosyllabic as he was _____.
    a. garrulous
    b. heterodox
    c. prescient
    d. fractious

ped	*(foot or child)*	orthopedist, pedagogue, centipede, expedition, pedestrian, pedestal	*Latin*
mort	*(death)*	mortal, mortician, mortified, immortality, mortuary, moribund	*Latin*
carn	*(flesh)*	carnivorous, incarnate, reincarnated, carnival, carnation, carnage	*Latin*
psych	*(soul)*	psychology, psychic, psychopathic, parapsychology, psychosis	*Greek*
ethno	*(race or culture)*	ethnocentrism, ethnic group, ethnography, ethnologist	*Greek*
gen	*(origin)*	genetics, hydrogen, progeny, engender, gene, ingenuous, indigenous	*Greek*
nat	*(born)*	prenatal, native, natural, nativity, nation, nascent, natal, perinatal	*Latin*
paleo	*(old)*	paleozoic, paleolithic, paleontologist, paleoanthropic, paleography	*Greek*
curs	*(run)*	cursive, discursive, incursion, precursor, cursory, cursorial, cursor	*Latin*
crypt	*(hidden)*	cryptic, cryptologist, crypt, cryptogram, encrypt, cryptesthesia	*Greek*
cad	*(fall)*	cascade, cadaver, cadence, cadenza, cadaverous, decadent	*Latin*
capit	*(head)*	decapitate, capital, recapitulate, capitulation, capitulum	*Latin*
loqu	*(talk)*	loquacious, circumlocution, eloquent, soliloquy, somniloquy	*Latin*
sacro	*(holy)*	sacrosanct, sacred, sacrifice, sacrament, sacrilege, consecrate	*Latin*
uni	*(one)*	unicycle, universe, united, union, uniform, unison, unique, unicorn	*Latin*
ness	*(quality)*	softness, redness, politeness, kindness, darkness, vagueness	*Old English*
alt	*(high)*	altitude, alto, altimeter, altar, altocumulus, altiplano	*Latin*
ics	*(art)*	politics, economics, aesthetics, graphics, ethics, calisthenics	*Greek*
iso	*(equal)*	isothermal, isometric, isosceles, isomer, isocracy, isotope	*Greek*
vert	*(turn)*	convert, revert, inverted, divert, vertex, controvert, extrovert, introvert	*Latin*
ate	*(cause)*	domesticate, implicate, create, procreate, insinuate, placate, dominate	*Latin*
cor	*(heart)*	core, concord, discord, misericord, cordial, courageous	*Latin*
ess	*(female)*	lioness, empress, princess, baroness, seamstress, governess	*Greek*
muta	*(change)*	mutant, mutation, mutagenic, mutable, transmutation, immutable	*Latin*
fug	*(flee)*	centrifuge, fugitive, tempus fugit, subterfuge, refugee, fugue	*Latin*

sub

under • beneath • below

The Latin stem **sub**, which we define as meaning *under*, actually can have a wide variety of meanings and is sometimes written as **suc, suf, sug, sum, sup, sur**, and even **sus** in order to blend with the stem that follows it. Though **sub** often means *under*, it can mean *beneath, below, lower, somewhat*, or even *inferior*. Here are some of the interesting words that contain **sub** in its various shades of meaning:

subcutaneous:	beneath the skin. He was troubled by a subcutaneous infection.
subduct:	to draw downward. She swam against the subduction in the offshore current.
sublunary:	under the moon. The lovers enjoyed a beautiful sublunary dance.
sublimate:	to express acceptably. The urge of the id can find creative sublimations.
submontane:	at the foot of the mountains. The submontane vegetation was more lush.
subtle:	not obvious. Subtle clues told her to avoid asking about the problem.
subvert:	to overthrow. They worked to subvert the established regime.
substratum:	foundation. His peaceful humility was founded on a substratum of religion.
subsistence:	bare survival. They survived at a subsistence level by gathering food.
subaqueous:	underwater. The subaqueous habitation gradually developed into a city.
subservient:	obsequious. The toady's subservient fawning irritated her.
subtrahend:	number subtracted. The deduction was a fearful subtrahend from the check.
surreptitious:	done in secret. The plans were made at a surreptitious meeting in the Alps.
suffuse:	to fill with color. Becky Thatcher's face was suffused with embarrassment.
suffrage:	voting. Women's suffrage began very late in American history.
succinct:	brief and clear. Her succinct description impressed them all.
suggest:	to mention. He suggested a solution, but no one listened.
suffocate:	to smother. Small businesses were being suffocated by federal regulations.
suspend:	to hang. The bridge was suspended from massive cables.
sustain:	maintain. They were unable to sustain their initial enthusiasm.
summon:	order to appear. The peremptory summons was ignored.

1. The **orthopedist** went on an African **expedition**.

2. The **mortician** was **mortified** at the sight of the **mortal** wound.

3. The **carnivorous** beasts of Venus are **reincarnated** after death.

4. The **psychologist** viewed the **parapsychologist** with suspicion.

5. **Ethnocentrism** is disturbing to all **ethnic** groups.

6. The **geneticist's** hobby was studying **pathogenic** substances.

7. **Prenatal** care is important to **natives** in **natural** environments.

8. The **paleontologist** was an expert on the **Paleozoic** Era.

9. The **discursive** speech gave only **cursory** attention to the problem.

10. The **cryptologist** worked all night to break the enemy secret code.

11. The **cadaver** was discovered near the rushing **cascade**.

12. **Decapitation** was once a common form of **capital** punishment.

13. The **loquacious** bore answered every question with a **circumlocution**.

14. The hero's **sacrifice** was a **sacrosanct** memory.

15. The **United** Planets of the **Universe** soon celebrate their **union**.

16. The sky's **redness** and the clouds' **softness** were beautiful.

17. The broken **altimeter** no longer measured the **altitude**.

18. Computer **graphics** enhance books on **politics** and **economics**.

19. The **isothermal** piedmont region escaped the extremes of temperature.

20. The new **convert** soon **reverted** to his previous views about **advertisement**.

21. To **calibrate** one's response is to **obviate** one's apology.

22. The extreme **discordance** of viewpoints prevented **concord**.

23. The **lioness** ate the **empress** but not the **princess**.

24. The post-war **mutants** lived in a **mutagenic** atmosphere.

25. "*Tempus fugit*," said the escaped **fugitive** caught in the whirling **centrifuge**.

Pictured on the left are wooden auloi, which were two pipes that were played together at one time by one player. Reeds were inserted in the end of the pipes. They are often pictured on Greek vases such as the one here from Sparta (note the long hair on the pipe player). The auloi apparently produced a sound like an oboe. The Spartans marched into battle to the tune of these instruments.

They would advance on the enemy slowly in a disciplined line that often struck fear into their adversaries, who on many occasions fled before battle was joined. Apparently the slow and measured pace of their advance was particularly frightening. The hoplites of other armies often ran into battle, charging their enemy at a trot or full run, as the Athenians had at Marathon. One reason to run into battle was to limit exposure to arrows, javelins, and sling shot; it was not desirable to shoot arrows or fling javelins if your hoplites were within inches of the enemy, but until the lines came together, advancing troops were easy targets. Another reason to charge into battle might be to engage before fear or prudence could overtake the warrior. However, the Spartans came slowly, unafraid of arrows and javelins and sling shot and certain of their courage in the impending engagement. If their enemies lost their nerve and fled, the Spartans did not pursue. In ancient battles the huge casualties occurred once the line was broken and one side fled; the fleeing soldiers were cut down from behind by their pursuers. By not giving chase, the Spartans allowed their opponents to think better of the fight and to escape with their lives, an outcome they would not be assured once battle was joined. The Spartans won many battles without a fight on the strength of their discipline and the sound of their auloi.

SPARTAN CHARACTER

Dr. Thomas Milton Kemnitz

Spartan men did not work, either in trades or in agriculture. The existence of Helot serfs allowed the Spartans to devote themselves to affairs of state, to physical fitness, to preparing for battle, and to discussions of topics of interest to them. Apparently a great deal of the education of the youth and the conversation of the adults was about what was and was not proper conduct. An enormous premium was put on character in Sparta; only physical prowess and character distinguished one Spartan from another.

Sparta was often praised by the ancient Greeks for many of its qualities. Philosophers such as Socrates, Plato, and Aristotle found much to admire. First and foremost was its emphasis on the character of the individual. Sparta was held in high esteem for the calm order of its society, which often contrasted with the disorder of other polities, particularly with the unruly behavior of the Athenian Assembly and juries. The absence of ostentatious display and luxury appealed to many. Some ancient writers praised the quality of the unadorned furniture that came from Sparta. The *Agoge* was thought to develop good and virtuous citizens. The prohibitions on overindulgence appealed to many; the self-control the Spartans exercised was widely admired. Others were taken with the economy of language with which the Spartans expressed themselves. Never was the conciseness more evident than when Philip of Macedonia sent a message to Sparta inviting it to submit to his *hegemon* and saying that if he entered Laconia, he would raze Sparta. The Spartans responded with a succinct single word: "If."

Sparta avoided many problems and wars because it did not have a class of people who desired to enrich themselves by plunder. When the Spartans fought, their objectives were generally clear and relatively limited, and they were successful. The Spartan organization created a remarkably effective war machine because it had the only full-time soldiers. Generation after generation of Spartans went undefeated in battle. The army of the Greeks during the second Persian invasion was under Spartan leadership because the Spartans were the professionals and were most proficient at warfare. Indeed, their participation was so important that Themistocles ceded to Sparta the command of the navy, though Sparta had few ships, and when battle came on the seas, it was Themistocles and the Athenian ships that were the most important.

It is remarkable that most of what Sparta valued was transient and has vanished. There is nothing left of their music or dance, their physical fitness or athletic prowess, their courage or their capacity to endure pain or their abilities in war. Character is important, and we know a great deal about the character of many ancient Greeks; in this capacity the Spartans stand out and were acknowledged by their contemporaries to be outstanding. But their furniture has vanished along with their simple houses. Their city was without great monuments, so there is less to see than at other ancient sites. There is very little Spartan literature.

Sparta was clearly a preeminent city. The Spartans had the attention and respect of their fellow Hellenes. It was as men of war and statecraft and character that they were respected, and for that we have the testimony of others. The Spartans lived in Laconia, from which we get the adjective *laconic* to describe a person of few words. The Spartans were people of few words, and they left even fewer as their legacy.

600–490 B.C. Archaic Period	490–323 B.C. Classical Period	485 B.C. Sparta receives a prophecy at Delphi	483 B.C. Silver find at Athenian mines; decision to build the navy	481 B.C. Greek polities meet to form defensive strategy

emotion

1. How would you feel if you were forced to **capitulate** (Imagine the circumstances for yourself.)? How would you feel if someone were forced to capitulate to you?

2. Imagine your emotions if **mutagenic** substances were discovered in your drinking water—substances that could be traced to a nearby toxic waste dump. Who would you seek out for actions and explanations?

aesthetics

1. What sounds do these words suggest: **unison, carnival, darkness, centrifuge, refugee, sacrifice, Paleozoic, calisthenics,** and **universe**?

2. Is your artistic appreciation **ethnocentric**? Can you think of another—especially a very different—culture whose art you deeply admire?

synthesis

1. Pick an example word in List #10, and use at least three other words from the list to define the word you picked.

2. Make a **cryptogram** using words from List #10. To make it more difficult, use words from one field of thought only—use words from biology, or history, etc.

divergence

1. How many *cracy* or *archy* words can you think of that are names for different forms of government? Don't forget **isocracy**, a government in which each person has an equal amount of power to every other person. Once you have remembered as many as you can, see how many forms of government you can invent, such as the **dormocracy**: the government that seems to be asleep! Invent as many new governments as you can.

2. Have you ever been trapped by someone who wanted to talk about a subject you wished to avoid? Or who wanted to ask a question you didn't want to answer? How many clever **subterfuges** can you think of to escape such a situation? As an example: "I'd love to talk to you now, but I left a poodle in the petwash."

Apollo was the god of music and dance, and on this Athenian-made, red-figure cylix, we see him playing a kithara. The kithara was a stringed instrument more solemn in tone than the lyre. Apollo is seated on a square stool of a type frequently seen in vase illustrations; in front of him is an altar.

88

1. **SUBTERFUGE : FUGITIVE ::**
   a. circumlocution : orthopedist
   b. politics : economics
   c. lioness : empress
   d. ingenuous : indigenous

2. **UNICYCLE : UNIQUE ::**
   a. fugitive : refugee
   b. soliloquy : solitude
   c. extrovert : introvert
   d. concord : discord

3. **DIALOGUE : SOLILOQUY ::**
   a. altimeter : altitude
   b. mutagen : mutation
   c. colloquy : monologue
   d. aesthetics : graphics

4. **DOMINATION : CAPITULATION ::**
   a. decapitate : recapitulate
   b. natal : perinatal
   c. pedagogue : pedestrian
   d. rule : surrender

5. **AESTHETICS : ETHICS ::**
   a. convert : revert
   b. sacrosanct : sacred
   c. art : morals
   d. economics : psychopathic

6. **ETHNOLOGIST : ETHNIC GROUP ::**
   a. entomologist : altimeter
   b. psychologist : ethnography
   c. paleontologist : tyrannosaurus
   d. cryptologist : cryptogram

7. **CONSECRATION : SACRILEGE ::**
   a. mutagenic : immutable
   b. precursor : forerunner
   c. nascent : moribund
   d. paleozoic : paleontologist

8. **ELOQUENT : SOLILOQUY ::**
   a. ingenuous : progeny
   b. psychic : psychology
   c. incarnate : carnival
   d. grandiloquent : panegyric

9. **SOFTNESS : KINDNESS ::**
   a. roughness : ingenuousness
   b. somniloquy : discursive
   c. decadence : cadence
   d. cryptologist : encryption

10. **LIONESS : CARNIVOROUS ::**
    a. extrovert : loquacious
    b. convert : introvert
    c. sacrifice : sanguinary
    d. alto : cadenza

The auloi *were a favorite of both the Greeks and the Romans. The myth was that Athena was the originator of the* auloi, *but when she saw herself playing them reflected in a pond with her face distorted by her puffed-out cheeks, she thought she looked ugly and threw the pipes away. Immediately the satyr Marsyas snatched the pipes up and began to play them. He produced such a beautiful sound that he dared Apollo, the god of music, to a contest. The Muses were appointed judges, and they decided for Apollo, who punished Marsyas for his* hubris *by having him flayed alive. The Greeks had a wide-spread concern about* hubris—*excessive pride leading to defiance of the gods.*

1. A **Micropoem**: Has there been a recent **expedition** to the headwaters of the Amazon? A common characteristic of expeditions is suggested by the word itself: members of an expedition go out (*ex*) into the wild on foot (*ped*).

2. We all have had the displeasure of listening to **circumlocution**. That is when someone is talking (*loqu*) in circles (*circum*). But there are two main varieties of circumlocution. There is unintentional circumlocution, in which a person is talking in circles and doesn't realize it, and there is intentional circumlocution, in which someone talks in circles in order to avoid answering a question.

3. A **Micropoem**: A **subterfuge** is a clever evasion in which a person tries to avoid revealing something; it is an evasive trick, a stratagem. A literal interpretation of *subterfuge* might be to duck, in the sense of ducking a question, since *subterfuge* means to flee (*fug*) under (*sub*).

4. We say that a speech is **discursive** if it is rambling and digressive, if the speaker doesn't stick to the point. The literal meaning of *discursive*, however, is somewhat more exciting. A speech is discursive if it is a runaway, if it is out of control. The speaker has let the speech run (*curs*) away (*dis*) from him.

5. You wouldn't think that **hydrogen** would be an interesting word. Hydrogen is the name of the simplest and most common element in the universe, but on our planet we possess a wonderful hydrogen-based treasure: water. The importance of water to human life can hardly be exaggerated—even our bodies are mostly water. So when it was time to give hydrogen a name, the obvious choice was to name it after its most important role: hydrogen is the main ingredient in the creation (*gen*) of water (*hydro*). Hydrogen is the water-originator. No H, no H_2O.

6. One of the most biting terms of derision is the adjective **pedestrian**. We say that someone has pedestrian taste, or worse, a pedestrian mind. This means that the person simply never attains anything lofty or swift, graceful or elegant; he just slogs along on foot (*ped*), altitude zero, speed 1 mph.

7. The word **cadaver** is unusually poignant. All of our lives we live in the earth's gravitational field, and the vitality of our bodies allows us to resist that invisible force that constantly pulls down on us. We spend our lives exerting equal but opposite force to resist succumbing to gravity's mysterious forcefield. At the end of our lives, gravitation wins, and we fall (*cad*). A cadaver is a fallen person.

8. **Unique** is a perfectly self-explanatory word. It means precisely what its stem *uni* (one) implies. There is only one. Something cannot be rather unique; either it is one-of-a-kind and is unique, or there are other such cases, and it is not unique.

9. **Spanish Cognates**: One of the most important observations to gain from the study of the etymology of English vocabulary is that English and Spanish share thousands of words that are cognates—related words—that have common origins. Often, the English and the Spanish words share not only a stem but even more than one stem, and often in the same order. As examples, here are some English words from this lesson and their Spanish cognates:

   orthopedist : ortopeda
   reincarnated : reincarnado
   ingenious : ingenuo
   crypt : cripta
   cascade : cascada

   decapitate : decapitar
   unique : único
   ethics : ética
   indigenous : indígeno

In each case below, one of the choices was really the word used by the author in the sentence provided. All of the choices can be found in the example words on the first page of this lesson. Your challenge is to decide which word the author used. This is not a test; it is more like a game because more than one word choice may work perfectly well. See if you can use your sensitivity and intuition to guess correctly which word the author used. You may need a dictionary.

1. **From Nathaniel Hawthorne's *The House of the Seven Gables***

   I rejoice to hear so favorable and so _____ an account of my cousin Clifford.
   a. decadent
   b. loquacious
   c. ingenuous
   d. mutable

2. **From James Joyce's *A Portrait of the Artist as a Young Man***

   His life had grown to be a tissue of _____ and falsehood.
   a. subterfuge
   b. circumlocution
   c. capitulation
   d. eloquence

3. **From Mark Twain's *The Prince and the Pauper***

   He then walked up and down the room to keep his blood in motion, _____ as before.
   a. circumlocuting
   b. soliloquizing
   c. consecrating
   d. placating

4. **From Mary Shelley's *Frankenstein***

   How _____ are our feelings.
   a. mutable
   b. unique
   c. moribund
   d. nascent

5. **From Henry David Thoreau's *Walden***

   The tortoise and the frog are among the _____ and heralds of this season.
   a. ethnographies
   b. pedagogues
   c. pedestrians
   d. precursors

-i	(plural)	bacilli, fungi, nuclei, alumni, magi, octopi, gemini, homunculi, literati	*Latin*
jus	*(law)*	justice, justify, unjust, jus soli, justiciary	*Latin*
lum	*(light)*	luminary, luminous, illuminate, luminiferous, superluminous	*Latin*
ann	*(year)*	annual, superannuated, anniversary, annuity, perennial	*Latin*
apo	*(away)*	apotheosis, apogee, apoplexy, apology, aphelion, apostasy	*Greek*
sen	*(old)*	senile, senior, senator, seniority, senescent	*Latin*
sol	*(alone)*	solitude, solitary, solo, soliloquy, desolate, solipsism, solifidian	*Latin*
bas	*(low)*	bass, base, basic, basal, bassoon, debase, contrabase, abase, bas-relief	*Latin*
rogat	*(ask)*	interrogation, abrogate, derogatory, arrogate, supererogatory	*Latin*
parl	*(speak)*	parliament, parley, parlor, parlance, parlando	*Latin*
potent	*(power)*	potential, potentiometer, potentate, plenipotentiary, omnipotent	*Latin*
surg	*(rise)*	resurgence, insurgence, surge, surgent	*Latin*
log	*(word or reason)*	logic, neologism, philologist, logician, illogical, monologue	*Greek*
gram	*(writing)*	telegram, pentagram, hexagram, hologram, grammar	*Greek*
cant	*(sing)*	recant, cantata, incantation, descant, canticle, canto	*Latin*
reg	*(rule)*	regal, regiment, regulate, regent, interregnum, regicide, regime	*Latin*
pro	*(forward)*	provide, pronounce, program, prognosticate, prospect, prognosis, prolix	*Latin/Greek*
gyn	*(woman)*	androgynous, gynecologist, polygyny, misogynist, gynephobia	*Greek*
ag	*(to do)*	agile, agent, agency, agitate, aggression, aggrade	*Latin*
act	*(to do)*	transact, react, action, activate, abreact, counteract, interact	*Latin*
mob	*(move)*	mobility, mobile, immobile, mobilize, demobilize	*Latin*
sess	*(sit)*	session, sessile, insessorial, sessility, obsessed	*Latin*
fic	*(make)*	fortification, fiction, prolific, horrific, soporific	*Latin*
nounce	*(tell)*	denounce, pronounce, announce, renounce, enunciate	*Latin*
andro	*(man)*	androgynous, android (droid), androgens, androphobia, polyandry	*Greek*

trans

across • over • through

The Latin stem **trans**, which we define as meaning *across*, actually can have a wide variety of meanings and is sometimes shortened to **tra**. Though **trans** often means *across*, it can mean *over*, *beyond*, *through*, or *on the other side*. In chemistry, **trans** refers to isomers that have certain atoms or groups of atoms on opposite sides of a molecule. Here are some of the interesting words that contain **trans** in its various shades of meaning:

transalpine:	across the Alps. The Romans never suspected a transalpine invasion.
transect:	to cut across. The line he drew transected the polygon.
transitory:	not permanent. It was an intense but transitory romance.
transmute:	to change form. The transmutation in his personality amazed us all.
transpicuous:	clearly understandable. The transpicuous explanation settled the point.
transilient:	leaping from thing to thing. It was a day of abrupt, transilient changes.
transgress:	to overstep. Their reactions showed that he had transgressed some invisible line.
transfix:	to impale. Prufrock felt transfixed and wriggling on the wall.
transmigration:	reincarnation. They believed in the transmigration of souls.
transubstantiate:	change substance. She accepted the transubstantiation of the bread and wine.
travesty:	a farcical imitation. The grotesque travesty distorted his good intentions.
transverse:	crosswise. The transverse beam gave a cross-like appearance to the pillar.
transcribe:	write out. They carefully transcribed the conversation for distribution.
transpontine:	across the bridge. She gazed at the transpontine bustle across the Thames.
transpire:	to release vapor. The space suit recycled the body's transpired moisture.
transit:	passage. Something happened to the letters in transit; they never arrived.
transfigure:	change appearance. The frog was transfigured into a handsome prince.
traduce:	to defame. He was vilified and traduced by the obnoxious Philistines.
traffic:	wrongful trade. The traffic in surplus weapons benefited the rebel force.
trajectory:	flight path. He studied the trajectories of the cannon balls.
trance:	a fixed consciousness. He gazed at the board with a trance-like expression.

1. Do **bacilli** and **fungi** have **nuclei** in their cells?

2. Can a system of **justice** ever be **unjust**?

3. The **luminous** moonlight **illuminated** the **aluminum** sculpture.

4. The **superannuated** doorman celebrated his fiftieth **anniversary**.

5. Once the satellite reached its **apogee,** we could not find it with binoculars.

6. The **senior** class president befriended the not-so-**senile** old man.

7. On his **solo** transcontinental flight, he enjoyed the **solitude**.

8. **Basic** instructions are included with each new **bassoon**.

9. The **interrogation** was **derogatory** in tone.

10. Several members of **Parliament** had a **parley** in the **parlor**.

11. The **plenipotentiary** met twice with the **potentate**.

12. The **surge** of the sea portended the **resurgence** of violence.

13. The **philologist** delighted in inventing **neologisms**.

14. The **grammar** in the **telegram** was not correct.

15. During the holy man's **incantation**, the spirit began to appear.

16. There were no **regal** ceremonies in the **interregnum**.

17. The doctor's **prognosis** was not favorable.

18. The musician's **androgynous** appearance was widely imitated.

19. The secret **agent** spilled the deadly chemical **agent**.

20. There may be little time to **act** or **react**.

21. When the National Guard was **mobilized**, the **mobile** units were ready.

22. Dozens of chairs were arranged for the general **session**.

23. Is that wall supposed to be **beautification** or **fortification**?

24. **Pronounce** your **announcement** clearly.

25. The metal **android** grappled with the furry anthropoid.

analysis

1. What do you think the difference is between **misanthropy** and **androphobia** (a very rarely used word!)? Between **misanthropy** and **misogyny**? Break the words down and figure them out.

2. What is the difference between a **philosopher** and a **philologist**? Between a **regicide** and an **interregnum**?

evaluation

1. When Galileo published his discovery that the solar system was heliocentric, the church forced him to **recant**. Do you think there is ever a time when an institution or society has a right to prevent a truth from being known? Does national or social interest ever come into direct conflict with our interest in discovering truths? How can such questions be decided?

2. If you have made a firm, public commitment to some cause, do you have the right to **abrogate** your commitment if you begin to feel differently?

intuition

1. If you were the **Macrocosmic Potentate** and could make three changes in the universe—any three changes you wished—what would the changes be?

2. If you could shrink in size to one millimeter or even smaller and explore the world from a **microcosmic** perspective, what would you like to examine? What would **bacilli** and **fungi** look like on that scale?

emotion

1. Think about the subtle emotional connotations of the words **solo**, **solitude**, **solitary**, and **desolate**. What are the delicate shades of feeling that distinguish these words from each other and that allow you to choose among them in writing a poem or a short story?

2. If you could be **omnipotent** for a day, how would you feel? Scared? Excited? Stunned? What would your emotional response be?

The word acropolis *is a compound of two stems:* acro *meaning high, and* polis *meaning city. It literally was the high city of Athens where the Mycenaean rulers had built their palace, and it physically dominated Athens. Other Greek cities had similar features, and some of them called the highest hill the* acropolis.

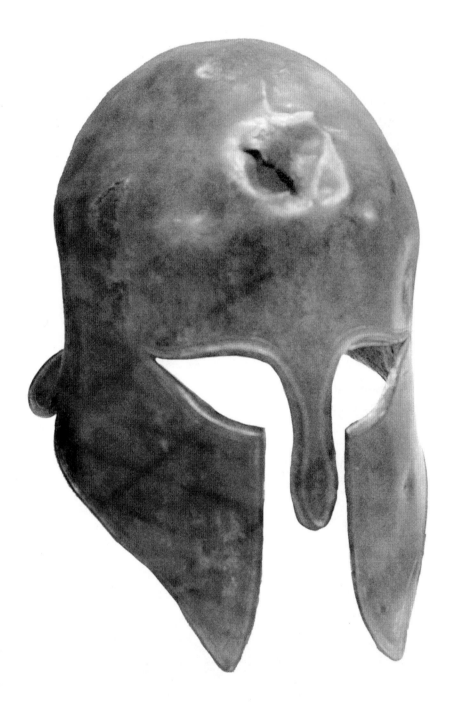

The owner of this Corinthian-type helmet may have sustained a blow from a javelin or a lance; a downward thrust from an opponent on horseback likely would have been fatal. Less lethal would have been a blow from lead shot or a stone from a sling shot. Had he been hit in the eye by shot or a stone, the blow would have been debilitating, if not fatal. The eyes were always one of the most vulnerable points for the hoplites, and many warriors' last sight was a very close-up view of the point of a missile—often an arrow or a javelin—that caused their demise.

ATHENS
Dr. Thomas Milton Kemnitz

Athens was the other significant city of ancient Greece. Unlike Sparta, which had been stable for two centuries when the Persians invaded, Athens was in the midst of fundamental alterations, both economic and constitutional. The Athenian economy had been agriculturally based, with farms stretching throughout Attica, a situation similar to the Spartan arable land throughout Laconia. Late in the sixth century, population pressures forced an increasing emphasis on trade and commerce in Athens, an avenue that Sparta was unable to take because of its constitution. Athens developed a merchant class and began to bring in craftsmen and traders from other parts of the Greek world. Already in the sixth century, Athens was the most populous polis and was becoming the leading city in Hellas in many endeavors. The red clay of Athens was superb for making pots, and Athenian pottery was eclipsing the wares of rival cities.

In the last years of the sixth century, Athens suffered a period of instability when its tyrant Hippias was overthrown. (Hippias fled to Persia, and it was he who chose Marathon as a landing point and arrived there with Darius in 490.) Cleisthenes and Isagoras emerged as rivals for power. Isagoras won the upper hand by appealing to the Spartan king Cleomenes I to help him expel Cleisthenes, whom he said was cursed. Cleisthenes left Athens, and Isagoras used his power to displace hundreds of other people from their homes on the basis that they also were cursed. When Isagoras attempted to dissolve the *Boule*, a council of aristocrats, it resisted and won support from the people, who forced Isagoras and his supporters to leave Athens. Cleisthenes was recalled, along with hundreds of exiles, and he assumed leadership of Athens. He began to set up a system of government that took advantage of the support of the *demos*, as the Greeks called the people. This was in 508/507 B.C., a year or two after a small town in Italy called Rome overthrew its king and established a republic. (Every Greek city operated on its own chronology, often numbering years by who ruled the polis. Putting the chronology of one city together with that of another is often exceedingly difficult or impossible. To add to the difficulties, the new year in some cities, including Sparta and Athens, fell in the summer, about the beginning of August.)

Cleisthenes organized Athens into ten "tribes" according to where they lived (their *deme*), replacing the traditional family clans. The *demes* were the basis of the government and were mirrored in a ten-month governing calendar, which was different from the religious calendar. Many offices in Athens would be filled by ten people, one from each *deme*, so there were ten generals, ten treasurers of the Delian League, etc. The system by which people were named was changed, so instead of getting a name based on one's father, a name was based on a *deme*. This is one reason why when the ancient Greeks talked about an individual, they usually included the information *son of so and so*, because that was the only way parentage information could be conveyed.

Cleisthenes also established legislative bodies run by individuals chosen by lottery—an interesting basis for democracy—rather than by kinship or heredity. He reorganized the *Boule* so that it had 500 members, fifty from each tribe. The members were not elected; they were selected annually by lottery from all eligible males age twenty-nine or older; the lottery meant that no one could control who served and who did not serve. Members from each *deme* served for one month during their year when they transacted day-to-day business. The members of the *Boule* took an oath Cleisthenes devised: "To advise according to the laws what is best for the people."

	Establishment of democracy in Athens	Battle of Marathon	Silver find at Athenian mines; decision to build the navy	Greek polities meet to form defensive strategy
600–490 B.C. Archaic Period	508/507 B.C.	490 B.C.	483 B.C.	481 B.C.

1. **BASE : ABASE ::**
    a. prolific : soporific
    b. mobile : immobile
    c. parley : parliament
    d. fortification : fortify

2. **TELEGRAM : PENTAGRAM ::**
    a. solifidian : desolate
    b. epistle : parallelogram
    c. solitude : solipsism
    d. apotheosis : renunciation

3. **ALUMNUS : ALUMNI ::**
    a. cantata : canticle
    b. luminous : superluminous
    c. phenomenon : phenomena
    d. mobilize : immobile

4. **PENTAGRAM : HEXAGRAM ::**
    a. senile : senior
    b. senescent : senile
    c. bilateral : trilateral
    d. prognosticate : prognosis

5. **REGIME : INTERREGNUM ::**
    a. apogee : perigee
    b. bassoon : base
    c. prose : fiction
    d. notes : intervals

6. **GYNEPHOBIA : ANDROPHOBIA ::**
    a. annual : perennial
    b. aphelion : perihelion
    c. bibliophile : agoraphobia
    d. misogyny : misanthropy

7. **PROLIX : PARLEY ::**
    a. superannuated : life
    b. regicide : interregnum
    c. react : counteract
    d. omnipotent : potentate

8. **PHILOLOGISTS : NEOLOGISMS ::**
    a. literati : fiction
    b. logician : apology
    c. magi : apostasy
    d. regent : regicide

9. **ABROGATE : TRANSACT ::**
    a. demobilize : mobilize
    b. aggression : justice
    c. philologist : philosopher
    d. bacilli : fungi

10. **MONOLOGUE : DIALOGUE ::**
    a. solo : symphony
    b. resurgence : insurgence
    c. nuclei : cells
    d. incantation : magi

The owl was native to the Acropolis, where it inhabited the caves and fissures of the rock. The Athenians adopted the bird and made it sacred to Athena. Many Athenian hoplites carried hoplons emblazoned with the white owl, and it was on one side of the Athenian silver coinage. The head of Athena was on the other side. Widely-circulated, the coins transmitted these images of Athens across the Mediterranean world.

1. A person of great power is sometimes known as a **potentate** (*potent*: power). What if a potentate requires an important business transaction to be made but cannot personally travel to conclude the transaction? In that event, the potentate may send a **plenipotentiary**, a person with full (*pleni*) power (*potent*) to transact any business.

2. Students are accustomed to studying and memorizing Hamlet's and Macbeth's famous **soliloquies**, but perhaps the students don't realize that they too give soliloquies every time they talk (*loqu*) while alone (*sol*).

3. A **Micropoem**: Imagine a music teacher telling a student to sing a song again until he sings it correctly. This is the somewhat humiliating idea behind the word **recant**. When Galileo asserted that the solar system was heliocentric (sun-centered), he was forced to recant by the church. Literally, he was forced to sing (*cant*) the tune again (*re*)—this time geocentrically.

4. Many scientific terms such as **apogee**, **aphelion**, **perigee**, and **perihelion** are self-defining—one need only understand their construction. The moon reaches apogee when it is farthest away (*apo*) from the earth (*geo*). The earth reaches aphelion when it is farthest away (*apo*) from the sun (*helio*). Perigee and perihelion are the opposite terms and simply mean near (*peri*) to the earth and sun. What does Halley's Comet look like at perihelion?

5. Some people have trouble keeping the terms **fiction** and **nonfiction** straight. It is easy to remember which is which, however, once you realize that fiction is the stuff we make (*fic*). Fiction is made-stuff, and nonfiction is not-made-stuff!

6. Some of the younger **senators** might be momentarily nonplussed (baffled) to learn that the word *senator* is closely related to the word **senile**. A **senate** was originally a council of old men who used the wisdom of age to deliberate. In modern times not all senators are old (*sen*).

7. Consider the stems *logy* and *log*. It is convenient to separate them and to maintain that *logy* means science, while *log* means either word or reason. But are these ideas really as distinct as they seem? Probably not. There are profound connections and areas of overlap among words, reason, and science. Could there be reason without words, or is reasoning a form of wording? Isn't science primarily the intense use of reason to create and arrange words? Don't almost all words using *log* or *logy* bear some deep relationship to all three definitions? It is important to make convenient distinctions, but it is also important to explore profound relationships.

8. **Supererogatory** is an interesting, double-edged word. It means above (*super*) what is asked (*rogat*). One can perform saint-like supererogatory services to mankind, or one can be wasteful and superfluous in performing needless supererogatory repetitions of an experiment.

9. **Spanish Cognates**: One of the most important observations to gain from the study of the etymology of English vocabulary is that English and Spanish share thousands of words that are cognates—related words—that have common origins. Often, the English and the Spanish words share not only a stem but even more than one stem, and often in the same order. As examples, here are some English words from this lesson and their Spanish cognates:

justice : justicia	parliament : parlamento	androgynous : andrógeno
luminary : luminaria	omnipotent : omnipotente	agile : ágil
senile : senil	neologism : neologísmo	android : androide

In each case below, one of the choices was really the word used by the author in the sentence provided. All of the choices can be found in the example words on the first page of this lesson. Your challenge is to decide which word the author used. This is not a test; it is more like a game because more than one word choice may work perfectly well. See if you can use your sensitivity and intuition to guess correctly which word the author used. You may need a dictionary.

1. **From Robert Louis Stevenson's *Treasure Island***

   The captain had been struck dead by thundering _____.
   a. apoplexy
   b. senescence
   c. omnipotence
   d. incantation

2. **From Charles Dickens's *David Copperfield***

   There was a black barge, or some other kind of _____ boat, not far off.
   a. luminiferous
   b. sessile
   c. superannuated
   d. supererogatory

3. **From William Makepeace Thackeray's *Vanity Fair***

   Honest William was left as George's _____ in London, to transact all the business.
   a. soporific
   b. plenipotentiary
   c. potentate
   d. luminary

4. **From John Milton's *Paradise Lost***

   Raphael, the affable Arch-angel, had forewarn'd Adam by dire example to beware _____.
   a. interrogation
   b. solipsism
   c. apostasy
   d. bacilli

5. **From Walt Whitman's *Leaves of Grass***

   Sprouts take and accumulate, stand by the curb _____ and vital.
   a. prolific
   b. supererogatory
   c. superannuated
   d. prolix

Battles and men at war were important, but the domestic, commercial, civic, and religious aspects of Greek life are as interesting.

an-	*(without)*	anemia, anechoic, anaerobic, anorexia, anarchy	*Greek*
ab	*(away)*	abnormal, abjure, absent, abrogate, abrupt, abduct, abdicate	*Latin*
mel	*(song)*	melody, melodrama, melodeon, melodious, melodia	*Latin*
aden	*(gland)*	adenoid, adenine, adenoma, adenovirus	*Greek*
aer	*(air)*	aerobic, aerie, aerosol, aerial, aerobes, aerodynamics, malaria	*Greek*
alb	*(white)*	albumen, alba, album, albino, albinism, albedo	*Latin*
ase	*(enzyme)*	permease, galactosidase, proteinase, luciferase	*Greek*
epi	*(on)*	epicenter, epidemic, epigram, epidermis, epigraph, epitaph	*Greek*
hum	*(earth)*	humus, exhume, posthumous, humble, humiliate, human	*Latin*
-be	*(life)*	microbe, aerobe, anaerobe	*Greek*
bon	*(good)*	bonny, bonanza, bon mot, bonus, bon vivant, bonhomie, bona fide	*Latin*
struct	*(build)*	construct, destruct, substructure, instruction, structure, infrastructure	*Latin*
chlor	*(green)*	chlorophyll, chlorine, chloroplasts, chlorella	*Greek*
cyan	*(blue)*	pyocyanin, cyanide, cyan, cyanophyta, cyanosis, cyanotype	*Greek*
cyt	*(cell)*	erythrocyte, leucocyte, cytology, cytoplasm, melanocyte	*Greek*
diplo	*(double)*	diplococcus, diploid, diplomacy, diplopoda, diplopia	*Greek*
dys	*(bad)*	dysentery, dyslexia, dystrophy, dysfunction, dysphonia	*Greek*
eco	*(house)*	ecology, economy, ecosystem, ecotone, economist, ecologist	*Greek*
emia	*(blood)*	bacteremia, anemia, hypoglycemia, toxemia	*Greek*
enter	*(intestine)*	enteritis, dysentery, gastroenteritis, enterozoan	*Latin*
erythro	*(red)*	erythrocyte, erythroblastosis, erythrism, erythromycin	*Greek*
idio	*(peculiar)*	idiot, idiosyncrasy, idiomorphous, idiom, idiot savant	*Greek*
exo	*(out)*	exotoxin, exogenous, exodus, exorbitant, exorcism, exotic, exobiology	*Greek*
im	*(not)*	impossible, impassable, improbable, imperfect, immobile, impecunious	*Latin*
fil	*(thread)*	filiform, filicineae, filament, filaria, filigree, defile	*Latin*

super

over • above • higher

The Latin stem **super**, which we define as meaning *over*, actually can have a wide variety of meanings, including *above*, *higher*, *on top of*, *greater*, or *surpassing*. The stem **supra** is a close relative. Here are some of the interesting words that contain **super** in its various shades of meaning:

superjacent:	lying on top of. They were unable to explore the superjacent structure.
superlunary:	beyond the moon. The craft sailed out to its superlunary orbit.
supernumerary:	extra. Her play was superfluous with supernumerary characters.
supernatant:	floating. They stared at the supernatant debris on the surface.
superfine:	too subtle. His argument was guilty of meaningless, superfine distinctions.
superordinate:	superior. There were superordinate issues that remained to be examined.
superpose:	to place above. Watson carefully superposed one model on top of the other.
supernal:	celestial. Einstein believed in a supernal consciousness, The Old One.
superscribe:	write on. The package arrived with his name superscribed at the top.
supervene:	to happen unexpectedly. Plans were suspended when tragedy supervened.
supersubtle:	too subtle. The point was supersubtle and was missed by the audience.
superable:	able to be overcome. Every difficulty, she felt, was superable.
superincumbent:	pressured from above. He succumbed to the boss's superincumbent demands.
superlative:	excelling all. Fischer's chess game possessed a superlative clarity and force.
superficial:	on the surface. The burn was superficial, but the wound to his pride was not.
superb:	majestic. This steep range of the Alps had a superb and rugged wildness.
supreme:	highest. The gold medal was the supreme accomplishment of her athletic life.
supraorbital:	above the eye. The Neanderthal skull had a massive supraorbital crest.
supersensible:	outside of sense perception. Tiresias possessed a supersensible vision.
supraliminal:	conscious. The subliminal fears overcame his supraliminal ideas.
supereminent:	extremely distinguished. The Nobel laureates form a supereminent class.

1.   The **anarchist** had a severe case of **anemia**.

2.   The **absentee** landlord was **abruptly abducted**.

3.   The **melodeon** played a sappy **melody** during the **melodrama**.

4.   The **adenovirus** was discovered in his **adenoids**.

5.   The pilot studied **aeronautics** and **aerodynamics**.

6.   The **albino** stared at the white pages of the blank **album**.

7.   **Luciferase** is the enzyme in the luminous organs of the firefly.

8.   Does Benjamin Franklin's tombstone **epitaph** contain a witty **epigram**?

9.   At the **exhumation**, the rich **humus** was removed from the **humble** grave.

10. **Microbes** are a favorite subject of biological studies.

11. The **bonny** lass discovered the **bonanza** by accident.

12. The **superstructure** was **constructed** in three days.

13. **Chlorine** from the pool damaged the **chlorophyll** in the plants.

14. He held the **cyanotype** to the light and admired the sharp, blue lines.

15. The **cytologist** watched the **leucocytes** and **erythrocytes** through the microscope.

16. She folded the **diploma** double and handed it to the waiting **diplomat**.

17. His **dyslexia** made it difficult for him to read words.

18. The **ecologist** was fascinated with the living things in the **ecosystem**.

19. The senator had **hypoglycemia**, not **anemia**.

20. A specialist in **dysentery** and **enteritis** explained the rare intestinal ailment.

21. The blood's **erythrocytes** are generated by **erythroblasts** in the bones.

22. The **idiot savant** was a handicapped artist with **idiosyncrasies**.

23. The crowd made a sudden **exodus** when the **exorcism** began.

24. The journey is **impossible** because the roads are **impassable**.

25. The gold **filigree** in her jewelry resembled the bright **filaments** in a light bulb.

The paraphernalia of Athenian democracy, justice, and civil life have survived, including jury identification strips, the blocks into which they fit, the wheels for casting verdicts, and such items as official weights and measures and water clocks for timing speeches. More than 100,000 vases and pieces of pottery from ancient Greece exist, but the daily life of the democracy is absent from them. They offer no depictions of the Assembly in session, orators in full flight of persuasion, or visual representation of trials. But let a hoplite blow a trumpet, and the pottery decorator was there before the last note. The heroism of warfare was regarded as noble, the daily life of a democracy too mundane to use for decoration.

Jury identification strip

This is part of a large device to select jurors by accepting or rejecting randomly an entire horizontal row of jury identification strips, which were inserted into the slots.

THE ATHENIAN DEMOCRACY
Dr. Thomas Milton Kemnitz

Athenian democracy was unlike ours in that it had no government and no elected representatives who passed laws. It was direct in that the people voted to make laws rather than electing representatives to do so. Its central body was the Assembly, composed of all the adult male citizens who had completed military training and were more than eighteen years old. It met at least once in each of the ten months of the state calendar. The Assembly held public discussion of all issues; it passed the laws, determined policy, and directed military operations. A new president of the *Boule* was chosen by lottery every day. It was the role of the *Boule* to propose laws to the Assembly. The bills proposed could be rejected, passed, or returned for amendments by the Assembly. Participation in the Assembly was not mandatory, but it seems to have been remarkably widespread. People who did not participate were called *idiotes*—from which our term *idiots* derives.

The judicial system was no less democratic than the law making. Up to 600 jurors from each *deme* were chosen for trials. Athenians eligible to sit on juries had thin brass strips with their names on them; they were inserted into a stone or wood holder, and entire rows were either accepted or rejected. There were no prosecutors or lawyers for the defense. Every participant but the accused was there voluntarily. Magistrates were drawn by lot from the *demes*. Trials were speedy; none lasted more than a day. Private trials about such matters as debts might take only an hour or so. By the middle of the fifth century, jurors were paid for their service but paid very little—only an amount significantly less than a craftsman could make in a day. Public trials might have very large juries of up to 6,001 jurors. The jurors cast their ballots by putting wheels with axles into a pot. The hollow axle was a vote for the plaintiff, the solid one a vote for the defendant or for acquittal. The jurors could hide their vote by covering the end of the axle with a thumb and forefinger. If the person who brought the charges did not receive at least twenty percent of the votes, he had to pay a fine for bringing an action that was manifestly frivolous.

The Assembly annually chose a board of ten generals who were in fact the most important people in the Athenian firmament. They came from the elite and were the wealthiest and best educated of the city. They tended to dominate the affairs of the democracy. Legislation was proposed by citizen initiators, who were from the foremost families of the city and were often the generals. But they did not control the Athenian democracy. The assignment of offices, councils, magistrates, and juries by random lots meant that important posts could be filled by anyone, and the elites could not control the choice. The immense size of juries meant that the outcome of trials was a reflection of the popular will rather than the desires of the wealthy, and it made the outcome of those trials far more unpredictable than the elites would have liked.

600–490 B.C. Archaic Period	508/507 B.C. Establishment of democracy in Athens	490–323 B.C. Classical Period	483 B.C. Silver find at Athenian mines; decision to build the navy	481 B.C. Greek polities meet to form defensive strategy

aesthetics

1. Sometimes it is possible to relish a word purely for its artistic merit, for the poetic image it conveys. The enzyme that allows a firefly's tail to glow in the dark, giving rise to spooky and wondrous summer evenings, is called **luciferase**: the devil's enzyme.

2. Imagine living in an **aerie**. How would your sense of the world, of its sounds, temperatures, colors, smells, and textures change from season to season? Why do people become fire tower operators, perched alone in tiny rooms atop high observation towers on mountain peaks?

synthesis

1. Use ten words from List #12 in a paragraph on the human body.

2. Suggest three life experiences that might combine to make someone become an **anarchist**.

divergence

1. How many things can you think of that will always be **impossible**? How many things can you think of that are **immobile**? **Impassable**?

2. Think of as many important steps as you can for specialists from the Center for Disease Control to take at the outbreak of a virulent **epidemic**.

analysis

1. We **adjure** our friends to do something, meaning that we earnestly urge them to do it. We **abjure** our former beliefs, meaning that we renounce them or give them up. Analyze the difference between these two words. Remember that to analyze something is to break it into its components and to examine the components one at a time.

2. Analyze the words **gastroenteritis** and **hypoglycemia**.

evaluation

1. It is a common principle of international **diplomacy** that nations do not search the **diplomatic** pouches of other nations. It is also common to grant the **diplomats** of other nations diplomatic immunity from prosecution for crimes. Finally, it is common to allow the foreign diplomats safe passage out of one's country—even in time of war. Should we continue to observe these policies?

This red-figure cylix is one of the very few that show what might have been an outdoor scene from the Athenian streets: a boy carrying two amphorae using a yoke to distribute the load across his shoulders. It was made in Athens about 510 B.C.

1. **ANAEROBIC : AEROBIC ::**
    a. enteritis : dysentery
    b. nontoxic : toxic
    c. filament : filigree
    d. bonus : bonanza

2. **MICROBE : MICROSCOPE ::**
    a. astronomer : telescope
    b. cyanophyta : chloroplasts
    c. astronomy : astrophysics
    d. spectrum : spectrometer

3. **ALBINO : ALBINISM ::**
    a. melodrama : cubism
    b. red hair : erythrism
    c. exodus : influx
    d. melodia : melody

4. **ENTEROZOAN : DYSENTERY ::**
    a. protozoan : protozoa
    b. erythrocyte : leucocyte
    c. pneumococcus : pneumonia
    d. diplococcus : anorexia

5. **EPIGRAM : EPIGRAPH ::**
    a. *bon mot* : inscription
    b. epitaph : phonograph
    c. diplomacy : bonhomie
    d. atrophy : dystrophy

6. **IMPECUNIOUS : PENNILESS ::**
    a. humus : earth
    b. defile : pollute
    c. construct : destruct
    d. bonny : pretty

7. **CYTOPLASM : LEUCOCYTE ::**
    a. enterozoan : protozoan
    b. building : parking lot
    c. language : idiom
    d. substance : object

8. **BON VIVANT : ASCETIC ::**
    a. instruction : construction
    b. cytology : cytoplasm
    c. idiot savant : talent
    d. sybarite : spartan

9. **ABJURE : ADJURE ::**
    a. renounce : entreat
    b. denounce : pronounce
    c. abrogate : annul
    d. abdicate : relinquish

10. **ANARCHY : NIHILISM ::**
    a. gerontocracy : pointillism
    b. exobiology : hedonism
    c. ecology : romanticism
    d. monarchy : absolutism

Domestic scenes showing women or girls in many aspects of daily life were common on pottery in the Greek world. This red-figure hydria (water jug) shows the poetess Sappho reading to a small group. It was produced in Athens about 430 B.C. One of the women on the right holds a lyre, which was often strummed when poems were read, a practice that explains the origins of the term lyric poetry.

107

1. Some have said that knowledge is power, but to the **aeronautical** engineer who is attempting to design a new aircraft by using the principles of **aerodynamics**, air (*aer*) is power (*dyna*). The pressure of air against the wings is powerful enough to lift the aircraft into the sky.

2. A **Micropoem**: Concerned citizens sometimes feel that our nation's **economy** would improve if we applied the same common sense to our financial and monetary laws that thrifty individuals have always applied to the economical laws (*nomy*) of the house (*eco*).

3. What does the word **diplomacy** have to do with the idea of double (*diplo*)? Diplomacy is largely the art of producing and conveying important state documents that, in ancient times, were known for being folded double.

4. Some words have forbidding exteriors but inside are simple and pretty. **Chlorophyll** is the green material within plants that is responsible for photosynthesis. The word *chlorophyll*, however, means only green (*chlor*) leaf (*phyll*).

5. What do an **idiom** and an **idiosyncrasy** have in common? Peculiarity. The stem *idio* means peculiar. An idiosyncrasy is a peculiar way of behaving, and an idiom is a way of speaking that is peculiar to one group or to an individual.

6. We think of **instruction** as teaching, and we imagine classrooms and blackboards. But the true relatives of the word *instruction* are words such as **destruction**, **structure**, and **construction**. *Struct* means build, and in that sense, instruction is a wonderfully poetic word; it means to build (*struct*) within (*in*) the mind. The insight contained in this word sheds light on the idea that it isn't really a teacher who makes learning occur; it is the student. The teacher can help to make learning possible, but only the student can build a structure within herself. No one else can build something within you.

7. **Spanish Cognates**: One of the most important observations to gain from the study of the etymology of English vocabulary is that English and Spanish share thousands of words that are cognates—related words—that have common origins. Often, the English and the Spanish words share not only a stem but even more than one stem, and often in the same order. As examples, here are some English words from this lesson and their Spanish cognates:

    abrupt : abrupto
    abdicate : abdicar
    posthumous : póstumo
    microbe : microbio
    infrastructure : infraestructura
    cytoplasm : citoplasma
    ecology : ecología
    hypoglycemia : hipoglicemia
    exodus : éxodo

A child's commode

In each case below, one of the choices was really the word used by the author in the sentence provided. All of the choices can be found in the example words on the first page of this lesson. Your challenge is to decide which word the author used. This is not a test; it is more like a game because more than one word choice may work perfectly well. See if you can use your sensitivity and intuition to guess correctly which word the author used. You may need a dictionary.

1. **From John Knowles's *A Separate Peace***

   We had been a(n) _____ , leaderless band.
   a. melodious
   b. anaerobic
   c. impecunious
   d. idiosyncratic

2. **From George Orwell's *Animal Farm***

   This _____ set the table in a roar.
   a. melodeon
   b. *bon mot*
   c. epitaph
   d. idiom

3. **From James Hilton's *Lost Horizon***

   Barnard's wise-cracking _____ was of the kind he would have cultivated with a butler.
   a. epigram
   b. bonhomie
   c. abjuring
   d. anarchy

4. **From Sir Walter Scott's *Ivanhoe***

   Go to the Grand Master, _____ the order to his very teeth.
   a. exhume
   b. abjure
   c. abrogate
   d. abdicate

5. **From Oscar Wilde's *The Picture of Dorian Gray***

   You cut life to pieces with your _____ .
   a. abrogations
   b. epigraphs
   c. epigrams
   d. melodramas

Detail from a red-figure cylix of a woman with a flower

109

chrom	*(color)*	chrome, chromatic, chromatin, chromosome, polychrome, monochrome	*Greek*
form	*(shape)*	coliform, formation, formative, formula, uniform, oviform, reform	*Latin*
sequ	*(follow)*	consecutive, sequence, sequel, obsequious, consequence, subsequent	*Latin*
glyc	*(sweet)*	glycemia, glycerin, glycerol, glycogen, hypoglycemia, glucose	*Greek*
hemo	*(blood)*	hemoglobin, hemorrhage, hemophilia, hemolysis, hemoid, hemostat	*Greek*
ultima	*(last)*	ultimate, ultimatum, penultimate, Ultima Thule, ultimogeniture	*Latin*
infra	*(beneath)*	infraorbital, infrared, infrasonic, infra dig, infralapsarianism	*Latin*
leuko	*(white)*	leukocyte, leukemia, leucocytosis, leucite, leucoplast, leucocratic	*Greek*
lys	*(break down)*	hemolysis, electrolysis, electrolyte, analysis, dialysis, lysis	*Greek*
meso	*(middle)*	mesophilic, mezzotint, mesomorph, Mesozoic, Mesopotamia, mesophyll	*Greek*
milli	*(thousandth)*	millimeter, millipede, milligram, milliliter, million, millimicron	*Latin*
mem	*(remember)*	memory, memorandum, commemorate, memorial, memo, memoir	*Latin*
gress	*(step)*	congress, egress, digress, progress, aggression, regress, ingress	*Latin*
labor	*(work)*	labor, laborious, collaborate, laboratory, elaborate, labored	*Latin*
myo	*(muscle)*	myocardium, myology, myoglobin, myogram, myocarditis, myotomy	*Greek*
vac	*(empty)*	vacant, vacuum, vacation, evacuate, vacuous, vacuole, vacuity	*Latin*
oligo	*(few or small)*	oligosaccharide, oligarchy, oligocarpous, Oligocene, oligoclase	*Greek*
ose	*(sugar)*	lactose, fructose, sucrose, glucose, dextrose, dextroglucose	*Greek*
osis	*(condition)*	neurosis, psychosis, ichthyosis, erythroblastosis, thrombosis, meiosis	*Greek*
tude	*(state of)*	pulchritude, multitude, solitude, turpitude, rectitude, aptitude, similitude	*Latin*
patho	*(disease)*	pathogenic, psychopath, sociopath, pathological, idiopathic	*Greek*
phag	*(eat)*	phagocyte, bacteriophage, geophagy, anthropophagite, sarcophagus	*Greek*
phor	*(carry)*	euphoria, conidophore, metaphor, chromatophore, dysphoria, anaphora	*Greek*
phyt	*(plant)*	phytotoxin, sporophyte, neophyte, gametophyte, phytochrome	*Greek*
phyll	*(leaf)*	chlorophyll, phyllotaxis, phyllopod, phyllophagous, monophyllous	*Greek*

com/con

together • with • (intense)

The Latin stem **com**, which we define as meaning *together*, also can mean *with*, often appears in its **con** variation, and is sometimes seen as **col**, **cor**, and even **co**. Though **com** usually means *together*, it also can be used as an intensifier for the stem it precedes. Here are some of the interesting words that contain **com** in its various shades of meaning:

commodious:	spacious. Finally, they moved into a more commodious apartment.
compadre:	close friend. The two compadres, Tom and Huck, sauntered down the path.
compendious:	brief but complete. She had prepared a compendious study of the precedents.
commute:	to lessen in severity. The death sentence was commuted to life imprisonment.
complacent:	self-satisfied. Their complacent smugness left them oblivious to criticism.
complicity:	being an accomplice. Manson was accused of complicity in the terrible crime.
complement:	that which completes. The predicate nominative complements the subject.
comprise:	to consist of. The rest of the assault team was comprised of local Sherpas.
con brio:	with spirit. The passage was played *con brio*, and the audience cheered.
concave:	hollow. Mosquitoes hatched where the concave rock had collected rain water.
concord:	agreement. A brief spirit of amity and concord marked the opening day.
concierge:	a doorkeeper. They were greeted aloofly by the condescending concierge.
conciliate:	to placate. In anger, he refused to make any gesture to conciliate his opponent.
condone:	to pardon or overlook. Dr. King urged us to forgive but not to condone.
confabulate:	to talk informally. They confabulated excitedly in the hallway.
conflagration:	a destructive fire. The firebombing of Dresden created a deadly conflagration.
consonant:	in accord. The action was not consonant with the standard of ethics.
corvée:	forced labor. The Chinese government built the dams by a system of corvée.
corroborate:	to confirm. No corroborating testimony supported Flaubert at his trial.
collect:	to gather together. The numismatist collected coins.
colleague:	a coworker. She consulted her colleagues before revising the exam.

1. **Polychrome** sculptures have more colors than **monochrome** ones.

2. The **formation** of troops in **formal uniforms** was impressive.

3. Three **consecutive sequels** were of no **consequence**.

4. His **hypoglycemia** made him watch his diet.

5. The patient's **hemophilia** made it difficult to stop the **hemorrhage**.

6. The expedition's **Ultima Thule** was the north pole.

7. She felt that it was *infra dig* to eat fried chicken with her fingers.

8. **Leukemia** produces an excessive number of **leucocytes**.

9. If **hemolysis** breaks down red blood cells, what does **analysis** do?

10. Did **mesons** strike **Mesopotamia** in the **Mesozoic** Era?

11. Would you walk a **millimeter** to drink a **milligram** of milk?

12. The **memo** helped him **remember** the **commemoration** ceremony.

13. Don't **digress**; discuss **progress** with members of **congress**.

14. The **collaborators** spent **laborious** nights in the **laboratory**.

15. The **mycardiograph** showed the jogger's **myocardium** to be strong.

16. The **evacuation** left **vacancies** in the **vacation** resort.

17. The elite members of the **oligarchy** decided national policy in secrecy.

18. Did the **fructose** from the apples raise his **glucose** level?

19. Unfortunately, the **neurosis** developed into a **psychosis**.

20. The celebrity's **pulchritude** was only equaled by his **turpitude**.

21. The **pathological** behavior of the **psychopath** was **pathetic**.

22. The **anthropophagites** welcomed the plump visitor with broad, sharp smiles.

23. Why is a pigment cell called a **chromatophore**?

24. The young artist was a **neophyte** in the New York art scene.

25. Why is the arrangement of leaves on a stem known as **phyllotaxis**?

intuition

1. If you suddenly found yourself pursued by Paleolithic hirsute **anthropophagites**, how could you escape?

2. Imagine the life forms of the **Mesozoic** Era, 150,000,000 years ago. What life forms do you see? Look the Mesozoic Era up in the library, and see how close your imagination was to reality.

emotion

1. What is **euphoria**? When was the last time you felt euphoria?

2. What emotions do you associate with the following words: **collaboration**, **vacation**, **evacuate**, and **ultimatum**?

aesthetics

1. Would you rather make art that is **monochrome**, **polychrome**, or **chromed**?

2. If you could redesign the **uniforms** (Why do they call them uniforms?) of the White House guards, and if you wanted to make the uniforms wild and creative, what would you design?

synthesis

1. Use the facts you know about **Mesopotamia** to generate a theory about why it became a cradle of civilization.

2. Why is a beginner called a **neophyte**?

divergence

1. List as many species as you can think of that are **phyllophagous**.

2. How many situations can you think of in which a human being could be described as a **neophyte**?

The women's quarters of the house were called the gynaikonitis, and activities of many sorts that took place there were pictured on vases. A surprising number of vases show women juggling or holding balls.

113

When one political faction attempted to ostracize the leader of the other faction, it was important to be prepared with the necessary ostracon so the desired votes could be cast. These were among the thousands of pieces of pottery prepared for ostracizing Themistocles, which was done successfully by Cimon and his faction in the late 470s. Hundreds of them were found in a well near the Acropolis.

PUNISHMENT IN ATHENS
Dr. Thomas Milton Kemnitz

Athenian democracy clearly frightened the elites who ruled the other Greek city states. The assumption elsewhere was that the poorer masses would be swayed by the wisdom of the wealthier; in Athens the elites were at risk if they incurred the anger of the ordinary citizens.

Punishment could be meted out to anyone whose actions angered the city, and those who were entrusted with the leadership of troops or expeditions could face trial and punishment. Because Athens did not have an elaborate system of jails, punishments consisted of fines, banishment, or execution. Street crime was harshly punished. A thief caught in the act or with the evidence might come before a magistrate, and the consequence of being found guilty or admitting to the crime was execution. A person was attached to wood planks by a set of iron shackles, including one around his neck that could be tightened to strangle him. It is not clear if death came this way or by leaving him to die slowly. Toward the end of the fifth century, those who could afford it could purchase hemlock and drink that, as Socrates chose to do. Most of the more affluent were expected to flee Athens rather than be executed.

Public trials were held for those who angered the people by their failures. Office holders were held accountable, and dereliction of duty was punished by execution. It was not good to lose a battle, and sometimes winning was not much better. Nor was it good to be a treasurer of the Delian League when funds were missing. On one occasion each of the ten treasurers was called to explain missing funds, and each was executed when he could not. After the ninth man had been executed, it was found that in fact no funds were missing but rather an accounting error had been made. The last treasurer was thereby spared from the fate his fellows had suffered.

To prevent a single person from perverting the democratic process, a provision allowed for a ten-year banishment of anyone by a vote of the Assembly; ballots were cast by writing on pieces of pottery called *ostracon*. Themistocles used the nascent institutions of democracy for his purposes, and he was opposed at almost every turn by Aristides, who was backed by the aristocrats of Athens. Eventually Themistocles managed to get the Assembly to vote to ostracize Aristides, who was forced to leave the city. After the battle of Thermopylae, Themistocles had the Assembly bring back everyone who had been ostracized to aid Athens in its fight against the Persians. About eight years after the Persians had been expelled from Greece, in 472 or 471 B.C., Themistocles lost such a vote and was himself ostracized, never to see Athens again. He apparently liked adulation, and his boastfulness, as well as his opposition to Sparta, annoyed enough Athenians that they ostracized the great hero who had saved all of Greece. After spending some years in Argos aiding the Athenian cause against Sparta, Themistocles was forced to flee to Persia, where ironically he wound up an honored guest of Xerxes, who remembered the messages Themistocles had sent him during the second Persian invasion, interpreting them as truly friendly.

Punishment in Athens was not a matter of justice as we understand it but rather a way of venting anger. After the Battle of Arginusae in 406, the victorious Athenian admirals were recalled, and six of the eight returned to Athens. They were accused of failing to rescue the sailors whose ships had been sunk. They explained that a storm had made it impossible to effect the rescue. That was not sufficient to deal with the anger of the people, and the admirals were all executed; the next year it was hard to find commanders for the fleet. The great historian Thucydides was ostracized because an expedition he led arrived too late to achieve its objective.

490–323 B.C. Classical Period	472/471 B.C. Themistocles ostracized	454 B.C. Delian treasury moved to Athens	430 B.C. Plague in Athens	406 B.C. Victory at Arginusae; six admirals executed

1. **OLIGARCHY : NEUROSIS ::**
   a. monarchy : reform
   b. plutocracy : economy
   c. democracy : uniform
   d. gerontocracy : psychosis

2. **ANALYSIS : DIALYSIS ::**
   a. evaluation : hemolysis
   b. bacteria : bacteriophage
   c. neophyte : phytotoxin
   d. congress : digress

3. **POLYCHROME : MONOCHROME ::**
   a. solitude : multitude
   b. neurosis : psychosis
   c. square : line
   d. ultimogeniture : primogeniture

4. **HEMORRHAGE : HEMOSTAT ::**
   a. path : gate
   b. water : dam
   c. film : sequel
   d. cell : vacuole

5. **ICHTHYOSIS : NEUROSIS ::**
   a. dermatitis : psychosis
   b. psychopath : sociopath
   c. ultimate : penultimate
   d. euphoria : dysphoria

6. **OBSEQUIOUS : DOMINEERING ::**
   a. rectitude : turpitude
   b. flatter : fawn
   c. mezzotint : polychrome
   d. slave : master

7. **PULCHRITUDE : UGLINESS ::**
   a. multitude : host
   b. supersonic : infrasonic
   c. ichthyosis : neurosis
   d. neophyte : beginner

8. **MESOZOIC : MESOPOTAMIA ::**
   a. Paleozoic : laboratory
   b. Cenozoic : dinosaur
   c. Cretaceous : geophagy
   d. Jurassic : Iberia

9. **ANTHROPOPHAGY : HUMAN ::**
   a. sarcophagus : burial
   b. geophagy : earth
   c. bacteriophage : virus
   d. collaborate : labor

10. **OLIGARCHY : MONARCHY ::**
    a. group : person
    b. person : group
    c. soliloquy : monologue
    d. *infra dig* : infrared

Many interior domestic scenes are found on vases designed for use in marriage ceremonies or for holding cosmetics or jewelry. This red-figure nuptial lebes (probably used for sprinkling the bride with water) shows a nursery scene with an obviously healthy baby.

1. An **elaborate** scheme is a carefully worked (*labor*) out (*ex*) scheme, one executed with great care and exactness.

2. Do you have a fondness for the occasional sesquipedalian (foot-and-a-half-long) word? How about **infralapsarianism**? That is the religious doctrine (*ism*) that, except for the elect few, all human beings will fall (*laps*) below (*infra*) to eternal misery.

3. What does **Mesopotamia** have in common with the hippopotamus? The river. Mesopotamia is the land between (*meso*: middle) the Tigris and Euphrates rivers (*potamus*), and a hippopotamus, according to some astonished ancient Greek traveler, is a sort of big river (*potamus*) horse (*hippo*). Ride 'em, Plato.

4. Is the diagnosis **myocarditis**? That is an inflammation (*itis*) of a muscle (*myo*) in the heart (*card*) wall. Many medical terms are understandable to a lay person who is familiar with common Greek and Latin stems because medical terms are created in such an intentional, logical way. This makes it much easier for a doctor to remember the thousands of words he or she needs in a profession that is heavy-laden with specialized vocabulary.

5. When you see a word with *path* in it, you must decide whether *path* means feeling, as in **sympathy**, **empathy**, and **telepathy**, or whether *path* means disease, as in **pathological**, **psychopath**, and **sociopath**.

6. A **Micropoem**: It is the task of the president to **execute** the law. What is the precise meaning of the word *execute*? It is to follow (*sequ*) out (*ex*) the directions fully.

7. Have you been asked to **analyze** something, but you didn't quite understand what analysis was? **Analysis** is the process of loosening (*lys*) something up (*ana*) into its separate parts. One begins with a unified entity and separates it into its components. **Synthesis** is the opposite process: one begins with a number of discrete items and combines them into a single entity. Analysis loosens (*lys*); synthesis brings together (*syn*). Can you analyze the word **gastroenteritis**? Can you synthesize divergent views into a single policy?

8. **Spanish Cognates**: One of the most important observations to gain from the study of the etymology of English vocabulary is that English and Spanish share thousands of words that are cognates—related words—that have common origins. Often, the English and the Spanish words share not only a stem but even more than one stem, and often in the same order. As examples, here are some English words from this lesson and their Spanish cognates:

   chromatic : cromático
   consecutive : consecutivo
   commemorate : conmemorar
   ingress : ingresar
   laborious : laborioso
   collaborate : colaborar
   glucose : glucosa
   psychopath : sicópata
   euphoria : euforia

This white-ground cosmetic pot shows a woman processing wool.

117

In each case below, one of the choices was really the word used by the author in the sentence provided. All of the choices can be found in the example words on the first page of this lesson. Your challenge is to decide which word the author used. This is not a test; it is more like a game because more than one word choice may work perfectly well. See if you can use your sensitivity and intuition to guess correctly which word the author used. You may need a dictionary.

1. **From James Watson's *The Double Helix***

   His talk was far from _____ and stood out sharply from the rest.
   a. pathological
   b. chromatic
   c. vacuous
   d. formative

2. **From Charlotte Brontë's *Jane Eyre***

   You have no right to preach to me, you _____.
   a. neophyte
   b. vacuole
   c. memo
   d. leukocyte

3. **From H.G. Wells's *The Invisible Man***

   The pistol snapped its _____ shot.
   a. subsequent
   b. chromatic
   c. monochrome
   d. penultimate

4. **From Thomas Hardy's *The Return of the Native***

   A profile was visible against the dull _____ of cloud around her.
   a. monochrome
   b. formula
   c. dextrose
   d. myopia

5. **From Mary Wollstonecraft's *Vindication of the Rights of Woman***

   When we hear of some daring crime, it comes full on us in the deepest shade of _____.
   a. metaphor
   b. turpitude
   c. consequence
   d. egress

pleo	*(more)*	pleomorphic, pleonasm, pleochroic, Pliocene, pleophagous, pleopod	*Greek*
pod	*(foot)*	pseudopod, arthropod, diplopoda, cephalopod, podiatrist, gastropod	*Greek*
soror	*(sister)*	sorority, sororicide, sororize, sororal	*Latin*
-a	*(plural)*	data, phenomena, bacteria, Cephalopoda, phyla, effluvia, trivia, Nematoda	*Greek*
val	*(worth)*	valiant, valid, equivalent, devaluate, evaluate, ambivalent, covalent	*Latin*
para	*(beside or near)*	parable, parapsychology, parabola, paradigm, paradox, paraphrase	*Greek*
dom	*(rule)*	dominate, predominant, dominion, domineering, subdominant, domain	*Latin*
erg	*(work)*	energy, ergonomics, erg-second, ergatocracy, exergonic, synergy	*Greek*
rhiz	*(root)*	rhizoid, rhizome, rhizomorphous, rhizophagous, rhizanthous	*Greek*
sapro	*(rotten)*	saprophytic, saprophyte, saprogenic, saprolite, saprophilous	*Greek*
schizo	*(divide)*	Schizomycetes, schizophrenia, schism, schizocarp, schizoid, schizopod	*Greek*
hippo	*(horse)*	hippopotamus, hippodrome, hippogriff, hipparch, eohippus	*Greek*
som	*(body)*	somatic, chromosome, lysosome, somatoplasm, psychosomatic, somatology	*Greek*
spor	*(seed)*	endospore, sporophyte, sporangia, Sporozoa, sporogenesis, macrospore	*Greek*
sta	*(stop)*	hemostat, stasis, station, stationary, status quo, apostasy, hypostatize, static	*Latin*
rhodo	*(rose)*	rhododendron, rhodolite, Rhode Island, rhodium	*Greek*
taxis	*(arrangement)*	syntax, chemotaxis, taxidermy, phyllotaxis, taxonomy, ataxia	*Greek*
vol	*(will)*	volunteer, malevolent, benevolent, volition, involuntary	*Latin*
frat	*(brother)*	fraternity, fraternal, fratricide, fraternize	*Latin*
trich	*(hair)*	monotrichous, trichina, trichocysts, trichinosis, trichosis	*Greek*
troph	*(nourishment)*	autotroph, eutrophication, atrophy, dystrophy, trophism	*Greek*
tox	*(poison)*	toxin, toxoid, nontoxic, antitoxin, detoxification, toxicity, phytotoxins	*Greek*
sect	*(cut)*	dissect, intersection, vivisection, bisect, section, sectarian, sector	*Latin*
zygo	*(yoke)*	zygote, zygospore, zygodactyl, zygomorphic, zygoid, zygoptera	*Greek*
zym	*(ferment)*	enzyme, zymology, zymurgy, zymogenesis, zymoscope, zymogen	*Greek*

dis

away • apart • not • cease

The Latin stem **dis**, which we define as meaning *away*, actually can have a wide variety of meanings and is sometimes shortened to **di** or **dif**. Though **dis** often means *away*, it can mean *apart, not, cease, opposite of, lack of*, or even *fail*. Here are some of the interesting words that contain **dis** in its various shades of meaning:

disavow:	disclaim. Iago disingenuously disavowed any suspicion of Desdemona.
disclose:	to reveal. She heroically refused to disclose her friends' names to McCarthy.
discord:	conflict. Discord among the Hausa, Fulani, and Ibo divided Nigeria.
disembosom:	to reveal oneself. The pitiful monster disembosomed himself to his maker.
disfigure:	to deform. Snow, Auden wrote, disfigured the public statues.
dislodge:	to drive out. Lee's army could not dislodge Union forces from their positions.
disgruntle:	to peeve. Jove was disgruntled by the bellicose Ares.
disorient:	to confuse. Henry Fleming was disoriented by the blow.
dissimulate:	to pretend. Prospero glared at the odious and dissimulating Caliban.
distraught:	extremely upset. Heathcliff was distraught with grief over Catherine's death.
dissipate:	to scatter. At last the storm began to dissipate, and the sea began to calm.
disseminate:	to distribute widely. Luther's theses were disseminated all over Europe.
dissuade:	to persuade against. Calpurnia could not dissuade Caesar from going.
disputant:	one who debates. In Plato's *Dialogues*, Socrates is the major disputant.
disparage:	to belittle. Blind and disparaging remarks were made about Lincoln's speech.
disrepute:	disgrace. Gandhi's *Satyagraha* placed British imperialism in disrepute.
disquiet:	to make uneasy. At first Macbeth was disquieted by the witches' prophesy.
dispirit:	to depress. The gladiator's victory dispirited the Roman crowd.
disparity:	difference in amount. The disparity in their ages was no obstacle to her.
dissever:	separate. Southern states attempted to dissever themselves from the Union.
distaste:	aversion. Mr. Hyde's truculent visage engendered a feeling of distaste.

1. A **pleochroic** crystal shows different colors from different directions.

2. The **podiatrist** couldn't treat the injured **arthropod**; he only treated humans.

3. The **sorority** was located between two fraternities.

4. The **data** revealed not one phenomenon but several **phenomena**.

5. The **valedictory** address contained **valid** arguments and **evaluations**.

6. The **parapsychologist** told a **parable** that contained a **paradox**.

7. The baron was **dominant** over his entire **dominion**.

8. Do the workers in this country want a meritocracy or an **ergatocracy**?

9. **Rhizophagous** jungle animals dig up and feed on delicious **rhizomes**.

10. **Saprogenic** bacteria soon caused the material to decay.

11. The **schism** in the party could not be healed before the election.

12. In Mesopotamia, the **hippopotamus** is allowed to use the **hippodrome**.

13. Did his **chromosome** problem have a **psychosomatic** cause?

14. The **Sporozoa** are protozoa that multiply by **sporogenesis**.

15. The people in the **station** voted to preserve the **status quo**.

16. The **rhododendron** was in bloom on the high mountainsides.

17. The **taxidermist** was interested in the **taxonomy** of animal species.

18. The new **volunteer** had a curious, **malevolent** expression.

19. The candidate tried to **fraternize** with the local politicians.

20. **Trichinosis** is a disease caused by the **trichina** worm.

21. His muscles had begun to **atrophy** from disuse.

22. The high **toxicity** of the **toxin** made a powerful **antitoxin** necessary.

23. **Dissection** is legal, but **vivisection** is not.

24. A **zygote** is the cell produced by the union (yoking) of two gametes.

25. If **zymology** is the science of enzymes, why is **zymurgy** winemaking?

The seated woman is making a wreath.

analysis

1. Analyze—by examining the words—the ideas inherent in these facts: Plants are **autotrophic**. **Eutrophication** clogs ponds. **Atrophy** shrinks limbs. Muscular **dystrophy** ruins lives.

2. Explain the logic of the names **arthropod**, **cephalopod**, and **gastropod**.

evaluation

1. If a country had to choose between becoming a **plutocracy** and becoming an **ergatocracy**, which would be the most intelligent choice?

2. Should trained scientists involve themselves in studies of **parapsychology**?

intuition

1. A writer of novels needs a **malevolent** image or symbol to use for the stitched emblem emblazoned on the backs of the leather jackets worn by a street gang. What images come to your mind?

2. If you were a **taxidermist**, what animal would you enjoy working on? What animal would you dread working on?

emotion

1. What are your emotional responses to the practice of **vivisection**?

2. What are some emotional problems and misunderstandings that could result in a tragic **fratricide**?

aesthetics

1. What would be a surprising, whimsical, creative material to use in making a humorous sculpture of a **hippopotamus**?

2. If you had the magical ability to put the clouds in any shapes and patterns you wished and to fill the sky with chosen colors, what would your **predominate** patterns and color schemes be?

The white owl appeared on the shields of Athenian hoplites, on buildings in Athens, and on some Athenian-made pottery.

1. **ERGATOCRACY : GERONTOCRACY ::**
   a. elderly : manual
   b. hard hat : cane
   c. fraternity : fraternal
   d. eohippus : horse

2. **STATUS QUO : REVOLUTION ::**
   a. form : metamorphosis
   b. taxidermy : animal
   c. autotroph : heterotroph
   d. vivisect : dissect

3. **APOSTASY : ZEALOTRY ::**
   a. predominant : superior
   b. fanaticism : commitment
   c. betrayal : loyalty
   d. psychology : parapsychology

4. **BISECT : DISSECT ::**
   a. dominate : divide
   b. multiply : factor
   c. intersect : vivisect
   d. detoxify : poison

5. **ZYMURGY : CHEMISTRY ::**
   a. topiary : gardening
   b. gastropod : cephalopod
   c. wine : bouquet
   d. cell : chromosome

6. **VOLUNTEER : VOLITION ::**
   a. traitor : confession
   b. deserter : desertion
   c. apostate : commitment
   d. equivalence : ambivalence

7. **PHENOMENA : PHENOMENON ::**
   a. fraternize : fraternity
   b. benevolent : benevolence
   c. fungi : fungus
   d. saprophyte : saprogenic

8. **SOMATIC : PSYCHOLOGICAL ::**
   a. fracture : neurosis
   b. resentment : arthritis
   c. body : vestment
   d. parabola : ellipse

9. **PARADIGM : PROTOTYPE ::**
   a. conceptual : physical
   b. malevolent : benevolent
   c. schizophrenia : neurosis
   d. rhizophagy : anthropophagy

10. **AMBIVALENT : AMBIGUOUS ::**
    a. evaluate : devaluate
    b. feeling : meaning
    c. conflict : tranquility
    d. somatic : psychosomatic

This is a red-figure scene of a wine-drinking party, when Greek men might get together and talk. Their name for such a session was symposium, which is the term used in the modern world for an academic gathering to discuss a specific topic. Greek houses were configured with a front room containing seven couches: two along each of three walls, and one couch and a door on the fourth wall. There the companions would spend late afternoons and evenings in drinking and discussion.

LATE BRONZE AGE	1600–1100 B.C.	Mycenaean culture flourishes
	c. 1184	Fall of Troy
	c. 1150	Destruction of Mycenaean cities
DARK AGE	1100–900 B.C.	Greek migration to the islands, Ionia
GEOMETRIC PERIOD	900–700 B.C.	
	776	Earliest known Olympic games
ORIENTALIZING PERIOD	700–600 B.C.	
ARCHAIC PERIOD	600–490 B.C.	
	508/507 B.C.	Establishment of democracy in Athens
CLASSICAL PERIOD	490–323 B.C.	
	490	Battle of Marathon
	485	Sparta receives a prophecy at Delphi
	483	Silver find at Athenian mines; decision to build the navy
	481	Greek polities meet to form defensive strategy
	480	Persian invasions; Battles of Thermopylae, Salamis
	479	Greek victories at Plataea, Mylcale
	478/477	Delian League formed
	472/471	Themistocles ostracized
	469 or 466	Battle of Eurymedon
	464	Earthquake at Sparta; Helot revolt begins
	461	Cimon ostracized
	454	Delian treasury moved to Athens
	449	Peace with Persia negotiated
	447–438	Parthenon built
	438–432	Pediment statues erected
	437–432	Propylaea erected
PELOPONNESIAN WARS	431–404 B.C.	
	430	Plague in Athens
	429	Death of Pericles
	427–424	Temple of Athena Nike erected
	421	Peace of Nicias
	421–405	Erechtheion erected
	415–413	Expedition to Sicily
	415	Alcibiades defects
	407	Alcibiades returns to Athens
	406	Victory at Arginusae; six admirals executed
	405	Destruction of Athenian fleet on shore
	404	Athens surrenders
	399	Socrates condemned
	371	Thebes defeats Spartan army
	359	Philip becomes king of Macedonia
	337	Philip founds Greek League
	336	Philip assassinated; Alexander assumes throne
	334	Alexander crosses Hellespont
	323	Alexander dies
HELLENISTIC ERA	323–146	
	146	Rome conquers Greece

THE ATHENIAN NAVY

Dr. Thomas Milton Kemnitz

Themistocles was the champion of the Athenian navy. When ridiculed for his distinct lack of graces, he said that he could not tune a lute or play a harp, but he could make a small and obscure city great and glorious. It was he who conceived the strategy that made Athens a great city: to rely upon sea power, leaving land warfare to other polities. This strategy was followed by those who came after him for almost two centuries. It was Themistocles who convinced the Athenians to spend the bounty from the silver find on ships instead of giving a little to every citizen. The navy was popular with the poorer people in Athens because it provided employment. Athenians were paid to row, paid to train, and paid to fight. By contrast, land warfare was a wealthy man's game; each man had to supply his armor, his shield, his helmet, his breastplate, his greaves, his sword and scabbard, his lances, not to mention his plume. It cost a lot of money, and there was no pay. To serve in the Athenian navy, all a volunteer had to supply was his rower's cushion, and he got paid for each day. Themistocles deliberately cultivated the working people to win votes in the Assembly for his strategy of building triremes. Where Themistocles led, every great leader of ancient Athens followed; the navy and democracy were the key to retaining power in Athenian politics, as well as the key to Athenian predominance in the Greek world.

Most of the working population of Athens had family members employed in the navy, either rowing or in building and maintaining the ships or the dockyards, which were the major public works of Athens in the first half of the fifth century B.C. The ships were highly vulnerable to the Teredo worm, known as ship worm, in fact a form of saltwater clam without a shell that bores into wood and eventually destroys it. The ships had to be stored on shore when not in use and had to be coated with pitch or tar to protect the wood from the Teredo worm; all of the Athenian triremes had dry dock space that was protected by a roof. The sails, an auxiliary form of power, required constant maintenance. The ropes, masts, rudders, and girding ropes all had to be maintained; the Athenian trireme was held together by two huge ropes eighteen inches in diameter that ran from stem to stern; they needed special maintenance, and two spares were carried on every journey. The largest roofed building in all of Greece was a 400-foot-long storehouse in Pireaus for the sails and ropes of the fleet. The ships were highly decorated with statues, ornamental eyes, and other art. Every ship had 170 men on the oars plus an additional thirty who were in other capacities, and Pericles kept at least sixty triremes at sea for eight months of the year. It was very expensive to maintain the Athenian navy, and most of that money went into the hands of the working people of Athens.

The trireme was an unseaworthy ship designed only to fight. The lowest oars were just above the waterline, and they took on water in choppy seas. Most naval battles were fought in the morning when the sea was calm. Triremes did not put to sea in the winter months; they did not have space for provisions other than water, and they had no place to rest or sleep. They had to put into land each night to feed the crews and allow them to rest. Greek fleets were seldom out of sight of land, and most naval battles took place near shore. The Greeks could swim, so survival after a sinking was possible. Some enemies like the Persians generally did not know how to swim, and for them a ship sinking was likely to be fatal. One often-used tactic of all combatants was to have hoplites on shore near a naval battle to save their own men and kill or imprison any of the enemy who made it to land. The navy was so important to Athens that information about it can be found in much of the surviving literature, including many plays.

Establishment of democracy in Athens	Silver find at Athenian mines; decision to build the navy	Greek polities meet to form defensive strategy	Themistocles ostracized	Delian treasury moved to Athens
508/507 B.C.	**483 B.C.**	**481 B.C.**	**472/471 B.C.**	**454 B.C.**

1. After more than 2,000 years, we still ponder the famous **paradox** of Socrates, who knew that he knew nothing. We use the word *paradox* to refer to a seemingly self-contradictory statement that nevertheless is regarded as true. Why does the word *paradox* have that meaning? Because in a paradox, the two contradictory-sounding opinions (*dox*) are placed right beside (*para*) each other. Zeno's paradox is that if you continually move half the distance toward something, you will never reach it!

2. In the operating room, the surgeon asks for a **hemostat**. The nurse hands her a metal tool that looks like a combination of scissors and tweezers. What is the purpose of a hemostat? To stop (*sta*) the bleeding (*hemo*).

3. There are democracies (people/rule), plutocracies (wealthy/rule), meritocracies (meritorious/rule), and hagiocracies (saints/rule). What is an **ergatocracy**? The workers (*erg*) rule.

4. The art by which specialists make wine or brew beer is known as **zymurgy**. Why? Because both require fermentation: zymurgy is the technology (*urgy*) of fermentation (*zym*).

5. A **Micropoem**: When you study biology, pity the poor **cephalopod**; it was born with its feet (*pod*) in its head (*cephalo*)!

6. Place a single cell in a slide, and put it under the microscope. Turn on the light. What do you see? Not much, because the light is bright, and the structures in the cell are translucent (clear). Now add a colorful die to the solution that the cell is in. Certain structures inside the cell will absorb the color well so that you can study them. These bodies (*som*) that absorb the color (*chrom*) well are called the **chromosomes**, the color-bodies.

7. We say that green plants are **autotrophic**, which means that they are self-nourishing (*auto*: self, *troph*: nourishment). But in what sense are plants self-nourishing, since they seem to need water and fertilizer? The answer is that the water and minerals a plant takes in are not food. These things are simply inorganic substances that a plant changes into food by **photosynthesis**. Remember that *syn* means together; the plant's cells put these substances together (synthesize them). Since the plant uses light to effect this synthesis, the process is called *photosynthesis*. So a plant is self (*auto*) nourishing (*troph*) because it uses light (*photo*) to put food together (*syn*).

8. A **Micropoem**: The word **apostate** is graphically descriptive. An apostate is a person who forsakes his party, church, or cause. But there is a microdrama within the word: we see the apostate alone, standing (*sta*) away (*apo*) from the group he has deserted. An apostate is an away-stander. Note that both the stems, *apo* and *sta*, have alternate meanings. *Apo* may mean away or up, and *sta* may mean stand or stop.

9. The noun **paradigm** is pronounced para-DIME, not para-DIJUM. Be sure that you pronounce this word correctly!

10. **Spanish Cognates:** One of the most important observations to gain from the study of the etymology of English vocabulary is that English and Spanish share thousands of words that are cognates—related words—that have common origins. Often, the English and the Spanish words share not only a stem but even more than one stem, and often in the same order. As examples, here are some English words from this lesson and their Spanish cognates:

paradigm : paradigma	taxonomy : taxonomía	toxin : toxina
paraphrase : parafrasear	fraternity : fraternidad	sector : sector
static : estático	trichinosis : triquinosis	enzyme : enzima

In each case below, one of the choices was really the word used by the author in the sentence provided. All of the choices can be found in the example words on the first page of this lesson. Your challenge is to decide which word the author used. This is not a test; it is more like a game because more than one word choice may work perfectly well. See if you can use your sensitivity and intuition to guess correctly which word the author used. You may need a dictionary.

1. **From James Watson's *The Double Helix***

   He had _____ feelings about the value to biology of Pauling-like structural studies.
   a. ambivalent
   b. static
   c. equivalent
   d. malevolent

2. **From Ralph Ellison's *Invisible Man***

   The _____ sounds became a quiet drone.
   a. sectarian
   b. fraternal
   c. somatic
   d. static

3. **From Jack London's *White Fang***

   He continued to go forward of his own _____.
   a. taxonomy
   b. schism
   c. volition
   d. paradigm

4. **From Rachel Carson's *Silent Spring***

   The balance of nature is not a(n) _____; it is fluid, ever shifting, in a constant state of adjustment.
   a. status quo
   b. paradox
   c. hippodrome
   d. apostasy

5. **From Charles Dickens's *David Copperfield***

   That restlessness of limb...is not an infrequent _____ in youths of his age.
   a. paradigm
   b. volition
   c. phenomenon
   d. atrophy

tropo	*(turn)*	heliotrope, troposphere, tropism, trophy, phototropism, apogeotropism	*Greek*
gastro	*(stomach)*	gastronomy, gastroscope, gastropod, gastroenteritis, hypogastric	*Greek*
arthro	*(joint)*	arthritis, arthropod, arthralgia, arthrospore, arthroscopic	*Greek*
ventri	*(belly)*	ventriloquist, ventral, ventricle, dorsoventral, ventriculus	*Latin*
dors	*(back)*	dorsal, dorsoventral, dorsum, dorsal fin	*Latin*
macro	*(large)*	macrobiotic, macrocephalic, macrocosm, macron, macroscopic	*Greek*
dextro	*(right or clockwise)*	dextrose, dextral, dexterity, dexterous, dextrorotation	*Latin*
brachy	*(short)*	brachycephalic, brachypterous, brachycranic, brachylogy	*Greek*
brachio	*(arm)*	brachiopod, brachiation, brachiate, brachium	*Greek*
branchio	*(gills)*	branchiopod, branchiate, branchia	*Greek*
kin	*(motion)*	kinetic, kinescope, hypokinesia, hyperkinetic, telekinesis	*Greek*
phylo	*(kind)*	phylum, phylogeny, phyla, phylogenesis, subphylum	*Greek*
blasto	*(embryo)*	blastocyst, blastogenesis, erythroblast	*Greek*
dactylo	*(finger)*	pterodactyl, dactylic, dactylology, dactylography	*Greek*
phos	*(light)*	phosphorus, phosphene, phosphoroscope, phosphoresce	*Greek*
gon	*(angle)*	pentagon, tetragon, decagon, hexagonal, diagonal, orthogonal	*Greek*
lite	*(mineral or fossil)*	perlite, cryolite, halite, coprolite	*Greek*
vore	*(eating)*	omnivore, herbivore, carnivore, voracious, devour, fructivorous	*Latin*
holo	*(whole)*	holocaust, hologram, holometabolous, holograph, holophrastic, holistic	*Greek*
haplo	*(single or simple)*	haploid, haplopia, haplosis, haplology	*Greek*
opia	*(sight)*	myopia, hyperopia, hemeralopia, synopsis, diplopia, biopsy	*Greek*
lent	*(full of)*	corpulent, virulent, turbulent, excellent, succulent	*Latin*
ef	*(out)*	effusive, effulgent, efflux, efficacy, effeminate, effluvium, effluent	*Latin*
ium	*(an element)*	radium, sodium, uranium, germanium, iridium, einsteinium	*Latin*
dicho	*(in two parts)*	dichotomy, dichotomize, dichogamous, dichotomist	*Greek*

ex

out • beyond • without

The Latin stem **ex** is a relative of the Greek stem **exo**, and though we define **ex** as meaning *out*, it actually can have a wide variety of meanings, such as *beyond, without, upward, forth,* or even *thoroughly*. **Ex** is often shortened to **ef, e, ec,** or **es** before certain other letters. Here are some of the interesting words that contain **ex** in its various shades of meaning:

exalt:	to glorify. Since his ignominious death, Mozart has been exalted.
excogitate:	to think out. Newton solved the problem through lengthy excogitations.
exigent:	critical. The famine in the Sudan had developed into an exigent crisis.
exiguous:	meager. They scratched out an exiguous existence from the thin soil.
exordium:	the opening of a speech. She began with a moving exordium on human rights.
expurgate:	to censor. Bowdler even expurgated objectionable passages from Shakespeare.
expedient:	advantageous. Borgia's tactic may not have been ethical, but it was expedient.
effrontery:	impudence. The teacher gazed at Scout, amazed at her effrontery.
effigy:	a crude likeness. The crowd burned a scarecrow-like effigy of Quisling.
effete:	weak. He had declined into an effete simulacrum of his former self.
efface:	to erase. A thousand seasons had effaced the words from the stone.
eccentric:	unconventional. The eccentric tycoon lived in disregard of all convention.
essay:	to attempt. He essayed a precarious route across the rock face.
excerpt:	a selected passage. The excerpt was carefully chosen to distort his meaning.
exotic:	strangely beautiful. Her exotic beauty haunted him for many years.
explicate:	to explain completely. Yeats explicated his own passage from "Lake Isle."
extol:	to praise. Mark Antony came not to bury Caesar but to extol his virtues.
extrinsic:	not inherent. Foreign language study has extrinsic as well as intrinsic merits.
exhume:	to unearth. The distraught Lincoln had his son's body exhumed one last time.
exile:	banishment. The emperor forced Ovid to live in exile from Rome.
exhilarate:	to invigorate. The arctic wind exhilarated his senses as he urged the dogs on.

1. In the **tropics**, the leafy **heliotropes** turn toward the sun.

2. The **gastrologist** studies the stomach; the **gastronome** prepares the food.

3. The aged **arthropod** suffered from **arthritis** and **arthralgia**.

4. The popular **ventriloquist** had a heart operation on his left **ventricle**.

5. **Dorsiventral** leaves have distinct upper and lower surfaces.

6. The universe is sometimes referred to as the **macrocosm**.

7. Are right-handed people really more **dexterous**?

8. **Brachypterous** insects have short wings.

9. **Brachiate** trees have widely spreading branches in pairs, like arms.

10. The **branchiopods** are underwater crustaceans that breathe through gills.

11. The **hyperkinetic** little boy did not possess **telekinesis**, fortunately.

12. The vertebrate species Homo sapiens belongs to the Chordata **phylum**.

13. Reproduction by budding is also called **blastogenesis**.

14. If fingerprinting is **dactylography**, is sign language **dactylology**?

15. If you press your closed eyelids, you will see **phosphenes**.

16. What is the difference between a pentagram and a **pentagon**?

17. **Perlite** is a volcanic glass that resembles obsidian.

18. The **voracious carnivore devoured** the small **herbivore**.

19. The glowing **hologram** could be viewed from all sides.

20. The diploid structure divided into two **haploid** structures.

21. Far-sightedness is sometimes known as **hyperopia**.

22. For the **corpulent** boy, dieting was a **turbulent** and strenuous mental effort.

23. The **effeminate** host made an **effort** not to be **effusive**.

24. Which element does society more harm: **uranium** or **sodium**?

25. There is a sharp **dichotomy** between your ideas and mine.

synthesis

1. Invent a neologism that could serve as a general term to describe all of the following: a **pentagon**, a **tetragon**, a **hexagon**, a **decagon**, an **octagon**. The term **polygon**, of course, already exists, so you will have to think about these geometric constructions in a different way.

2. What can you think of that **arthropods**, **gastropods**, and **protozoans** have in common?

divergence

1. A science fiction writer is working on a novel about a planet where **pterodactyls** still fly. In order to avoid monotony, the writer needs dozens of good descriptive adjectives to describe the pterodactyls. How many can you think of? Remember that the most creative ideas often arise after the obvious suggestions have been quickly exhausted and the thinking gets hard.

2. Can you think of practical uses for **hologram** technology?

analysis

1. Guess the meanings of the following words by breaking them down into their component stems: **haplopia**, **dichotomy**, **macrocosm**, **effusive**, and **apogeotropism**.

2. What is the difference between **arthritis** and **arthralgia**?

evaluation

1. If you were searching for a biological metaphor to describe corporate America's relationship to the rest of the country, would you choose **carnivorous** or **symbiotic**? Why?

2. Do you think that authorities have the right to use **dactylography** as evidence against students who vandalize public school property?

intuition

1. If you designed an unusual dummy for a **ventriloquist**, what would it be?

2. What trick would you play on a friend if you had the power of **telekinesis**?

The Temple of Hephiastos as seen from the Acropolis

The Athenian treasury is the only nearly complete building still standing at Delphi. The purpose of the building was to store the treasures that the Athenians brought to Delphi as offerings to the gods. On the pedestals along the wall on the left side of this picture, the Athenians displayed their trophies from the Battle of Marathon: Persian shields, weapons, banners, and other emblems.

CIMON AND A RICHER ATHENS
Dr. Thomas Milton Kemnitz

Cimon, like Themistocles, adopted the strategy of using the navy to make Athens preeminent. Cimon's father was Miltiades, the Athenian general who had played a decisive part in winning the battle at Marathon and who the next year led an Athenian expedition to attack Greek islands that were thought to have supported the Persians. His fleet attacked the island of Paros but failed to take it. Miltiades suffered a severe leg wound and became incapacitated. His failure prompted an outcry on his return to Athens, enabling his political rivals to exploit his fall from grace. Charged with treason, he was sentenced to death, but the sentence was converted to a fine of fifty talents. Unable to pay it, he was incarcerated and, according to Herodotus, soon died of infection from his wound. Only a year earlier he had won for the Athenians one of the most glorious victories in the history of the world! Miltiades's son Cimon was left with his father's debt.

Cimon played an important part in the Athenian victory over the Persians at the Battle of Salamis in 480 B.C. Thereafter he became the leading general, *strategos*–from which we get *strategy*–of the Delian League, and for nearly two decades he led fleets that attacked the Persians and others and brought a huge amount of plunder to Athens. When charges were brought against him for accepting a bribe, he said, "Never have I been an Athenian envoy to any rich kingdom. Instead, I was proud, attending to the Spartans, whose frugal culture I have always imitated. This proves that I don't desire personal wealth. Rather, I love enriching our nation with the booty of our victories." Cimon had shown his admiration for Sparta by naming one of his sons (who would later command the Athenian fleet) Lacedaemonius, after the land where Sparta is situated.

Cimon enriched Athens spectacularly. Once at dinner he described what he thought was the cleverest thing he had ever done. After the capture of Sestos and Byzantium by the Athenians and their allies in 479 and 478 B.C., Cimon was pressed by the allies to divide the spoils, including a great number of prisoners. He ordered the prisoners stripped naked, put all their goods and clothes in a pile, and gave the allies the choice of the naked prisoners or their possessions. The allies chose the possessions, which included substantial gold and silver jewelry and many rich fabrics. For a time all the Athenians had was a large number of naked men unfit for work. But then the prisoners' relatives began to arrive to ransom them for great sums of money. The ransom money enabled Cimon to give his fleet four months' pay and send a fortune to Athens for the public treasury.

Cimon's most successful venture in generating booty was his victory over the Persians at the Battle of the Eurymedon. Cimon's forces destroyed or captured the entire Persian fleet of more than 200 triremes and overran and captured the Persian camp with an enormous booty of gold and silver. With the riches that were his personally, Cimon created a number of shady walks in Athens by planting plane trees. He rebuilt the south wall of the Acropolis, restored many buildings that had been destroyed by the Persians, and laid the foundations for the long walls that ran from Athens to Piraeus and that formed the basis for the defense of Athens in later decades. Personally, he emanated charity; he tore down the walls around his gardens and farms to allow people to come and take crops as they needed, kept an open table at dinner for the hungry of his *deme*, and often was accompanied around Athens by a youth with a cup full of coins that were given to working people and craftsmen.

Battle of Marathon	Persian invasions; Battles of Thermopylae, Salamis	Greek victories at Plataea, Mylcale	Battle of Eurymedon	Cimon ostracized
490 B.C.	480 B.C.	479 B.C.	469 or 466 B.C.	461 B.C.

1. **MACROCOSM : TELESCOPE ::**
   a. microcosm : microscope
   b. microscope : telescope
   c. television : film
   d. gastroscope : gastropod

2. **HAPLOID : DIPLOID ::**
   a. arthropod : cephalopod
   b. monocular : binocular
   c. dichotomy : dichotomist
   d. phyla : phylum

3. **CORPULENT : ENDOMORPH ::**
   a. virulent : metamorphosis
   b. svelte : ectomorph
   c. obese : rotund
   d. mesomorph : mesophyll

4. **SUCCULENT : ESCULENT ::**
   a. edible : inedible
   b. juicy : fruit
   c. edible : juicy
   d. juicy : edible

5. **SYNOPSIS : ELABORATION ::**
   a. synthesis : hypothesis
   b. sketch : outline
   c. introduction : conclusion
   d. summary : development

6. **HYPOKINETIC : HYPERKINETIC ::**
   a. monochrome : polychrome
   b. dichotomy : trichotomy
   c. normal : abnormal
   d. paucity : surfeit

7. **KINETIC : HYPERKINETIC ::**
   a. growth : hypertrophy
   b. voracious : carnivore
   c. phylum : subphylum
   d. telekinesis : motion

8. **FRUCTIVOROUS : GEOPHAGOUS ::**
   a. herbivorous : plant
   b. chloroplast : chlorophyll
   c. apple : dirt
   d. eat : hunger

9. **VENTRAL : DORSAL ::**
   a. fin : tail
   b. side : back
   c. back : forward
   d. belly : back

10. **EFFUSIVE : INDOLENT ::**
    a. effulgent : bright
    b. demonstrative : lazy
    c. refulgent : lazy
    d. turbulent : turbid

The Panathenaia was an annual Athenian celebration held in July/ August to celebrate the birthday of Athena; every four years the Magna Panathenaia included the procession to the statue of Athena depicted on the Parthenon frieze. Competitive events included singing, music, dancing, athletics, horse and boat racing, and a relay race with a torch. Prizes included a special amphora with a depiction of Athena armed with spear and shield standing between two columns on one side and a depiction of the event for which the prize was awarded on the other side. Athena's shield bears the image of a famous statue that shows the tyrant slayers whose actions eventually led to the establishment of Athenian democracy. This black-figure amphora was one of the trophies.

1. Close your eyes, and press your eyelids with your hands. Small lights will appear and dance about. The lights will have various shapes. These lights (*phos*) that appear (*phen*) are called **phosphenes**. You sometimes see phosphenes when you stand up too fast.

2. The **ventriloquist** who entertains you on the television may be more skilled than you realize, if his name means anything. Literally, a ventriloquist is a belly (*ventri*) talker (*loqu*)! Do they make chapstick for the stomach?

3. What is the difference between **arthritis** and **arthralgia**? Arthritis is the inflammation (*itis*) in the joints (*arthro*) that causes the joints (*arthro*) to hurt (*algia*). Did you hear the one about the **arthropod** who had arthritis?

4. In the Mesozoic Era, 150,000,000 years ago, **pterodactyls** with forty-foot wingspans sailed over what is now called Arizona. Today the giant flying reptiles are reduced to petrified bone fragments in the hot desert sand. Why were the pterodactyls called *pterodactyls*? Because of the claws or fingers (*dactylo*) that appeared on their wings (*pter*). (I know what you're thinking, but you'd never get it housebroken!)

5. A **Micropoem**: Tough luck for the poor snails and other **gastropods**, which have to slide around all day on their stomachs (*gastro*). Or is it on their foot (*pod*)? Or on their stomach-foot? Just thinking about it makes one glad to be a biped.

6. More and more American films are about young people who have the power of **telekinesis**, which allows them to do terrible, violent things to other people just by thinking. Telekinesis means that you have the ability to move (*kin*) objects from far (*tele*) away. The very idea of tele-powers stirs one's creative fantasies; if only I could be televoracious, for instance, I would practice and practice.

7. What is the difference between the **microcosm** and the **macrocosm**? A microcosm is the small (*micro*) universe (*cosmo*) inside (for example) a drop of pond water; a macrocosm is the large (*macro*) universe of galaxies.

8. You might think that **trophy** contains the stem *troph* (nourishment), but it doesn't. The stem for *trophy* is *tropo* (turn), and it represents the award received for turning the enemy in battle, for forcing the enemy to reverse direction and retreat. Modern athletic trophies are cultural evolutions of the ancient trophies won on the fields of battle.

9. A **synopsis** is simply a summary, a brief review. It is a way of bringing everything together (*syn*) so that it can be seen (*opia*) at a glance.

10. Why does *gon* mean angle? It's a variation of the Greek *gony* (knee). A triangle has three knees, a rectangle four knees!

11. **Spanish Cognates:** One of the most important observations to gain from the study of the etymology of English vocabulary is that English and Spanish share thousands of words that are cognates—related words—that have common origins. Often, the English and the Spanish words share not only a stem but even more than one stem, and often in the same order. As examples, here are some English words from this lesson and their Spanish cognates:

gastronomy : gastronomía	microbiotic : microbiótico	corpulent : corpulento
trophy : trofeo	herbivore : herbívoro	effusive : efusivo
arthritis : artritis	myopia : miopia	dichotomy : dicotomia

In each case below, one of the choices was really the word used by the author in the sentence provided. All of the choices can be found in the example words on the first page of this lesson. Your challenge is to decide which word the author used. This is not a test; it is more like a game because more than one word choice may work perfectly well. See if you can use your sensitivity and intuition to guess correctly which word the author used. You may need a dictionary.

1. **From James Barrie's *Peter Pan***

   In time it lost its _____, and became hard as a stone.
   a. synopsis
   b. succulence
   c. dichotomy
   d. virulence

2. **From H.G. Wells's *The War of the Worlds***

   This spoiled child of life thought his weak tears in some way _____.
   a. efficacious
   b. dichotomous
   c. diagonal
   d. voracious

3. **From Kate Chopin's *The Awakening***

   There was a soft _____ in the east.
   a. arthralgia
   b. holocaust
   c. turbulence
   d. effulgence

4. **From H.G. Wells's *The Time Machine***

   I never met people more _____ or more easily fatigued.
   a. indolent
   b. omnivorous
   c. effusive
   d. dexterous

5. **From Mary Shelley's *Frankenstein***

   I perused, for the first time, those poets whose _____ entranced my soul.
   a. effusions
   b. effluvia
   c. heliotropes
   d. macrocosms

Anglo	*(English)*	Anglophile, Anglophobe, Anglican, Anglicism, Anglo-Saxon	*Latin*
ist	*(one who)*	artist, funambulist, anthropologist, solipsist, centrist, atheist, sophist	*Greek*
saur	*(lizard)*	dinosaur, pterosaur, tyrannosaurus, stegosaurus, saurian, plesiosaur	*Greek*
pithec	*(ape)*	pithecanthropus, australopithecus, dryopithecus, oreopithecus	*Greek*
calli	*(beautiful)*	calligraphy, calliope, calisthenics, calliopsis, callithumpian	*Greek*
austro	*(south)*	australopithecus, Australia, austral, Austronesia, austromancy	*Latin*
cephalo	*(head)*	cephalic, cephalopod, cephalothorax, microcephalic, encephalitis	*Greek*
chiro	*(hand)*	chiromancy, chiropody, chiropteran, chiropractor	*Greek*
caust	*(burn)*	caustic, holocaust, cauterize, caustically, causticity	*Greek*
terr	*(land)*	extraterrestrial, subterranean, Mediterranean, terrain, terra firma	*Latin*
cata	*(down)*	catapult, catastrophe, catacombs, catalepsy, cataclysm, cataract	*Greek*
jur	*(swear)*	abjure, adjure, perjure, jury, jurisdiction, jurisprudence, jurist	*Latin*
flu	*(flow)*	confluence, fluid, influence, fluent, superfluous, effluent, fluvial	*Latin*
here	*(stick)*	coherence, adhesive, adhere, inherent, incoherent	*Latin*
pos	*(put)*	position, deposit, superimpose, transpose, depose, imposition	*Latin*
mund	*(world)*	mundane, transmundane, intermundane, mundanity, mundo	*Latin*
cracy	*(government)*	autocracy, democracy, aristocracy, plutocracy, meritocracy	*Greek*
mania	*(madness)*	kleptomania, egomania, pyromania, dipsomania, megalomania	*Greek*
ize	*(make)*	victimize, harmonize, temporize, mobilize, fossilize, polarize, bowdlerize	*Greek*
antho	*(flower)*	anthology, anthozoan, anthocyanin, anthophilous, anther	*Greek*
algia	*(pain)*	neuralgia, analgesic, arthralgia, hemialgia, algometer, algophobia	*Greek*
somn	*(sleep)*	insomnia, somniferous, somnolent, somnambulate, somniloquy	*Latin*
quadr	*(four)*	quadruped, quadratic, quadrant, quadruplet, quadrilateral, quadriplegic	*Latin*
err	*(wander)*	error, erratic, knight-errant, erroneous, erratum	*Latin*
sine	*(without)*	sinecure, sine qua non, sine die, sine prole	*Latin*

in

in • into / not • without

The Latin stem **in**, which we define as meaning *in* or *not*, actually can have a wide variety of meanings and is sometimes changed to **il**, **ir**, or **im** in order to blend with the stem that follows it. Though we say for convenience that **in** means *in* or *not*, we might better regard these as two prefixes, one meaning *in*, *into*, *with*, *on*, *toward*, or as an intensive, and the other meaning *not*, *without*, or *no*. Here are some of the interesting words that contain **in/in** in their various shades of meaning:

incarnate: in the flesh. The egotist thought he was excellence incarnate.

inane: foolish. She grew tired of his inane objections to foreign customs.

incendiary: starting fire or strife. Trotsky's speech had an incendiary effect on the mob.

inclement: stormy. The game was postponed due to inclement weather.

incuse: stamped in. An incuse portrait of Alexander was stamped on the coin.

incubate: to develop. Whitman observed people as poems incubated in his mind.

inexpugnable: unconquerable. The position at Masada was nearly inexpugnable.

infrangible: unbreakable. Infrangible bonds bound Romeo and Juliet.

inhume: to bury. Jerry Cruncher exhumed bodies almost as fast as they were inhumed!

inhibit: to repress. The grandmaster inhibited her opponent into unwonted errors.

inquisition: harsh investigation. McCarthy's inquisitions make him a modern Torquemada.

innervate: stimulate to action. The near fall innervated him to new heights of effort.

insolent: egregiously disrespectful. The divergent idea was mistaken for insolence.

insomnia: sleeplessness. The vampire blamed his night-doings on chronic insomnia.

intaglio: an incised design. Unlike a cameo, the intaglio design was cut into the stone.

illative: producing an inference. He used illative words, such as *therefore*.

irreconcilable: incompatible. Irreconcilable differences proved to be their undoing.

immobile: motionless. Newton saw that an immobile object tends to remain immobile.

impalpable: too subtle to touch. The ideas were impalpable like smoke and eluded him.

impavid: fearless. An impavid need for experience drove her to join the expedition.

impeccant: blameless. A special prosecutor must have an impeccant record.

1.   He is a member of the **Anglican** church, but he is not an **Anglophile**.

2.   The **anthropologist** studies human cultures the world over.

3.   The **pterosaur** and pterodactyl were both flying **dinosaurs**.

4.   Fossilized **Pithecanthropus** and **Australopithecus** skeletons were discovered.

5.   Her **calligraphy** is ornate, like the music of the **calliope**.

6.   The **austral** winds raised dust storms over the dry **Australian** outback.

7.   The **microcephalic** boy held the **cephalopod**, a nautilus, in both hands.

8.   The physician accused the **chiropractor** of practicing **chiromancy**.

9.   The survivor of the **holocaust** made a **caustic** comment about social Darwinism.

10. The **extraterrestrial** admired the high **terrain** and the **subterranean** grottoes.

11. The **cataract** after the **cataclysm** caused a **catastrophe** in the **catacombs**.

12. The lying criminal **perjured** himself as the **jury** listened.

13. A fortunate **confluence** of **influences** made him **fluent** in Spanish.

14. The senator's **adherents** thought the opponent's speech was **incoherent**.

15. The corrupt ruler was **deposed** when his foreign bank **deposits** were discovered.

16. His **mundane** conversation bored her to tears.

17. Do we want a **democracy** and a **meritocracy** or a **plutocracy** for the **aristocracy**?

18. The host's **egomania** kept him from noticing the **kleptomania** of his guest.

19. He was **victimized** by his own ignorance of his civil rights.

20. The **anthology** article discussed the **anthozoans**, including the sea anemones.

21. The over-the-counter **analgesic** didn't help her **arthralgia** much.

22. The mayor's **somniferous** speech put even the **insomniac** to sleep.

23. The **quadruped** from Neptune gave birth to **quadruplets**.

24. The **knight-errant's error** was to save the dragon from the maiden.

25. A **sinecure** in the bureaucracy was the *sine qua non* of his dreams.

This head of Zeus is a striking representation of the pointed beard style of Greek men.

The ostracon above is one used against Cimon. This one says Cimon on the top line, and below it is the name of his father, Miltiades. The maker of this ostracon was maliciously rubbing it in, remembering that a little more than twenty-five years earlier, Cimon's father had suffered punishment at the hands of the people of Athens. The Greeks used the letter kappa in the names of Cimon and Pericles. (For this book I have followed the style of spelling more familiar to most readers.)

THE ECLIPSE OF CIMON
Dr. Thomas Milton Kemnitz

Part of the story of fifth-century Athenian democracy is of contending parties led by notable individuals, all of whom were ostracized. Aristides led the aristocratic faction in opposition to Themistocles, who was successful in ostracizing Aristides. Themistocles recalled Aristides and others after the battle of Thermopylae when he needed everyone in Athens working in concert to defeat the Persians. Within a decade, the aristocratic party embraced the young Cimon and used him to focus opposition to Themistocles. The aristocratic party was partial to Sparta and its values and emphasis on a land army of hoplites. The more democratic party emphasized the navy as the basis of Athenian power and was suspicious of Sparta. Cimon was a highly successful admiral, and his naval successes made him and his party of elites more palatable to the general populace and enabled his faction to ostracize Themistocles.

The Athenian aristocrats had a distinctive style because they wore their hair long in the fashion of Spartan men. In Sparta married women wore their hair short, but as we have seen, the men had long hair, often braided with hair clips. In Athens we know that gold hair clips were one of the features of the party of the few. The less privileged Athenians wore their hair short; most Athenian men wore beards trimmed to a point. Philosophers and others wishing to convey a deliberate disdain for fashion wore shaggy beards. Spartan and Athenian fashion differed in that Spartan men shaved their upper lips; Athenian men did not.

Eventually Cimon made a mistake that allowed others to impeach him. Pericles and his party tried to prosecute him for accepting bribes from Alexander I of Macedon, and Cimon was acquitted, but eventually his admiration for Sparta led to his downfall. In 462 B.C., he sought the support of Athens's citizens to provide help to Sparta when the Helots revolted. Although others maintained that Sparta was Athens's rival for power and should be left to fend for itself, Cimon won his point. He led 4,000 hoplites to Spartan territory, but the expedition ended in humiliation for Cimon and for Athens when the Spartans expelled him and his army because they feared the democratic principles of the Athenians. Apparently men in Cimon's army were genuinely shocked by the harsh treatment of the Helots, who were, after all, Greek. This insulting rebuff turned popular sentiment in Athens against Cimon. He was ostracized for ten years beginning in 461 B.C., and his pro-Spartan stance was rejected.

Although all he had done for Athens was insufficient to protect him from ostracism, Cimon had shown the way to a more beautiful, powerful, and richer city. His victories over the Persians had brought many cities and islands into the Delian League, which was key to Athenian power. His flexibility in allowing Delian League members to stop sending ships and men and to send money instead increased Athens's wealth and relative power. In the three decades after his ostracism, Athens would benefit enormously from following his path.

As long as Cimon was ascendant in Athens, relations with Sparta were good. His well-known admiration of Sparta was sufficient to blunt any apprehension the Spartans might have felt about Athens's growing power and prestige. It is hard to dislike a polity headed by a man who admires you so much that he names his son after your territory. But acrimony replaced harmony very soon after Cimon was expelled from Athens, and the two polities were quickly in a state of hostilities. Eventually Cimon had to be brought back to arrange peace with Sparta.

	Cimon ostracized	Delian treasury moved to Athens	Peace with Persia negotiated	Parthenon built
490–323 B.C. Classical Period	461 B.C.	454 B.C.	449 B.C.	447–438 B.C.

emotion

1.   What differences of emotion would there be between a **megalomaniac** and the people around a megalomaniac?

2.   What emotions do **caustic** comments produce?

aesthetics

1.   If you like to draw, draw a **Pithecanthropus**, or some fantasy **quadrupeds**, or an **anthozoan**.

2.   If you were to create a piece of "found" art by simply painting a common, **mundane** object, what object would you paint, and what colors would you use?

synthesis

1.   A **monomaniac** is obsessed (*mania*) with one (*mono*) thing. Can you think of a famous monomaniac, either fictional or historical?

2.   Use five words from List #16 in a satirical paragraph about an incident of **kleptomania**.

divergence

1.   A large asteroid has broken from its orbit and is heading for earth. What possible solutions could there be to avert this **catastrophe**? Generate ideas until you feel that you have some creative and workable solutions to choose from.

2.   How many kinds of art are there? Are there human activities that are not referred to as art but should be?

analysis

1.   Explain the difference between a **soliloquy** and a **somniloquy**.

2.   What is the difference between **egomania** and **megalomania**?

This bronze discus is one of many that have been uncovered by archaeologists. The Greeks had no standard weight or size for a discus. The modern discus weighs about a pound less than the average weight of those used by the ancient Greeks. This discus depicts an engraved figure of an athlete holding a measuring cord.

1. **PLUTOCRACY : MERITOCRACY ::**
   a. government : society
   b. money : merit
   c. democracy : president
   d. autocracy : monarchy

2. **PYROMANIA : MATCH ::**
   a. dipsomania : glass
   b. dipsomania : drink
   c. kleptomania : thief
   d. megalomania : megalopolis

3. **SUPERFLUOUS : INCISIVE ::**
   a. confluence : dispersion
   b. unnecessary : trenchant
   c. mundane : worldly
   d. Anglophile : Anglophobe

4. **SOLIPSIST : PAINTER ::**
   a. philosophy : aesthetics
   b. sophistry : honesty
   c. hermit : eremite
   d. ascetic : hedonistic

5. **MUNDANE : COSMIC ::**
   a. continent : ocean
   b. planet : star
   c. world : universe
   d. ordinary : earth

6. **CATACOMBS : BURIAL ::**
   a. *sine qua non* : essential
   b. fork : utensil
   c. Mediterranean : terrain
   d. cabinet : storage

7. **TERRA FIRMA : HYDROSPHERE ::**
   a. funambulism : somnambulism
   b. fish : bird
   c. terrestrial : marine
   d. water : fire

8. **ENCEPHALITIS : BRAIN ::**
   a. arthropod : joint
   b. infection : fracture
   c. neuralgia : pain
   d. arthritis : joint

9. **BOWDLERIZE : EXPURGATE ::**
   a. extraterrestrial : subterranean
   b. abjure : adjure
   c. truncate : cut off
   d. anthology : poems

10. **CEPHALOTHORAX : STEGOSAURUS ::**
    a. analgesic : arthralgia
    b. abdomen : duck
    c. cephalopod : plesiosaur
    d. head : body

This black-figure amphora depicts the pankration, a brutal mix of boxing and wrestling with few rules except the contestants were forbidden to bite their opponents or to gouge their eyes out. The figure on the right is the referee. The stick he holds was used to tap or hit a fighter to get him to cease a prohibited action; it clearly would have been hazardous for referees to try to separate the fighters the way their modern counterparts do. This was one of the prize amphorae from the Panatheniac games.

1. A **Micropoem**: An **anthology** of modern poetry is a collection of poetry from many different poets, carefully selected in order to present poems of high quality. An anthology is a good way to become familiar with many famous poems and with differences in style among poets. Even the word *anthology* is poetic. In fact, *anthology* contains a quiet but beautiful metaphor, for the literal meaning of *anthology* is to make a study/collection of (*logy*) the flowers (*antho*). An anthologist collects the flowers of literature.

2. When we say that there has been a **confluence** of ideas or a confluence of trends, we are taking an image from geography, from the lowlands where the rivers flow (*flu*) together (*con*).

3. Imagine taking the trouble to put something together from many different places, only to find that you didn't put it together well enough, and now the pieces are dropping off and falling, one at a time. This is the image we relish when we say that an argument is **coherent** or **incoherent**. If an argument is coherent, it sticks (*here*) together (*co*). The stuff that makes an argument stick together is a mixture of consistency and logic.

4. The usual order of events is that we have to take time in order to do things. But sometimes it is the opposite. Sometimes we try to stall or delay, and so we have to think of things to do in order to make time. To do so is to **temporize**, literally to make (*ize*) time (*tempor*).

5. **Jurisdiction** is a big, stately word. It means the legal power to hear disputes and to interpret the law. The literal meaning of the word is exactly that; the person with jurisdiction can say (*dict*) what the law (*jur*) requires.

6. Even careful speakers sometimes confuse two similar words, **abjure** and **adjure**. To abjure a belief is to disclaim it, to renounce it. To adjure someone is to earnestly command or request him or her. How can these two words, like two insects that strikingly resemble each other through protective coloration, be told apart? The answer is in the prefix. *Abjure*, to renounce, means swear (*jur*) away (*ab*). *Adjure*, to entreat, means swear (*jur*) to (*ad*). I abjure my former political beliefs, but I adjure you not to forsake yours.

7. What does **calisthenics** mean? The art (*ics*) of becoming beautiful (*calli*) and strong (*sthen*)!

8. Under the ocean there are beautiful, flowery, plant-like organisms such as sea corals and sea anemones. But are they plants? The answer is in their name; they are the **anthozoans**, the flower (*antho*) animals (*zo*).

9. Some words provide almost mystical insight. Do we **influence** each other? Then we flow (*flu*) into (*in*) each other as we exchange ideas, thoughts, emotions, and reactions. We allow our selves to flow into each other.

10. **Spanish Cognates**: One of the most important observations to gain from the study of the etymology of English vocabulary is that English and Spanish share thousands of words that are cognates—related words—that have common origins. Often, the English and the Spanish words share not only a stem but even more than one stem, and often in the same order. As examples, here are some English words from this lesson and their Spanish cognates:

Anglicism : Anglicismo
atheist : ateísta
calligraphy : caligrafía
microcephalic : microcefálico
extraterrestrial : extraterrestre
holocaust : holocausto
coherence : coherencia
anthology : antología
somniferous : somnífero

The stone finish line of the stadium at Delphi was just a few steps short of a stone wall.

In each case below, one of the choices was really the word used by the author in the sentence provided. All of the choices can be found in the example words on the first page of this lesson. Your challenge is to decide which word the author used. This is not a test; it is more like a game because more than one word choice may work perfectly well. See if you can use your sensitivity and intuition to guess correctly which word the author used. You may need a dictionary.

1. **From Kenneth Grahame's *The Wind in the Willows***

   The Badger's _____, not to say brutal, remarks may be imagined.
   a. analgesic
   b. somnolent
   c. caustic
   d. erroneous

2. **From Harriet Beecher Stowe's *Uncle Tom's Cabin***

   Are they swayed and perverted by the _____ of worldly policy?
   a. perjuries
   b. sophistries
   c. confluences
   d. somniloquies

3. **From Ralph Ellison's *Invisible Man***

   So don't waste time with _____ questions.
   a. superfluous
   b. fluent
   c. incoherent
   d. somnolent

4. **From F. Scott Fitzgerald's *The Great Gatsby***

   The quality of Wilson's _____ muttering changed.
   a. caustic
   b. incoherent
   c. erratic
   d. adhesive

5. **From Benjamin Franklin's *Autobiography***

   Thus I corrected that great _____ as well as I could.
   a. cataclysm
   b. plutocracy
   c. sinecure
   d. erratum

This vase depicts a two-horse chariot passing a finishing post.

lingu	*(tongue)*	bilingual, linguist, lingua franca, linguine, language	*Latin*
mot	*(move)*	motor, motivation, demote, emotion, motion, promote, motile, commotion	*Latin*
nav	*(ship)*	navy, naval, navigate, circumnavigate, unnavigable	*Latin*
und	*(wave)*	inundate, undulate, undulatory, undulation	*Latin*
flect	*(bend)*	reflect, inflection, genuflect, deflect, reflection	*Latin*
coron	*(crown)*	corona, coronation, coronary, coroner	*Latin*
aur	*(gold)*	aureate, auriferous, Aurora, auric	*Latin*
liter	*(letter)*	literature, illiterate, preliterate, literati	*Latin*
rat	*(think)*	rational, ratio, irrational, ratiocinate, rationalize	*Latin*
sis	*(condition)*	arteriosclerosis, osmosis, mitosis, meiosis, catharsis, symbiosis	*Greek*
par	*(equal)*	parity, disparity, par, compare, incomparable, disparate	*Latin*
mens	*(measure)*	commensurate, immense, incommensurable, mensurable, dimension	*Latin*
mony	*(condition)*	acrimony, patrimony, matrimony, ceremony, parsimony	*Latin*
quin	*(five)*	quintet, quintillion, quintuplet, quintuple, quintessence, quindecagon	*Latin*
socio	*(society)*	sociology, sociable, socialism, sociopath, dissociate	*Latin*
ovi	*(egg)*	oviducts, oviparous, ovipositors, ovoviviparous, ovisac, oviform, ovary, oval	*Latin*
phasia	*(speech)*	aphasis, dysphasia, apophasis	*Greek*
pter	*(wing)*	pterodactyl, helicopter, pterosaur, archaeopteryx, chiropteran	*Greek*
phen	*(appearance)*	phenomenon, phenotype, phosphenes, fancy, fantasy	*Greek*
hist	*(tissue)*	histopathology, histolysis, histology, histogenesis	*Greek*
glott	*(tongue)*	epiglottis, polyglot, glossolalia, glottal, monoglot, glossectomy	*Greek*
phan	*(appearance)*	phantom, epiphany, diaphanous, sycophant, cellophane, theophany	*Greek*
peri	*(near or around)*	perimeter, perihelion, perigee, periphery, periodical	*Greek*
pot	*(drink)*	potable, potion, potation, potatory, compote, symposium	*Latin*
via	*(road)*	via, viaduct, trivia, via avion, obviate, obvious, via media	*Latin*

syn

with • together

The Greek stem **syn**, which we usually define as meaning *together*, is sometimes altered to **sym**, **syl**, **syz**, or **sys** in order to blend with the stem that follows it. Though **syn** often means *together*, it can mean *with*, *at the same time*, or even *by means of*. Here are some of the interesting words that contain **syn** in its various shades of meaning:

syncline:	a rock downfold. The bones were discovered in the limestone syncline.
syncope:	dropping sounds. Through syncope, *Gloucester* becomes *Gloster*.
symposium:	conference. The symposium on the rain forest had little effect on the fires.
synonym:	a word of similar meaning. He argued that there were no true synonyms.
synapse:	nerve connection. The neural impulse shot through the synapses.
symphysis:	bone junction. The two halves of the jaw had grown together at the symphysis.
symptom:	an indication. The doctor felt a chill when she learned of his symptoms.
syncretism:	reconciliation of religions. The theological purists rejected all syncretism.
systaltic:	dilating and contracting. The normal systaltic heartbeat pattern was disrupted.
syzygy:	pair of opposites. At lunar syzygy, the moon was exactly opposite the sun.
syllogism:	conclusion from premises. There was an error in his specious syllogism.
syllabus:	course outline. Dr. Adamson reviewed her syllabus with the students.
symbiont:	an organism in symbiosis. The rhinoceros liked his blue-feathered symbiont.
synchronous:	simultaneous. At 4:30 a.m., synchronous explosions rocked the sleeping city.
syncopate:	shift rhythm. They played the "Closer Walk" theme in syncopated time.
synecdoche:	part for whole. By the synecdoche of "daily bread," he meant food.
systemic:	affecting the whole organism. It was a virulent systemic infection.
symmetry:	correspondence of opposites. In psychological symmetry, he loved her, too.
sympathy:	agreement of feeling. The old enemies met in a historic new sympathy.
synthesis:	combination. The synthesis of tensor calculus and physics was space-time.
syndetic:	connective. The surrounding tissue had a syndetic effect on its contents.

1. The **linguine-loving linguist** knew the *lingua franca*.

2. **Motile** microorganisms have powers of spontaneous **motion**.

3. The **navy circumnavigated** the globe by precise **navigation**.

4. The **undulant** waves soon **inundated** the low regions.

5. As she **genuflected**, she saw her **reflection** in the glass.

6. A hazy **corona** circled the moon the night before the **coronation**.

7. The goddess of the golden dawn, **Aurora**, held the **auriferous** rocks.

8. At the party the **literati** discussed the glories of **literature**.

9. The **rational** person will not **rationalize** his wrongs away.

10. Singing was an emotional **catharsis** for the vocalist.

11. There was a **disparity** between his story and the facts.

12. Are the rewards of the job **commensurate** with the duties?

13. We must decide whether we wish to live in **harmony** or **acrimony**.

14. The **quintet** played Mozart to a group of **quinquagenarians**.

15. The **sociopath** used his knowledge of **sociology** for evil purposes.

16. **Ovoviviparous** fishes produce eggs that hatch inside the mother's body.

17. The **dysphasia** resulted from injury to the speech center of his brain.

18. The stunned shepherd watched the **pterodactyl** fly off with his ram.

19. Are you studying these **phenomena** or this **phenomenon**?

20. **Histology** is the study of the structure of plant and animal tissues.

21. The famous **polyglot** spoke seventeen languages.

22. Soft light came through the **diaphanous** curtains.

23. The moon's **perigee** and the earth's **perihelion** are both tomorrow.

24. The magic **potion** was too vile to be **potable**.

25. His resignation **obviated** the need for impeachment proceedings.

evaluation

1. Should high schools require all students to become **bilingual** as a graduation requirement?

2. Should executives who challenge corporate policies be **promoted** or **demoted**?

intuition

1. You are in a **helicopter**, trying to land under dangerous circumstances. What are the dangerous circumstances?

2. On a voyage to study a newly discovered **preliterate** tribe in Borneo, your ship runs into a storm in the Indian Ocean, and suddenly your **navigation** equipment fails. What has happened to the navigation equipment?

emotion

1. What do you think is the **emotional** structure in most highly **self-motivated** people?

2. What **emotions** are common causes of **irrationality**?

aesthetics

1. What could an aesthetically-minded city do to turn its highway **viaducts** into works of modern art?

2. Can you think of an aesthetic use for **linguine**?

synthesis

1. Explain the common concept among the words **diaphanous**, **diameter**, and **dialogue**.

2. What do **emotion** and **promotion** have to do with **motion**?

This black-figure amphora *was a prize for winning the two-horse chariot race in the* Magna Panathenaia.

Pericles was said to have had an exceptionally elongated head, which contemporary playwrights and others ridiculed. This is reputed to be the reason he was particularly fond of the Athenian general's helmet.

THE EMERGENCE OF PERICLES

Dr. Thomas Milton Kemnitz

Pericles and Ephialtes led the democratic party that ostracized Cimon. With their success, Ephialtes in 461 systematically altered Athenian democracy to remove some of the institutions that favored the aristocrats. A member of the aristocratic party assassinated Ephialtes, and Pericles stepped forward and held sway for three decades. They would be years that left an enduring mark in world history.

Plutarch tells us that when Pericles entered political life, "he immediately altered his mode of life; was never seen in any street except that which led to the market place and the national Assembly, and declined all invitations to dinner and such like social gatherings, so utterly that during the whole of his long political life he never dined with one of his friends." Pericles was cultivating a reputation, and as Plutarch explains, "solemnity is wont to unbend at festive gatherings, and a majestic demeanor is hard to keep up when one is in familiar intercourse with others." The threat of ostracism hung so much over Pericles that he "feared to make himself too common even with the people, and only addressed them after long intervals—not speaking upon every subject, and, not constantly addressing them, but ... keeping himself ... for great crises, and allowing his friends and other orators to manage matters of less moment." The result of Pericles's lofty style and aloof conduct was that he earned the sobriquet "Olympian," meaning godlike.

Pericles was recognized in his day as a great leader, and twenty-five centuries later it is clear that he was one of the greatest leaders of any democracy. He did everything possible to make himself someone whose speech would be respected and whose behavior was beyond reproach. He was the son of the politician Xanthippus, who, although ostracized in 485/484 B.C., returned to Athens to command the Athenian contingent in the Greek victory at Mycale just five years later. Pericles came from a leading family on his mother's side also; she was a descendant of Cleisthenes, who established the Athenian democracy in 508/507. Pericles was well-educated; he developed, as Plutarch records, "a lofty style of oratory far removed from vulgarity and low buffoonery, and also a calmness of demeanor and appearance which no incident could disturb as he was speaking, while the tone of his voice never showed that he heeded any interruption." One incident told about him is that "some low worthless fellow" spent an entire day heaping abuse on Pericles as he conducted urgent business, even following him home still disparaging him. When he reached his door, Pericles, rather than responding with acrimony, ordered one of his servants to take a torch and light his tormentor's way home because it was dark.

Pericles was rich and of noble birth, and because of the experience of his father, he feared being ostracized and was not motivated to participate in public affairs when he was young. He proved a brave and daring soldier. After Aristides died, Themistocles had been ostracized, and Cimon was away on distant campaigns, Pericles entered public affairs on the democratic side, where he was welcomed as a counterweight to Cimon. But no Athenian politician was immune from the threat of ostracism; to the left is an *ostracon* prepared for an unsuccessful attempt to ostracize Pericles.

Establishment of democracy in Athens		Sparta receives a prophecy at Delphi	Cimon ostracized	Parthenon built
508/507 B.C.	490–323 B.C. Classical Period	485 B.C.	461 B.C.	447–438 B.C.

1. **UNDULATORY : PLACID ::**
   a. flux : stasis
   b. literate : literati
   c. reflection : refraction
   d. tranquil : smooth

2. **COMMENSURATE : INCOMMENSURATE ::**
   a. disproportionate : inadequate
   b. proportionate : sufficient
   c. disproportionate : insufficient
   d. proportionate : incommensurable

3. **SOCIABLE : HERMIT ::**
   a. egregious : blatant
   b. gregarious : eremite
   c. tractable : sociopath
   d. irate : buffoon

4. **PARSIMONY : PRODIGALITY ::**
   a. spending : saving
   b. literate : preliterate
   c. stinginess : wastefulness
   d. promotion : demotion

5. **POLYGLOT : MULTILINGUAL ::**
   a. language : *lingua franca*
   b. potation : potable
   c. periphery : diameter
   d. phenomenon : phenomena

6. **POTABLE : ESCULENT ::**
   a. water : food
   b. boat : land
   c. glass : cup
   d. simony : parsimony

7. **PERIHELION : PERIGEE ::**
   a. heliotropic : heliocentric
   b. aphelion : apogee
   c. histology : tissue
   d. obviate : prevent

8. **INUNDATE : DESICCATE ::**
   a. obviate : require
   b. navy : circumnavigate
   c. undulate : wave
   d. perihelion : perigee

9. **PERIHELION : PERIMETER ::**
   a. perigee : moon
   b. sun : perigee
   c. aphelion : diameter
   d. apogee : aphelion

10. **DIAPHANOUS : OPAQUE ::**
    a. translucent : transparent
    b. transparent : cellophane
    c. epiphany : recognition
    d. silk : wood

Plutarch was a Greek born about twenty miles from Delphi in 46 A.D. He traveled extensively and lived in Athens, and he became a Roman citizen before returning to his native town for most of his life. Plutarch wrote parallel lives of Greeks and Romans, matching individuals who seemed enough alike that he could discuss their characteristics in relationship to one another. He drew on all the sources he could, most of them now lost, and his biographies are often our only source for large parts of many individuals' lives. He was interested in illuminating the character of his subjects, and he focused on anecdotes that reveal personality rather than on chronological recitations of events.

1. A **Micropoem**: Pasta lovers beware. There is good news and bad news. The bad news is that **linguine** means little tongues, and **vermicelli** means little worms. The good news is that both terms refer to the shape of the pasta, not to the ingredients.

2. A **Micropoem**: A person who speaks many languages is a **polyglot**. But the literal meaning of the word is many (*poly*) tongued (*glot*). It is fortunate that the term is metaphorical, rather than anatomical! One is tempted to suggest that a true polyglot would make short work of an ice cream cone. And what if your blind date turned out to be a polyglot!

3. Why is a helicopter called a **helicopter**? Because as a helicopter goes up or down, its rotating wings (*pter*) describe a helix (*helico*) in the air.

4. To ask if the rewards of a job are **commensurate** with the responsibilities is to ask if what you get is on the same scale with what you give. It is to ask if the benefits and the requirements can be measured (*mens*) together (*co*).

5. A **phenomenon** is something that one observes and (usually) regards as remarkable. A green cloud would be an interesting meteorological phenomenon. The word *phenomenon* derives from the notion of something that appears or something that shines. The two stems *phen* and *phan* are actually variations of each other.

   There is a common mistake in usage that occurs with the word **phenomenon** and its plural, **phenomena**. People use the plural when they should use the singular, and vice versa. To say, "I saw an interesting phenomena" is like saying "I saw an interesting ducks." Just as we don't say *a ducks* or *those duck*, we shouldn't say *a phenomena* or *those phenomenon*.

6. To **obviate** the necessity of a trip is to make it unnecessary, to avoid the problem through anticipation. Literally, the word *obviate* means to look ahead for problems, spot them, and take the road (*via*) away (*ob*) before you reach them.

7. **Trivial** conversation is conversation of no importance. It is jabber, chatter. It is the sort of conversation that, in ancient times when people didn't travel in enclosed vehicles, used to arise when people met at intersections and stopped to talk. Trivial conversation is the sort to be found where three (*tri*) roads (*via*) cross. Trivial talk is crossroads talk.

8. **Spanish Cognates**: One of the most important observations to gain from the study of the etymology of English vocabulary is that English and Spanish share thousands of words that are cognates—related words—that have common origins. Often, the English and the Spanish words share not only a stem but even more than one stem, and often in the same order. As examples, here are some English words from this lesson and their Spanish cognates:

   bilingual : bilingüe
   promote : promover
   reflection : reflexión
   irrational : irracional
   compare : comparar
   immense : inmenso
   helicopter : helicóptero
   symbiosis : simbiosis

Oil lamps provided some light after dark in Greek homes.

In each case below, one of the choices was really the word used by the author in the sentence provided. All of the choices can be found in the example words on the first page of this lesson. Your challenge is to decide which word the author used. This is not a test; it is more like a game because more than one word choice may work perfectly well. See if you can use your sensitivity and intuition to guess correctly which word the author used. You may need a dictionary.

1. **From Frederick Douglass's *Narrative***

   Let darkness _____ with his crime hover over him.
   a. parsimonious
   b. navigable
   c. phenomenal
   d. commensurate

2. **From Mary Shelley's *Frankenstein***

   I…quickly lost him among the _____ of the sea of ice.
   a. genuflections
   b. epiphanies
   c. undulations
   d. literati

3. **From Emily Brontë's *Wuthering Heights***

   There was too great a(n) _____ between the ages of the parties to make it likely.
   a. disparity
   b. quintessence
   c. epiphany
   d. potation

4. **From Mary Wollstonecraft's *Vindication of the Rights of Woman***

   [He] is cajoled out of his humanity by the flattery of _____.
   a. matrimony
   b. *lingua franca*
   c. sycophants
   d. socialism

5. **From George Orwell's *1984***

   English is its chief _____ and Newspeak its official language.
   a. *lingua franca*
   b. inundation
   c. viaduct
   d. parsimony

Terracotta masks were used by actors in the Greek theater.

atmo	*(vapor)*	atmosphere, atmolysis, atmometer, atmospheric, atman	*Greek*
cardio	*(heart)*	cardiology, cardiovascular, cardiac, electrocardiogram	*Greek*
cosmo	*(world or universe)*	cosmos, cosmopolitan, cosmonaut, cosmology, microcosm	*Greek*
counter	*(against)*	counteract, counterproductive, counterpoint, counterinsurgence	*Latin*
cranio	*(skull)*	craniology, intracranial, craniotomy, cranium, dolichocranic	*Greek*
cyclo	*(circle)*	cyclone, cyclotron, bicycle, encyclopedia, recycle, cyclical	*Greek*
gno	*(know)*	agnostic, prognosis, gnostic, Gnosticism, diagnosis, topognosia, ignominy	*Greek*
oss	*(bone)*	ossify, ossuary, ossicle, osseous, ossiferous, ossein, ossification	*Latin*
xylo	*(wood)*	xylophone, xylograph, xyloid, xylophagous, xylose, xylotomy, xylem	*Greek*
monger	*(seller)*	fishmonger, warmonger, costermonger, ballad monger, phrasemonger	*Latin*
sept	*(seven)*	septangular, September, septuagenarian, septillion, Septuagint	*Latin*
xeno	*(stranger)*	xenophobia, xenolith, xenon, xenogenesis, xenodiagnosis	*Greek*
vas	*(vessel)*	vasoconstrictor, cardiovascular, vase, vessicle, vascular, vasectomy	*Latin*
fore	*(front)*	forehead, foreboding, forecast, forethought, foresail, forefront	*Old English*
ish	*(like)*	greenish, smallish, outlandish, snobbish, ghoulish, squeamish, mannish	*Old English*
less	*(without)*	fruitless, hopeless, motherless, bootless, pointless, hapless, feckless	*Old English*
baro	*(pressure)*	barometer, barograph, barometric, barogram, barometry	*Greek*
ferro	*(iron)*	ferronickel, ferromagnetic, ferrous, ferric, ferrite, ferroconcrete	*Latin*
quasi	*(somewhat)*	quasar, quasi-military, quasi-stellar, quasi-official, quasi-judicial	*Latin*
nesia	*(island)*	Micronesia, Polynesia, Melanesia, Austronesia	*Greek*
lepsy	*(attack)*	narcolepsy, epilepsy, catalepsy	*Greek*
let	*(little)*	booklet, piglet, aglet, hamlet, coverlet, omelet	*Latin*
nano	*(billionth)*	nanosecond, nanoplankton, nanosomia, nanogram	*Greek*
pico	*(trillionth)*	picofarad, picosecond, picogram	*Italian*
ideo	*(idea)*	ideograph, ideology, ideologue, ideogram, idée fixe, idealism	*Greek*

multi

many • more than two

The Latin stem **multi**, which we define as meaning *many*, can mean *consisting of many, affecting many, more than two, more than one,* or even *many times more than.* **Multi** is shortened to **mult** before vowels. Here are some of the interesting words that contain **multi** in its various shades of meaning:

multistage:	having several stages. The multistage rocket performed flawlessly.
multihued:	of many colors. The multihued foliage fell slowly to the ground.
multifarious:	diverse. It was a vigorous population of multifarious talents and interests.
multitude:	a large number. A multitude had assembled at the mount to listen.
multiform:	having many shapes. It was a multiform evolution from one shape to another.
multifid:	in many divisions. The multifid leaves had many divisions or lobes.
multifaceted:	having many aspects. It was a multifaceted problem, defying simple solutions.
multiparous:	bearing multiple offspring. The bears were multiparous and bore several cubs.
multidirectional:	in many directions. The anti-infantry weapon was a multidirectional explosive.
multilingual:	speaking many languages. Bilingual at first, he became multilingual in time.
multitudinous:	manifold. The red planet swarmed with multitudinous microscopic species.
multilateral:	many-sided. The multilateral negotiations were slow and frustrating.
multinational:	of many nations. The World Health Organization used multinational efforts.
multipartite:	of many parts. The ethnic groups wanted a multipartite division of the country.
multangular:	of many angles. The modern art museum was a sharp, multangular structure.
multiracial:	of many races. The United States is a vigorous, multiracial society.
multimillionaire:	having many millions. In his cupidity, he dreamed of being a multimillionaire.
multivariate:	of many variables. The complex system demanded multivariate analysis.
multicellular:	having many cells. The multicellular species fed greedily on the protozoans.
multiplicative:	multiplying. Through a strange multiplicative factor, the waveform intensified.
multistory:	having many stories. They looked for a multistory mansion to lease.

1. The **atmometer** measures the rate of evaporation of water.

2. The **cardiologist** studied the **cardiac** patient's **electrocardiogram**.

3. The orbiting Soviet **cosmonaut** had **cosmopolitan** views and tastes.

4. The command was **countermanded** by his British **counterpart**.

5. The **craniotomy** was performed by a skilled brain surgeon.

6. The **cyclone** hurled the **bicycle** fifty yards.

7. **Agnostics** are not usually attracted to **Gnosticism**.

8. Over the years, his habits had **ossified** beyond hope of change.

9. **Xylophagous** insects had eaten the antique **xylophone**.

10. The **costermonger** and the **fishmonger** shouted out prices to passersby.

11. **September** was the seventh month of the Roman calendar.

12. The flood of immigration stirred the **xenophobia** of the citizens.

13. The **cardiovascular** system responded gradually to the exercise.

14. The storm **forecast** filled her with **foreboding**.

15. The **smallish** object had a faint, **greenish** tint.

16. Their assault on the mountain summit proved **hopeless, bootless,** and **fruitless**.

17. Some think that high fashion is a **barometer** for stock market trends.

18. The company geologist studied the **ferrous** rock with care.

19. The **quasi-military** operation into Cambodia has failed.

20. We visited **Polynesia, Micronesia,** and **Melanesia**.

21. His uncontrollable **narcolepsy** made it hard for him to stay awake.

22. The **booklet** circulated through the **hamlet**.

23. The computation is made in less than a **nanosecond**.

24. There are a thousand **picoseconds** in one nanosecond.

25. The stubborn Chinese **ideologue** wrote his **ideas** in **ideograms**.

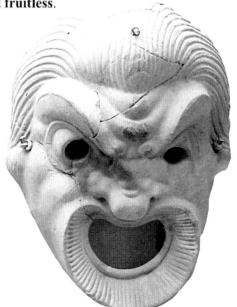

A terracotta theater mask

divergence

1. What would be the attitudes and viewpoints of a person with a **cosmopolitan** outlook?

2. How many cogent arguments can you think of to help someone overcome **xenophobia**?

analysis

1. How could you tell **xylophagous** and **phyllophagous** insects apart?

2. Analyze the word **vasoconstrictor**.

evaluation

1. Is someone who believes in a nuclear deterrent a **warmonger** or a realist?

2. Did American astronauts conduct joint space missions with Soviet **cosmonauts**?

intuition

1. You are sent through space in a craft that can travel at superluminous speeds to investigate a strange new phenomenon that is disrupting the principles of physics that regulate the **cosmos**. What is this strange phenomenon?

2. In a weird dream, you are shocked to find an article in an **encyclopedia**. What is the article about?

emotion

1. What emotions could be considered causes of **xenophobia**?

2. How would you feel if you were told that your efforts were **bootless**? Or that your mind was **xyloid**? Or that your attitudes had **ossified**?

The south wall of the Acropolis from the stage of the Theater of Dionysus. This is the wall that Cimon used his personal funds to have built.

1. **DIAGNOSIS : PROGNOSIS ::**
   a. sickness : health
   b. analysis : forecast
   c. ideology : ideologue
   d. prediction : weather

2. **BOOTLESS : FECKLESS ::**
   a. useless : feeble
   b. barefoot : unlucky
   c. shoe : vest
   d. ossicle : ossify

3. **AGNOSTICISM : CERTAINTY ::**
   a. costermonger : fruit
   b. cosmonaut : cosmology
   c. diffidence : confidence
   d. forecast : forethought

4. **FERRITE : PICOSECOND ::**
   a. pyrite : gold
   b. quartz : minute
   c. ossuary : bone
   d. month : nanosecond

5. **HAPLESS : LUCK ::**
   a. fruitless : results
   b. motherless : orphan
   c. bootless : useless
   d. feckless : ineffective

6. **MANNISH : MASCULINE ::**
   a. effeminate : feminine
   b. hero : heroine
   c. ideologue : dogma
   d. heterodox : orthodox

7. **FERROUS : AURIFEROUS ::**
   a. metal : nonmetal
   b. gold : ring
   c. iron : gold
   d. full of : lacking

8. **BALLADMONGER : POET ::**
   a. stellar : quasi-stellar
   b. claptrap : platitude
   c. literati : cognoscenti
   d. sophistry : philosophy

9. **IDEE FIXE : MONOMANIA ::**
   a. megalomania : diffidence
   b. xenophobia : cosmopolitan
   c. ethnocentrism : egalitarianism
   d. cardiovascular : circulatory

10. **INTRACRANIAL : CRANIUM ::**
    a. nucleus : cell
    b. brain : neuron
    c. surgeon : surgery
    d. fame : ignominy

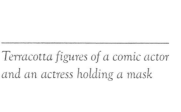

*Terracotta figures of a comic actor
and an actress holding a mask*

159

The Theater of Dionysus in Athens was the multiparous fount of theater as we know it. The Greeks made many contributions to Western civilization, including medicine and mathematics. But those were pursuits that could be undertaken almost anywhere, and the innovations did not occur in Athens. The theatrical arts thrive best in an atmosphere of freedom from censorship where a numerous and affluent audience can sustain it. Athens, uniquely in the classical Greek world, provided these ingredients, and from Athens came the elements of tragedy and comedy that form the basis of Western theater. The special front-row seats with backs were for the judges and were part of a fourth-century renovation of the facility.

PERICLES
Dr. Thomas Milton Kemnitz

Pericles arranged his life so that he was above suspicion on all accounts. He proved himself incorruptible when offered bribes. He inherited a large estate from his father, but he did nothing to increase it or to maximize his position to enrich himself. To counteract criticism of seeking to use his position for gain, Pericles developed a practice of taking all of the produce from his lands, selling it in the market at one time, and then using only that money for his household expenses. This did not please his family, who wanted more luxury than this mode of proceeding procured, and it was a source of contention between him and his sons. But Pericles was immune from the charge of in any way using his office to enrich himself, and that reputation stood him in good stead in the treacherous atmosphere of Athenian democracy.

Pericles used the treasury of Athens for the purpose of consolidating his support. First and foremost, he kept his adherents employed in the navy, either rowing or in building and maintaining the ships or the dockyards that were the major public works of Athens. In addition, Pericles began to pay jurors for their service; the pay was less than a skilled man could earn elsewhere, but it was something. Pericles was reported by Plutarch to have organized many festivals, parades, and spectacles for the people, and he established colonies in strategic places throughout the Mediterranean and sent multitudes of Athenians to populate them.

After Cimon was ostracized, a relative of his named Thucydides emerged as the leader of the party of the elites. This Thucydides was an older relative of Thucydides the great historian of the Peloponnesian Wars. We know very little of the politician Thucydides except that he endeavored to magnify the power of his aristocratic party by having its members sit together in the Assembly. Thucydides tried to organize an opposition to Pericles, but in this he was more of a nuisance than a deterrent.

In 454 Pericles took the highly controversial step of moving the Delian treasury from the island of Delos to Athens. He had been aggressive in using the Athenian navy to collect annual contributions from the members of the Delian League, whether they wanted to pay them or not; members of the League who tried to withdraw were invaded and forced to pay up. The Athenians had been successful in protecting the Greeks from the Persians, and now that the danger had largely passed, the allies saw no reason to continue to contribute. But Pericles had plans for the money, and so the Delian League became a protection racket in which its members were paying to be protected from Athens itself. Pericles, moreover, now asserted that the allies were in no position to question how Athens used the money so long as they were effectively protected. He intended to employ the treasury to beautify Athens. He had in mind a monumental building program that included a number of structures on the Acropolis, the high rock that dominates the city of Athens. After they had reclaimed their city when the Persians were driven out, the Athenians had decided to keep their ruined temples in the condition the barbarians had left them. For three decades they had looked at the ruins; now Pericles intended to rebuild them in spectacular fashion. And he was unapologetic about the means, saying that perhaps it was not right that Athens had acquired an empire, but it would be folly to give it up once it had come into existence.

Cimon ostracized	Delian treasury moved to Athens	Peace with Persia negotiated	Parthenon built	Pediment statues erected
461 B.C.	**454 B.C.**	**449 B.C.**	**447–438 B.C.**	**438–432 B.C.**

1. If you think for a moment about the many great cities of the world, cities on every continent and in every terrain and climate, and if you think of how it would change you to spend time traveling over the world, getting to know these great cities, to understand them, to feel at home in them, then you begin to understand the sense of the word **cosmopolitan**. To be cosmopolitan is to be sophisticated, traveled, knowledgeable about what is available. To be cosmopolitan is not to be provincial but to understand the things that people who know the cities (*polis*) of the world (*cosmo*) understand.

2. What is a **xylophone**? It is a series of wooden (*xylo*) bars of different lengths mounted on felt pads. When the wooden bars are struck, they make different sounds (*phon*), depending on the length of each bar. Though modern xylophones sometimes use metal bars, the word *xylophone* still means the sound of wood.

3. Perhaps the most derogatory term we have to describe a truly bad poet is the term **balladmonger**. It implies that the work isn't truly poetry at all but merely mediocre lyrics and that the poet isn't really an artist but a vendor (*monger*) trying to foist his bad words off on the public. *Balladmonger* is a fiercer term than **rhymester** or **poetaster**, which are also terms of derision for bad poets. Poetry tends to excite the emotions of those who wish to defend it. Emerson once pulled out all the stops in an effort to condemn the ostentatiously technical poetry of Edgar Allan Poe; Emerson called Poe "the jingle man."

4. A **Micropoem**: The word **atmosphere** contains an interesting feat of vision. Imagine what the atmosphere would look like from space if the rest of the earth became completely invisible. The resulting sight would be just what the word implies: an immense sphere of vapor (*atmo*) floating in space. The atmosphere is a vaporsphere.

5. **Spanish Cognates:** One of the most important observations to gain from the study of the etymology of English vocabulary is that English and Spanish share thousands of words that are cognates—related words—that have common origins. Often, the English and the Spanish words share not only a stem but even more than one stem, and often in the same order. As examples, here are some English words from this lesson and their Spanish cognates:

    atmosphere : atmósfera
    cosmopolitan : cosmopolita
    agnostic : agnóstico
    xylophone : xilófono
    cardiovascular : cardiovascular
    xenophobia : xenofobia

Not only are the forms of comedy and tragedy direct descendants of the Athenian theater, but the very terms theater, comedy, *and* tragedy *come to us almost unchanged from the Greek language of 2,500 years ago.*

In each case below, one of the choices was really the word used by the author in the sentence provided. All of the choices can be found in the example words on the first page of this lesson. Your challenge is to decide which word the author used. This is not a test; it is more like a game because more than one word choice may work perfectly well. See if you can use your sensitivity and intuition to guess correctly which word the author used. You may need a dictionary.

1. **From John Gardner's *Grendel***

   Merely rational thought leaves the mind incurably crippled in a closed and _____ system.
   a. ossified
   b. feckless
   c. foreboding
   d. xenophobic

2. **From John Hersey's *Hiroshima***

   He felt the strain of being a foreigner in an increasingly _____ Japan.
   a. microcosmic
   b. bootless
   c. narcoleptic
   d. xenophobic

3. **From William Shakespeare's *Othello***

   He robs himself that spends a _____ grief.
   a. septuagenarian
   b. bootless
   c. ferrous
   d. xenophobic

4. **From Virginia Woolf's *Mrs. Dalloway***

   Those _____ [were] not allowed to stand their barrows in the streets.
   a. cosmonauts
   b. cosmopolitans
   c. xenoliths
   d. costermongers

5. **From Maya Angelou's *I Know Why the Caged Bird Sings***

   I had accepted my plight as the _____, put-upon victim of fate and the Furies.
   a. osseous
   b. hapless
   c. narcoleptic
   d. cosmopolitan

ven	*(come)*	convene, convention, avenue, circumvent, advent, prevent, subvention	*Latin*
ichthy	*(fish)*	ichthyosaur, ichthyologist, ichthyoid, ichthyosis	*Greek*
pulse	*(drive)*	impulse, repulse, pulsate, impulsive	*Latin*
calor	*(heat)*	calorie, calorimeter, calorific, caloric	*Latin*
sol	*(sun)*	solar, solstice, solarium, solarize, solar plexus	*Latin*
strat	*(layer)*	stratigraphy, stratosphere, cirrostratus, strata, substratum, stratified	*Latin*
nuc	*(center)*	nucleus, nucleate, nuclide, nucleon, nucleotide, nucleoplasm	*Latin*
sat	*(enough)*	satisfy, dissatisfaction, saturate, insatiable, sate	*Latin*
protero	*(early)*	Proterozoic, proterandrous, proteranthous	*Greek*
mont	*(mountain)*	piedmont, Montana, Montevideo, montane, cismontane	*Latin*
kilo	*(thousand)*	kilometer, kiloton, kilowatt, kilogram	*Greek*
myria	*(many)*	myriad, myriapod, myriameter, myriarch, myriophyllum	*Greek*
tachy	*(quick)*	tachometer, tachycardia, tachylyte, tachygraphy	*Greek*
fiss	*(split)*	fissile, fission, fissipalmate, fissiped, fissure	*Latin*
cumu	*(heaped)*	accumulate, cumulus, cumulonimbus, cumulative	*Latin*
meteor	*(high)*	meteorite, meteoric, meteorograph, meteorology	*Greek*
hibern	*(winter)*	hibernate, hibernal, hibernaculum	*Latin*
di	*(two)*	diverge, dicotyledon, diencephalon, dilemma, catadioptric	*Greek*
bath	*(deep)*	bathymetry, bathyscaph, bathysphere, bathos, batholith	*Greek*
cirr	*(hair)*	cirrus, cirrostratus, cirriped, cirrocumulus	*Greek*
grav	*(heavy)*	gravity, gravid, gravimetric, gravamen, aggravate	*Latin*
solv	*(loosen)*	resolve, dissolve, absolve, solvent, insolvency	*Latin*
ophthal	*(eye)*	ophthalmologist, ophthalmoscope, ophthalmic, exophthalmic	*Greek*
oma	*(tumor)*	melanoma, carcinoma, hematoma, glaucoma	*Greek*
rub	*(red)*	rubric, rubious, rubicund, ruby, rubescent, rubella	*Latin*

spec

look • see

The Latin stem **spec**, which we define as meaning *look* or *see*, is sometimes seen as **spic** or **spect**. Since **spec** refers to vision, it appears in some of the most beautiful and descriptive words in our language. Here are some of the interesting words that contain **spec** in its various shades of meaning:

specimen:	an example. Unfortunately, the specimen died before it could be studied.
specific:	definite. They searched for the specific cause of the symptom.
special:	unique. The special theory of relativity was really something to see.
spectacle:	a remarkable sight. The spectacle in the Colosseum exhilarated the Romans.
specter:	an apparition. The sound of breathing rose as the glowing specter approached.
species:	a distinct variety. Undiscovered species are becoming extinct in the Amazon.
speculate:	to conjecture. She refused to speculate about the Egyptians' possible reply.
spectrum:	a continuous range. A spectrum of opinions characterized the diverse group.
re**spect**:	to hold in esteem. She looked at her friend with a new respect.
intro**spect**ion:	self-analysis. Macbeth lapsed into a chronic, melancholy introspection.
in**spect**:	examine critically. A probing inspection left little doubt about the error.
retro**spect**ive:	backward looking. The old songs put her in a pensive and retrospective mood.
su**spect**:	to believe guilty. Without specific reason, he began to suspect Raskolnikov.
tran**spic**uous:	easily understood. With transpicuous logic, Aristotle explained the cause.
specious:	false. The rationalizations for slavery were disingenuously specious.
per**spect**ive:	objective vision. The perspicuous essay showed she had not lost perspective.
pro**spect**:	an outlook. The prospect from Yeats's tower was inspiring.
a**spect**:	mien. "By your aspect, you appear to think so," Hamlet added.
spectator:	observer. The burning dirigible rained fire on the terrified spectators.
per**spic**uous:	clear. The essay was brilliantly perspicuous.

1. We **convened** at the Hilton on Third **Avenue**.

2. The **ichthyologist** removed the petrified **ichthyosaur** bones.

3. The **impulsive** commander **repulsed** the enemy.

4. The **calorimeter** measured the heat of the **calorific** reaction.

5. Heliophiles catch few **solar** rays at the winter **solstice**.

6. The bride and groom were not from the same social **stratum**.

7. There were **nucleotides** in the chromosomes of the cell **nucleus**.

8. He tried to **sate** his **insatiable** appetite for pizza.

9. Male **proterandrous** insects appear earlier in the season than females.

10. The **montane** vistas of **Montevideo** are as beautiful as those in **Montana**.

11. A **kilometer**, one thousand meters, is 0.62137 miles in length.

12. **Myriad** explanations exist of unidentified flying objects.

13. At the first sign of **tachycardia**, he was rushed to the hospital.

14. Is nuclear **fission** the opposite of nuclear fusion?

15. The **cumulus** clouds **accumulated** as the sun baked the sea.

16. The **meteorologist** reported that the **meteorite** did no damage.

17. The **hibernal** winds did not reach the **hibernating** bear.

18. The **dilemma** was whether to study the **dicotyledon** or the **diencephalon**.

19. The **bathymetry** of the Pacific was easily studied with the **bathyscaph**.

20. Barnacles and other **cirripeds** covered the marina's pilings.

21. The **gravamen** of the charges is that he left his post under fire.

22. The **solvent** did not **dissolve** the old paint on the brush.

23. The **ophthalmologist** treats the diseases of the eye.

24. The exposure to carcinogens produced **carcinomas** in the workers.

25. The red **rubric** at the beginning of the text was beautiful.

aesthetics

1. Describe a painting you would paint as a gift for an **ichthyologist**.

2. Would the silhouette of a **myriapod** make an interesting basis for the pattern in a graphics design?

synthesis

1. What words in List #19 would be used frequently by a **meteorologist**?

2. What courses—especially courses in different departments—do you think you would have to take in college to become an **ichthyologist**?

divergence

1. Think of some good ways to promote the **diffusion** of new ideas in spite of people's resistance to change.

2. What improvements in our lives would be possible if **meteorology** became a precise science, able to predict weather with perfect accuracy up to a year in advance?

analysis

1. What is the difference between **stratigraphy** and **tachygraphy**?

2. What is the difference between **cirrostratus** and **cirrocumulus** clouds?

evaluation

1. If the doctor's diagnosis is that the patient has a malignant **carcinoma**, and if her prognosis is that the patient has less than a year to live, are there any circumstances you can think of that would make it proper for the doctor not to tell her patient?

2. Should the United States attempt to abolish the social **stratification** structure, or should we leave the structure intact and let each person take responsibility for his or her own vertical mobility?

The Temple of Athena Nike

Rebuilding the south wall of the Acropolis had been a huge undertaking that Cimon had assumed at his own expense. It was a necessary precursor to the public works that Pericles pursued on the apex of the Acropolis.

Rebuilding in Athens took many other forms, such as the lovely Temple of Hephiastos, now the most complete existing Doric temple in Greece.

PERICLES THE BUILDER
Dr. Thomas Milton Kemnitz

Pericles's building program should be seen in the context of the rebuilding of Athens that had started in 479 when the Persians were expelled. Themistocles immediately had erected a wall to protect the city, over the objections of the Spartans, who did not want Athens to have walls. The wall of Themistocles was more than four miles long, some twenty-five feet high, and about ten feet wide; it had thirteen gates. Twenty years later Cimon laid the foundations of the long walls that connected Athens to its seaport at Pireaus, and he built the north wall. In the years from 446 to 443, Pericles had the long south wall built; the distance between the north and south walls was about 600 yards for much of the distance from Athens to Pireaus. In addition, other building projects were going on throughout Athens, including the construction of the lovely Doric Temple of Hephiastos in the Agora north of the Acropolis; its grace and beauty are still remarkable.

Among the buildings of Pericles was the Odeum on the south slope of the Acropolis. It was a huge roofed structure built of wood salvaged from Persian ships. Plutarch says that internally it "consisted of many rows of seats and many columns, and externally of a roof sloping on all sides from a central point, and was said to have been built in imitation of the king of Persia's tent." *Odeum* was the Greek word for singing contest. According to Plutarch, "Pericles used his influence to pass a decree for establishing a musical competition at the Panatheniac festival, and, being himself chosen judge, he laid down rules as to how the candidates were to sing, and play the flute or the harp." Next to the Odeum, the Theater of Dionysus was refurbished. Here it was that the great Greek playwrights of the fifth century–Sophocles, Euripides, Aeschylus, and Aristophanes– first staged their works, a spectacular epoch in the history of the theater.

Pericles was unapologetic about the value of his building program, according to Plutarch: "After the city had provided all that was necessary for war, it should devote its surplus money to the erection of buildings which would be a glory to it for all ages, while these works would create plenty by leaving no man unemployed, and encouraging all sorts of handicraft, so that nearly the whole city would earn wages, and thus derive both its beauty and its profit from itself. For those who were in the flower of their age, military service offered a means of earning money from the common stock; while, as he [Pericles] did not wish the less prosperous to be without their share, nor yet to see them receive it without doing work for it, he had laid the foundations of great edifices which would require industries of every kind to complete them; and he had done this in the interests of the working people, who thus, although they remain at home, would have just as good a claim to their share of the public funds as those who were serving at sea, in garrison, or in the field. The different materials used, such as stone, brass, ivory, gold, ebony, cypress-wood, and so forth, would require special artisans for each, such as carpenters, modelers, smiths, stone masons, dyers, smelters and moulders of gold, and ivory painters, embroiderers, workers in relief, and also men to bring them to the city, such as sailors and captains of ships and pilots for such as came by sea, and for those who came by land, carriage builders, horse breeders, drivers, rope makers, linen manufacturers, shoemakers, road menders, and miners. Each trade, moreover, employed a number of unskilled laborers, so that, in a work, there would be work for persons of every age and every class, and general prosperity would be the result."

Battle of Marathon	Persian invasions; Battles of Thermopylae, Salamis	Greek victories at Plataea, Mylcale	Battle of Eurymedon	Cimon ostracized
490 B.C.	480 B.C.	479 B.C.	469 or 466 B.C.	461 B.C.

1. **AGGRAVATE : IRRITATE ::**
   a. solar : stellar
   b. piedmont : foothills
   c. anger : peeve
   d. worsen : anger

2. **FISSION : FUSION ::**
   a. split : join
   b. nuclear : cellular
   c. synthesize : diverge
   d. convention : session

3. **BATHYSCAPH : HYDROSPHERE ::**
   a. dirigible : atmosphere
   b. depth : water
   c. fish : ocean
   d. physics : geometry

4. **ICHTHYOLOGIST : TROUT ::**
   a. zoologist : oak
   b. fish : bird
   c. astrophysicist : telescope
   d. microbiologist : euglena

5. **STRATA : STRATUM ::**
   a. layered : layers
   b. boats : boat
   c. fissure : interstice
   d. ruby : rubious

6. **SOLVENT : SOLUTE ::**
   a. solution : mixture
   b. paint : thinner
   c. mollification : anger
   d. cirrostratus : cirrocumulus

7. **RUBICUND : RUBESCENT ::**
   a. grown : growing
   b. red : rubious
   c. ruby : jewel
   d. moon : lunar

8. **RESOLVE : ABSOLVE ::**
   a. decide : exculpate
   b. meteorite : meteoric
   c. obey : circumvent
   d. solve : interpret

9. **DICOTYLEDON : RUBELLA ::**
   a. montane : alpine
   b. bathos : pathos
   c. melanoma : hematoma
   d. mesophyll : glaucoma

10. **MYRIAD : UNIQUE ::**
    a. sociable : solitary
    b. essay : monograph
    c. plentiful : sole
    d. myriapod : millipede

This statuette of Athena Promachos represents Athena holding her spear and shield (both now missing) as she fights in the front line to protect the city.

1. A **Micropoem**: **Ichthyosis** is a congenital disease that causes the sufferer's skin to harden and flake off. The name of the disease is unpleasantly descriptive because it means that the skin is in a fishy (*ichthy*) condition (*osis*).

2. The **Proterozoic** Age (a term that does not enjoy the vogue it once did among geologists) is a geologic time period that occurred between the Paleozoic and Archeozoic periods. It lasted from about 1,400,000,000 years ago until 620,000,000 years ago and is named after the fossils found in its sedimentary rock deposits. Only the simplest, most primitive fossils, including some invertebrates and marine algae, can be found in these rocks. The Proterozoic Era was the time of early (*protero*) animals (*zo*).

3. What is the difference between nuclear **fission** and nuclear **fusion**? It is simple to remember. Nuclear fission is the splitting (*fiss*) of the nucleus of a heavy atom like uranium, whereas fusion is the joining (*fus*: pour together) of the nuclei of lighter atoms like deuterium into heavier atoms like helium. Fission is a splitting; fusion is a pouring together.

4. In some books there is a title or heading that is set off from the rest of the text by being printed in red (*rub*). It is called a **rubric** after the traditional color used, even though today the rubric is sometimes printed in a color other than red.

5. In ancient Greece a **myriarch** was a commander (*arch*) of ten thousand (*myria*) soldiers. We still retain the stem *myria*, but we have relaxed the concept to mean not ten thousand but very many. The **Myriapoda** are the little critters with gobs of legs (*pod*), such as the centipedes and the millipedes.

6. Have you ever been **absolved** of guilt? That means that the guilt that was attached to you in other people's minds has been loosened (*solv*) and removed away (*ab*).

7. Have you ever encountered the two terms **pathos** and **bathos**? Pathos is the ability of a creative work to arouse a feeling (*path*) of sympathy or pity. If this emotion is overemphasized, too deep, or inappropriately deep (*bath*), we then call it bathos. Bathos is a too-deep pathos, an unrespectable sentimentality in a creative work.

8. **Spanish Cognates**: One of the most important observations to gain from the study of the etymology of English vocabulary is that English and Spanish share thousands of words that are cognates—related words—that have common origins. Often, the English and the Spanish words share not only a stem but even more than one stem, and often in the same order. As examples, here are some English words from this lesson and their Spanish cognates:

   prevent : prevenir
   impulse : impulso
   nucleus : nucleo
   montane : montañoso
   accumulate : acumular
   hibernate : hibernar
   aggravate : agravar
   glaucoma : glaucoma

The tortoise-shell lyre was held upright when played.

In each case below, one of the choices was really the word used by the author in the sentence provided. All of the choices can be found in the example words on the first page of this lesson. Your challenge is to decide which word the author used. This is not a test; it is more like a game because more than one word choice may work perfectly well. See if you can use your sensitivity and intuition to guess correctly which word the author used. You may need a dictionary.

1. **From Rachel Carson's *Silent Spring***

   Insects are finding ways to _____ our chemical attacks on them.
   a. solarize
   b. circumvent
   c. accumulate
   d. saturate

2. **From Jack London's *The Call of the Wild***

   Since his puppyhood he had lived the life of a(n) _____ aristocrat.
   a. impulsive
   b. sated
   c. myriad
   d. solvent

3. **From Ernest Hemingway's *The Old Man and the Sea***

   The _____ flecks of the plankton were annulled now by the high sun.
   a. myriad
   b. insatiable
   c. gravid
   d. rubescent

4. **From Nevil Shute's *On the Beach***

   The old man raised his flushed, _____ face in concern.
   a. rubicund
   b. ichthyoid
   c. calorific
   d. impulsive

5. **From Emily Brontë's *Wuthering Heights***

   He'll never be able to emerge from his _____ of coarseness and ignorance.
   a. cumulus
   b. nucleus
   c. bathos
   d. rubric

mela	*(black)*	melanin, melanite, melancholy, Melanesia, melanoma, melanocyte	*Greek*
vice	*(in place of)*	vice versa, vice president, vice consul, viceroy, vice-regent	*Latin*
foli	*(leaf)*	folio, foliolate, bifoliolate, foliation, defoliate, portfolio, folium	*Latin*
atom	*(vapor or particle)*	atomic, atomizer, atomize, atomism, subatomic, diatomic	*Greek*
orb	*(circle)*	orbit, exorbitant, orbital, orbicular, orbital decay, supraorbital	*Latin*
multi	*(many)*	multifarious, multitudinous, multilateral, multiped, multiply	*Latin*
ign	*(fire)*	ignite, igneous, ignis fatuus, ignition, reignite, ignescent, ignitron	*Latin*
moll	*(soft)*	mollify, emollient, mollusk, mollescent	*Latin*
lin	*(line)*	linear, delineate, lineation, lineal, rectilinear, lineage	*Latin*
hemi	*(half)*	hemisphere, hemialgia, hemiplegia, hemipterous, hemicrania	*Greek*
oo	*(egg)*	oophyte, oocyte, oology, oogenesis, oogonium, oophorectomy, oospore	*Greek*
grad	*(step)*	gradual, grading, retrograde, downgrade, gradualism, degrading	*Latin*
pneumo	*(lung or air)*	pneumogastric, pneumonia, pneumonectomy, pneumobacillus	*Greek*
radi	*(ray)*	radiation, radian, radial, radiolarian, radiance, irradiate	*Latin*
oscu	*(mouth)*	osculum, osculation, osculant, osculate	*Latin*
ob	*(against)*	obloquy, objurgation, obdurate, obsequious, oblique, obsolete, obstinate	*Latin*
vect	*(carry)*	convection, vector, invective, vectorial	*Latin*
digit	*(finger)*	prestidigitation, digital, digitation	*Latin*
gymno	*(naked)*	gymnasium, gymnastics, gymnosperm, gymnosophist	*Greek*
plasm	*(form)*	cytoplasm, endoplasm, ectoplasm, plasma, plasmodium	*Greek*
narco	*(sleep)*	narcotic, narcolepsy, narcotine, narcotism	*Greek*
vermi	*(worm)*	vermin, vermicelli, vermicide, vermivorous	*Latin*
lign	*(wood)*	lignite, lignify, ligneous, lignocellulose	*Latin*
dendr	*(tree)*	dendrology, dendroid, dendrochronology, dendrite, rhododendron	*Greek*
lachry	*(tear)*	lachrymose, lachrymatory, lachrymal	*Latin*

epi

on • upon • beside • among

The Greek stem **epi** is an important prefix in the English language. We usually define it as meaning *on*, but it can also mean *upon*, *beside*, *among*, *in front of*, or even *over*. In some words, **epi** is altered to **ep** or even **eph**. Here is a small selection of the interesting words that contain **epi** in its various shades of meaning:

epideictic:	for show. The openly epideictic speech was loudly applauded by the crowd.
episode:	a complete part. The forfeit was the latest enigmatic episode in Fischer's saga.
episcopate:	the position of a bishop. Within two years he had ascended to the episcopate.
epiphytotic:	epidemic in plants. The new virus had an epiphytotic virulence.
epilogue:	closing comment. Prospero's epilogue was a poignant moment for theater.
epicene:	effeminate. His manners and tastes manifested an epicene daintiness.
epitome:	a representative. Nero's evil deeds seemed the epitome of Roman decadence.
epizoon:	a parasite. The animal's skin had become a paradise for epizoa.
epoch:	an important period. Gorbachev's rule was an epoch in world history.
epode:	a poetic form. Short lines follow longer lines in Horace's epodes.
eponym:	a source-name person. Simon Bolivar is the eponym for the nation of Bolivia.
epigeal:	growing on the ground. Larger animals fed on the lush epigeal species.
epidermis:	outer skin. She specialized in treating diseases of the epidermis.
epistemic:	concerning knowledge. They debated a range of profound epistemic issues.
epistle:	a letter. The epistle to the Romans has received a certain fame.
epigone:	an inferior descendant. The founders were poorly imitated by their epigones.
epicenter:	center of an earthquake. The devastation was greatest at the epicenter.
epigenous:	growing on plant surface. Epigenous organisms covered the broad leaves.
epigraphy:	study of inscriptions. They needed a specialist in epigraphy to decipher the inscription.
epexegesis:	additional clarification. The brief epexegesis clarified the obscurity.
epigraph:	architectural inscription. "Bring to me your tired . . . ," began the epigraph.

1. The gloomy soul was unable to overcome her **melancholy**.

2. The **vice president** greeted the **vice consul,** and **vice versa**.

3. Agent Orange was a toxic **defoliant** used in the Vietnam War.

4. The **atomizer** was filled with a wonderful perfume.

5. **Orbicular** leaves are circular and flat.

6. Her **multifarious** nefarious deeds landed her in prison.

7. The *ignis fatuus* seemed to **ignite** and hover over the swamp.

8. We could do nothing to **mollify** the man's anger.

9. Quickly **delineate** your proposal.

10. **Hemiplegia** is paralysis of one side of the body.

11. The obsessed **oologist** painted his house robin's-egg blue.

12. We **gradually** became aware of the ship's **retrograde** motion.

13. The **pneumococcus** bacteria gave him **pneumonia**.

14. Skeletons of the microscopic **radiolarians** show **radial** symmetry.

15. The sponge expels water through its **osculum**.

16. He **objected** because the **object** caused the **obstruction**.

17. The **convection** current distributed the heat of the flames.

18. Houdini accomplished feats of **prestidigitation**.

19. The **gymnasium** is the perfect place for **gymnastics**.

20. An amoeba's **cytoplasm** includes **endoplasm** and **ectoplasm**.

21. The nodding man was a **narcotics** addict but also a victim of **narcolepsy**.

22. **Vermin** had gotten into the box of **vermicelli**.

23. **Lignocellulose** strengthens woody cells in plants.

24. The **rhododendron** fragments were useful to the **dendrochronologist**.

25. The cadet's **lachrymose** pleadings did not move the drill instructor.

intuition

1. In a dream you make friends with cool, leafy, **dendroid** creatures. Describe their personalities. What do dendroids do for fun?

2. What would a carbon **atom** look and sound like if you could shrink to the size of a **subatomic** particle and move in near the nucleus?

emotion

1. Describe the emotional state of a person delivering **invective** and a person receiving **invective**.

2. Describe the emotional environment that surrounds the telling of a **lachrymose** story.

aesthetics

1. For beauty in nature, few things surpass the delicate **radial** structures of the **radiolarians**. See if there is a book in the library that features photomicrographs of the radiolarians.

2. Many great artists have gone unrecognized during their lifetimes. Vincent Van Gogh sold almost nothing in the years that he painted, and if his brother Theo had not helped him along, he would have been hard-pressed to survive. Whistler received the **obloquy** of the art set for his paintings, which were then regarded as ludicrous nonsense and are now regarded as masterpieces. Read about these two aesthetically sensitive people and the problems that the world had taking in the new beauty that they were creating. Is our sense of beauty governed by the visual habits instilled in us by our social experience? How can we prepare ourselves to see new masterpieces for what they really are?

synthesis

1. What combination of factors do you think must be involved in a person's tragic surrender to **narcotic** addiction? What factors within the person's psychological makeup? What factors in the social environment?

2. What are some creative ideas for creating harmony and cooperation in our **multilateral** international political system?

Front view of the Propylaea with the Temple of Athena Nike on the right

1. **LACHRYMOSE : EUPHORIC ::**
   a. joyful : ecstatic
   b. tearful : miserable
   c. joyful : tearful
   d. tearful : joyful

2. **INVECTIVE : EULOGY ::**
   a. diatribe : excoriation
   b. malevolence : benevolence
   c. obsequious : slavish
   d. mollify : soften

3. **OOCYTE : OOLOGY ::**
   a. sanguine : melancholy
   b. egg : shell
   c. cell : science
   d. unilateral : multilateral

4. **PRESTIDIGITATION : ILLUSION ::**
   a. defoliation : leaves
   b. convection : heat
   c. friction : heat
   d. pneumonia : pneumobacillus

5. **DENDROCHRONOLOGY : AGE ::**
   a. sonar : distance
   b. radar : technology
   c. narcolepsy : sleep
   d. chronometer : watch

6. **LIGNEOUS : IGNEOUS ::**
   a. coal : wood
   b. fire : tree
   c. wood : fire
   d. *ignis fatuus* : lignocellulose

7. **OBLOQUY : REVILE ::**
   a. contumely : punishment
   b. ridiculous : derision
   c. discredit : infamy
   d. disgrace : condemn

8. **MULTIFARIOUS : MULTILATERAL ::**
   a. omnifarious : many-sided
   b. nefarious : wicked
   c. polygon : polyhedron
   d. ambivalent : ambiguous

9. **OBSTINATE : OBDURATE ::**
   a. oblique : slanting
   b. vermicide : vermin
   c. intractable : incorrigible
   d. multiply : divide

10. **VERMICELLI : VERMIVOROUS ::**
   a. worm : carnivorous
   b. eat : not eat
   c. noodle : fructivorous
   d. gymnasium : gymnastics

View of the Acropolis from the Agora on the north slope. From the left, the Erechtheion, the Parthenon, the Propylaea, and the Temple of Athena Nike.

Above, the Propylaea with the Temple of Athena Nike on the right, as seen from the foot of the Acropolis; and below, the Parthenon as seen from just inside the Propylaea. The large statue of Athena Promachos would have been to the left of the photograph below. The top of the Acropolis is an extensive building site in which considerable effort is being expended in attempting to undo the damage inflicted by previous restoration projects. Works have been going on at the Parthenon since 1975 (more than twice as long as it took to construct the building), with no end in sight. For two generations of visitors, much of the beauty of the building has been obscured by scaffolding.

THE ACROPOLIS AND ITS TEMPLES

Dr. Thomas Milton Kemnitz

When in 450 Pericles turned to the top of the Acropolis—the primary locus of Athenian religious life—he faced a desolate landscape of temples destroyed by the Persians thirty years earlier. The most sacred sites had been desecrated, but the ruins of the Temple of Athena Polias (protector of the polis) still held the statue of the goddess, as well as the treasury of Athens and of the Delian League. The wooden statue was Athens's single most sacred relic, said to have been cast down from heaven. When they abandoned Athens to the Persians in 480, the Athenians had taken the statue with them. The entry gate to the Acropolis also had been destroyed by the Persians. Pericles delegated the work of making the Acropolis the epitome of Athens's glory to his friend, the sculptor Phidias.

The first step Phidias took was to sculpt in bronze a colossal thirty-foot-high figure of Athena Promachos (foremost warrior). He placed it on a five-foot-high pedestal on the terrace of the ruined Temple of Athena Polias. Athena's gold spear tip and helmet were visible far out to sea, a welcome sight to returning Athenian sailors. This statue was moved to Constantinople about 800 years after it was erected, and from there it disappeared, its fate unrecorded.

The next step was to build the Parthenon, which took from 447 to 438. Greek temples existed to house the statues of gods; the Parthenon housed a new statue Phidias created of Athena Parthenos (the virgin). The Parthenon was built to the south and parallel to the ruined temple on a site where the Athenians had begun to build half a century earlier, only to have the Persians destroy the work in progress. When completed, the Parthenon also became the treasury.

With these two pieces in place, Pericles and Phidias were able to see the need for a gateway to the Acropolis, which they erected in the years from 437 to 432. Called the Propylaea, this entry was a mixture of Doric and Ionian styles and led visitors straight to the huge bronze statue of Athena Promachos and to the terrace and wall of the ruined temple.

To the south of the Propylaea and attached to it, the Athenians added (427 to 424) a small Temple of Athena Nike (victory). By then Pericles and Phidias were both dead, but the architects and builders and masons and other craftsmen they had worked with were still active and crucial to the ongoing building. The god in this case was a wooden statue of Nike without wings—said to keep the god from leaving Athens. The site was one that had been used for religious purposes for more than 500 years and had contained a previous temple of Nike that the Persians had destroyed. This was the first temple built entirely in the Ionian style.

Finally the Acropolis was adorned with the beautiful replacement for the ruined Temple of Athena Polias. The new building—known as the Erechtheion—was begun in 421 and was complete enough for the statue of Athena Polias to be moved to it in 407. Only then was the ruined Temple of Athena Polias completely destroyed. The Erechtheion was complex because the site was not level and because it housed a number of the most sacred relics of Athens. It is reasonable to assume that another wing of the building was intended, but construction was stopped when Athens surrendered to Sparta in 404. The Erechtheion was executed in the Ionian style, and its extraordinary porch of the caryatids is pictured on the back cover of this volume.

Parthenon built	Propylaea erected	Temple of Athena Nike erected	Erechtheion erected	Alcibiades returns to Athens
447–432 B.C.	437–432 B.C.	427–424 B.C.	421–405 B.C.	407 B.C.

1. The **Mollusca** are a large phylum of invertebrates named after their soft (*moll*) bodies. The **Mollusks** include such creatures as snails, squids, and octopi. We use the same stem in the word **mollify**. If a person has fierce anger, **obdurate** anger, then we try to make (*fy*) soft (*moll*) the anger that has hardened (*dur*) against (*ob*) us.

2. A **Micropoem**: Public blame and disgrace is sometimes called **obloquy**. Obloquy is horrible to experience, as the word implies: to suffer the obloquy of society is to have everyone talk (*loqu*) against (*ob*) you.

3. **Objurgation**, like obloquy, is bitterly unpleasant to receive. To be objurgated is to be berated, to be violently denounced, to be actually sworn (*jur*) against (*ob*).

4. If you are asked to **delineate** the options, don't drag out every fact and detail you know. Just give a precise summary, an outline. Put the lines (*lin*) down (*de*) without painting in the minutia.

5. Archaeologists studying Indian ruins in the American Southwest can often date a site to the exact year by using **dendrochronology**, or tree ring dating. Tree rings form a pattern: thick rings in wet years and thin rings in dry years. A careful examination of ring patterns has shown that trees (*dendro*) contain a record of time (*chron*) that can be used to study (*logy*) the past.

6. The circular (*orb*) paths that satellites follow around the earth are called **orbits**. Unfortunately, a satellite will not permanently follow the path it is placed in. **Orbital decay** refers to the gradual slowing and eventual falling of a satellite as a result of friction from the sparse molecules in the earth's upper atmosphere. Notice that *decay* literally means down/fall (*de*: down, *cad*: fall).

7. An **exorbitant** price is one that is outrageously high, unrealistic, completely out (*ex*) of the sphere (*orb*) of reason. It is a price that has escaped the gravity of sense that held it down to earth; it is out of **orbit**, off by itself.

8. **Spanish Cognates**: One of the most important observations to gain from the study of the etymology of English vocabulary is that English and Spanish share thousands of words that are cognates—related words—that have common origins. Often, the English and the Spanish words share not only a stem but even more than one stem, and often in the same order. As examples, here are some English words from this lesson and their Spanish cognates:

    vice versa : vice versa
    atomic : atómico
    delineate : delinear
    hemisphere : hemisferio
    irradiate : irradiar
    oblique : obliquo
    obstinate : obstinado
    digital : digital
    gymnasium : gimnasio

The Caryatid South Porch of the Erechtheion

In each case below, one of the choices was really the word used by the author in the sentence provided. All of the choices can be found in the example words on the first page of this lesson. Your challenge is to decide which word the author used. This is not a test; it is more like a game because more than one word choice may work perfectly well. See if you can use your sensitivity and intuition to guess correctly which word the author used. You may need a dictionary.

1. **From James Baldwin's *Go Tell It on the Mountain***

   She grinned, delighted at what she took to be a(n) _____ compliment.
   a. retrograde*
   b. obdurate
   c. oblique
   d. exorbitant

2. **From John Milton's *Paradise Lost***

   Canst thou with impious _____ condemn the just Decree of God?
   a. impulsive
   b. sated
   c. obloquy
   d. solvent

3. **From Kate Wiggin's *Rebecca of Sunnybrook Farm***

   Miranda was rather _____ by and pleased with the turn of events.
   a. ignited
   b. mollified
   c. osculated
   d. delineated

4. **From Natalie Babbitt's *Tuck Everlasting***

   The gentlest smile in the world displaced the _____ creases of his cheeks.
   a. melancholy
   b. lineal
   c. orbital
   d. obsequious

5. **From Charles Dickens's *David Copperfield***

   A sullen _____ disposition is, of all tempers, the worst.
   a. obdurate
   b. oblique
   c. mollescent
   d. lachrymose

equivocate	*(to hedge)*	The equivocating politician praised both groups.
superfluous	*(unnecessary)*	A superfluous comment is a waste of time.
bilateral	*(two-sided)*	The two nations formed a bilateral agreement.
unilateral	*(one-sided)*	The U.S. made a unilateral withdrawal.
circumspect	*(cautious)*	A circumspect reply is safer.
commensurate	*(of like measure)*	A big job needs a commensurate reward.
malevolence	*(evil intent)*	The creature cast a malevolent glare.
neophyte	*(beginner)*	She is a neophyte in the art world.
misanthropist	*(people-hater)*	The grouchy misanthropist wouldn't contribute.
bellicose	*(warlike)*	The bellicose tribe attacked without warning.
anthropomorphic	*(man-shaped)*	They believe in an anthropomorphic god.
captious	*(fault-finding)*	The captious remarks were not sincere.
neologism	*(new word)*	Create a neologism, like *televoracious*.
malediction	*(a curse)*	The convict's muttered malediction was inaudible.
incredulous	*(not believing)*	Her incredulous expression showed her feelings.
omniscient	*(all-knowing)*	You can't keep secrets from an omniscient god.
monomania	*(obsession with one thing)*	It was a hobby that became a monomania.
specious	*(false)*	You have a convincing but unfortunately specious argument.
excoriate	*(verbally flog)*	His speech excoriated the opponent.
prototype	*(first model)*	We saw an early prototype of the Mustang.
xenophobia	*(fear of foreigners)*	It is a hostile, xenophobic country.
benediction	*(blessing)*	The Pope's smiling benediction was televised.
amorphous	*(shapeless)*	A gray, amorphous mass was in the corner.
preponderance	*(bulk)*	The preponderance of the evidence indicates guilt.
magnanimous	*(great-minded)*	His magnanimous victory speech showed generosity.

inter

between • among • with

The Latin stem **inter** is one of the most commonly found prefixes in the English language. **Inter** means *between, among, with,* or even *mutual* or *reciprocal.* It is different in meaning from its relatives **intra** and **intro.** Here is a small selection of the interesting words that contain **inter** in its various shades of meaning:

interact:	to act reciprocally. The one interacts with the other, and each is changed.
intercalate:	to insert. We spent the evening intercalating the flyer into the newsletter.
interface:	a boundary plane. Ahab's sea surface was an interface between good and evil.
intermezzo:	short performance between acts. They went to the lobby during the intermezzo.
interim:	meantime. In the interim of Caesar's absence, the Gallic tribes had revolted.
interlope:	to intrude. She only intended to assist, not to interlope, in their affairs.
interpose:	to put between. A new barricade was interposed between troops and rebels.
interval:	a gap. A brief interval of silence occurred between the fusillades.
internuncio:	an envoy. The internuncio finally arrived, bringing the papal documents.
intervocalic:	between vowels. The witches' raspy intervocalics were insidious and evil.
intertribal:	among tribes. The emerging nation was wracked with intertribal conflicts.
intersperse:	to scatter among. Globular clusters were interspersed among the galaxies.
interpret:	to explain. The Apache guide nervously interpreted Geronimo's warning.
interplanetary:	between planets. Daily interplanetary travel became possible in 2123 A.D.
intertwine:	twist together. In King Lear, the main plot and subplots are intertwined.
intertidal:	shore between low and high tide. Fiddler crabs inhabited the intertidal zone.
intervale:	bottom land. He planted corn down in the intervale near the stream.
intermediary:	a go-between. The ambassador acted as official intermediary between them.
interdict:	prohibit. They attempted to interdict arms traffic on the high seas.
intergalactic:	between galaxies. Intergalactic gravity links Andromeda and the Milky Way.
intercultural:	among cultures. Future survival will require intercultural understanding.

The east end of the Parthenon, where the birth of Athena from the head of Zeus was depicted in the statuary on the pediment. It was at this end, away from the Propylaea, that the statue of Athena Parthenos with all its gold and ivory was housed. In the foreground are some of the pieces the restoration project has to fit into place.

THE PARTHENON

Dr. Thomas Milton Kemnitz

The great building of Pericles and of Athens—indeed one of the greatest buildings in all of Western civilization—is the Parthenon. The main structure was built in only nine years from 447 to 438, with another six years spent completing the sculptures on the pediments at each end. Five centuries later, the buildings on the Acropolis drew Plutarch's admiration, and 2,450 years later, they are venerated.

The marble for the buildings came from Mount Pentelikon, less than twelve miles from (and downhill all the way to) the base of the Acropolis. Rough blocks, a few weighing as much as ten tons, were cut and transported to the Acropolis. The blocks were finished at the building site. The sophistication of the finished workmanship is astonishing. Blocks were chiseled with hand tools to precise tolerances that were sometimes hundredths of an inch. No mortar was used in the building. Iron pins were used to hold the blocks in place, and then the pins were sealed with molten lead. Often it takes a magnifying glass to find the indentations for the pins; sometimes the fit between blocks is so precise than no joint shows nearly 2,500 years later. People working on the restoration of the Parthenon are certain that the Greeks had hand tools far superior to their modern counterparts in sharpness and durability. This is not as impossible as it sounds; some ancient metallurgy is sophisticated at a level we are still learning. With their more durable hand tools, Athenian stonemasons might have been able to complete work in half the time it takes modern masons.

The Parthenon is Doric in style. The columns were each made of twelve blocks of marble. Each piece was lowered into place using block and tackle; ropes were fastened to special protrusions on the stone. Once in place, the columns were cut with twenty flutes. The chiseling of the flutes is an art form; the restorers have no machine that can emulate what the original Athenian masons did. The labor cutting the flutes was probably equal to the labor of quarrying and moving the blocks of marble to the Parthenon site. The weight of each column is about fifty-five tons. Each column bulges about two inches in the middle—called *entasis*—a slight curve that gives the column the optical illusion of being perfectly straight. The corner columns are two percent greater in diameter than the others, because they are the ones seen against the sky, and they would appear to be thinner than the others if they were the same size. All of the columns are angled in slightly so that if they were continued upward, they would meet a mile above their base.

The base of the Parthenon is not perfectly flat but is slightly higher in the center than on the sides and ends. Again, the curve is necessary for the platform to appear flat. The roof is similarly curved. The precise measurements were laid out by lines drawn on the stone platform and the inner walls of the inner rooms, the *cella*, which were built (angled in slightly) before the columns were added and the roof put on. Every exposed part of the Parthenon was given a final embellishment of millions of tiny lines incised in a cross thatch so that the stone would not reflect the sun with an unbearable glare. The labor involved in this process is incalculable, but it is not an inconsiderable refinement in a climate with bright sun and for a people who had no sunglasses to reduce the glare.

Every part of the Parthenon was planned and built precisely with the viewer in mind. As perfect as the structure itself seems to be, it was in some respects only an elaborate stand for the sculptures that decorated it both internally and externally.

Peace with Persia negotiated	Parthenon built	Pediment statues erected	Propylaea erected	
449 B.C.	**447–438 B.C.**	**438–432 B.C.**	**437–432 B.C.**	**431–404 B.C.** Peloponnesian Wars

1. A **Micropoem**: Why does **equivocate** mean to hedge? Just as a hedge marks the point between two fields, a person who wishes not to answer a question can take the mid-point, giving equal (*equi*) voice (*voc*) to both sides of the issue. Someone who praises both camps in a dispute is equivocating.

2. Fault-finding comments are called **captious** because they are designed to catch (*cap*: take) you. They are full (*ous*) of catches (*cap*).

3. **Specious** does mean false, but not everything false is specious. Contrast *specious* with **veracious**. The veracious statement is full of truth, but the specious statement is full of (*ous*) looks (*spec*)! It is a good-looking false statement.

4. **Magnanimous** means great-minded, not in the sense of great intelligence but in the sense of greatness of spirit. Magnanimity is generosity, nobility of mind. Contrast *magnanimous* with **pusillanimous**—small-minded.

5. **Commensurate** refers to the way two things can be in or out of scale with each other, and it implies that they should be in scale. If we take on a big job, we want a big reward, not a small one. We expect our reward to be commensurate with our task. The two things should measure (*mens*) together (*co*).

6. **Excoriate** is not made of *ex* and *cor* (heart). It is made of *ex* and the Latin *corium*, meaning skin. To excoriate someone is, verbally, to skin him alive!

7. Before a motor company builds 200,000 new cars, it first (*proto*) makes a model and tests it. A **prototype** is a preliminary model built for testing and consideration. Once final decisions have been made, the company can proceed with full-scale production.

8. Why do we call a human beginner a **neophyte** (new plant)? We use the word *neophyte* in a metaphorical way. A beginner in the art world is like a baby plant that has just broken out of its seed and put forth little leaves. A neophyte in the art world is a brand new "baby" artist.

9. **Pronunciation Tips**

superfluous - soo PER flu us	malevolence - muh LEV o lence
specious - SPEE shus	equivocate - ee KWIV o kate
neophyte - neo FIGHT	omniscient - om NISH unt
xenophobia - zee no FO bee uh	incredulous - in KRED yoo luss
magnanimous - mag NAN i muss	

10. **Spanish Cognates**: One of the most important observations to gain from the study of the etymology of English vocabulary is that English and Spanish share thousands of words that are cognates—related words—that have common origins. Often, the English and the Spanish words share not only a stem but even more than one stem, and often in the same order. As examples, here are some English words from this lesson and their Spanish cognates:

equivocate : equivocar	malevolence : malevolencia	malediction : maldición
superfluous : superfluo	neophyte : neofita	incredulous : incrédulo
bilateral : bilateral	bellicose : belicoso	omniscient : omnisciente
unilateral : unilateral	anthropomorphic : antropomórfico	prototype : prototipo

The Word Within the Word • Classic Words #21

In each case below, one of the choices was really the word used by the author in the sentence provided. All of the choices can be found in the words on the first page of this lesson. Your challenge is to decide which word the author used. This is not a test; it is more like a game because more than one word choice may work perfectly well. See if you can use your sensitivity and intuition to guess correctly which word the author used. You may need a dictionary.

1. **From F. Scott Fitzgerald's *The Great Gatsby***

   That ashen, fantastic figure [glided] toward him through the __________ trees.
   a. captious
   b. superfluous
   c. amorphous
   d. unilateral

2. **From Jane Austen's *Emma***

   The consciousness of having done amiss had...made her __________ and irritable to a degree.
   a. captious
   b. malevolent
   c. omniscient
   d. specious

3. **From William Golding's *Lord of the Flies***

   Ralph had been deceived before now by the __________ appearance of depth in a beach pool.
   a. amorphous
   b. magnanimous
   c. bellicose
   d. specious

4. **From Alfred Lansing's *Endurance***

   The only __________ item Shackleton permitted was Worsley's diary.
   a. incredulous
   b. bellicose
   c. superfluous
   d. bilateral

5. **From Robert Louis Stevenson's *Treasure Island***

   I walked more __________ keeping an eye on every side.
   a. circumspectly
   b. malevolently
   c. omnisciently
   d. magnanimously

Erechtheion caryatid

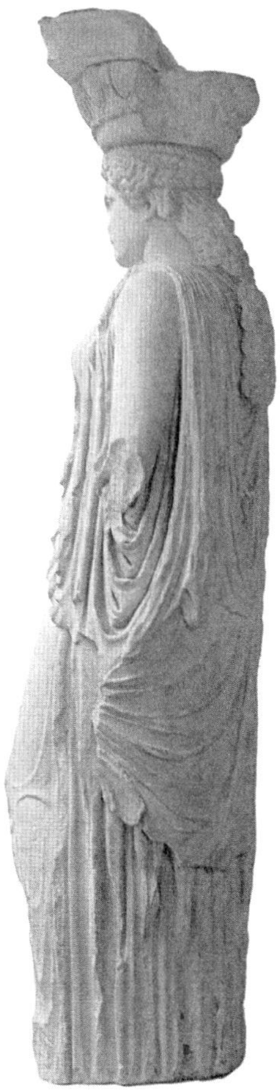

synthesis

Use **magnanimous**, **equivocate**, and **malevolence** in one sentence.

divergence

How many things can you think of that could be described as **amorphous**?

analysis

You might think that **excoriate** is a combination of *ex*, *cor*, and *ate*, but it isn't so. The *cor* in *excoriate* actually has a very different derivation and only happens to have the same spelling as the *cor* that we have studied. Look up the etymology of *excoriate* in a good dictionary, and explain why this word is used to describe extremely abusive denunciation or verbal whipping.

evaluation

Should the United States form its defense policy on a **unilateral** basis and let other nations deal with it as they wish, or should the United States work for a cooperative **bilateral** or **multilateral** defense policy through constant negotiations with other nations?

intuition

Can you think of an explanation for something, an explanation that is commonly accepted as true but that you suspect is **specious**?

emotion

What emotional reaction would you have if you arrived home, and your brother greeted you at the door with **captious** questions about where you had been?

aesthetics

Do you like abstract sculpture that is based on the human form in a vaguely **anthropomorphic** way but that is not finely detailed?

This is probably an accurate re-creation of the statue of Athena Parthenos by Phidias.

mollify	*(make soft)*	It can be difficult to mollify someone's anger.
ichthyologist	*(fish scientist)*	Up splashed a water-logged ichthyologist.
polyglot	*(multi-linguist)*	She is a brilliant polyglot who speaks seven languages.
diaphanous	*(semitransparent)*	Look through the diaphanous draperies.
somniferous	*(bringing sleep)*	The somniferous speech put him to sleep.
sinecure	*(an easy, lucrative job)*	He has a comfortable sinecure in his uncle's firm.
soliloquy	*(speech to oneself)*	Hamlet's famous soliloquy asks the great question.
adherent	*(supporter)*	The adherents of a militaristic foreign policy want war.
abjure	*(renounce)*	To abjure one's former beliefs is stressful.
caustic	*(burning)*	The caustic comments about her clothes hurt her.
confluence	*(a flowing together)*	The idea was formed by a confluence of other ideas.
depose	*(topple from power)*	He was deposed without violence.
egomania	*(self-obsession)*	The offensive egomaniac praised himself.
egregious	*(blatant)*	It was an egregious act of vandalism.
analgesic	*(painkiller)*	Take an extra-strength analgesic for the headache.
chiromancy	*(palm reading)*	Try to divine the future through chiromancy.
oligarchy	*(government by a few)*	The corrupt Greek oligarchy kept control.
intractable	*(stubborn)*	The bigot's intractable opinions were unchangeable.
intransigent	*(not compromising)*	The intransigent true believers wouldn't budge.
perfidious	*(treacherous)*	His perfidious cowardice made him infamous.
perspicuous	*(brilliantly clear)*	Her perspicuous essay won her the scholarship.
ingenuous	*(innocent and naive)*	The ingenuous—but not ingenious—girl believed it.
circumlocution	*(talking in circles)*	He used circumlocution to avoid answering the question.
gregarious	*(sociable)*	He has a friendly, gregarious personality.
discursive	*(rambling)*	It was an illogical, discursive speech.

To a spectator standing outside the Parthenon, the frieze, which was more than thirty-five feet in the air and inside the outer row of columns, might have seemed like the photograph above. Originally painted vivid colors, its scenes would have been easier to discern than this photograph suggests. Stripped of its paint and metal adornments and viewed at close range, it is evident that the Parthenon frieze was one of the great triumphs of Greek art. It initiated a new style of sculpture with free-flowing clothing and flexed bodies, an example of which is below.

THE SCULPTURE OF THE PARTHENON

Dr. Thomas Milton Kemnitz

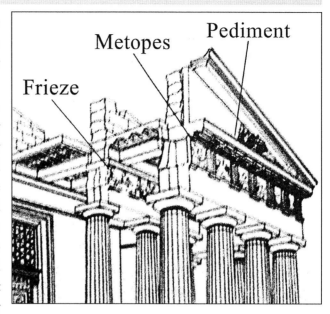

The Parthenon had four kinds of sculpture: the great statue of Athena Parthenos, the figures on the pediment, the metopes, and the inner frieze.

Phidias's statue of Athena was intended as spectacular thanks to the goddess for delivering the city from the Persians. Pericles foresaw political trouble about the amount of gold used in the statue and advised Phidias to incorporate into the design the ability to remove all of the gold to weigh it. When Pericles's political enemies attacked Phidias for embezzlement, he was able to demonstrate that all the gold was there. The gold weighed forty-four talents—the equivalent of about 2,400 pounds. The statue was more than thirty feet tall; its wood frame was covered in bronze, with gold and ivory for the arms and face.

The sculpture on the west pediment depicts the contest between Athena and Poseidon (god of the sea), vying to see which would be the patron god of Athens. On the east pediment is the birth of Athena from the head of Zeus. The surviving fragments from the pediment are some of the most natural and flowing of all Greek statuary.

The ninety-two metopes depict mythical battles on three sides and the Trojan War on the fourth. Each metope is a separate scene, and in their placement on the facade, they were separated by ornamental details. The metopes are in high relief, which means that most of the bodies stand out from the background. The metopes were on the outside of the building where they were easily seen.

The interior frieze was carved in low relief. A part of it is pictured on the front cover of this book. It is 524 feet long and about forty inches high and seems to represent a single event. The most likely explanation is that it depicts the first Panathenian, a sacred procession held every four years to present a specially woven cloak to the statue of Athena Polias. Perhaps the 192 men riding horses or in chariots commemorate the 192 venerated Athenians who lost their lives half a century previously at Marathon. The metopes were done in a style called *severe* that emphasized muscles and protruding veins but lack the freedom of movement of the frieze or of the even later pediment statuary, both of which are among the most beautiful of extant Greek sculpture.

The early Christians turned the Parthenon into a church and defaced the sculpture as idolatry, breaking noses here, excising entire faces there. Early in the nineteenth century, Lord Elgin, the British ambassador to the Ottoman Empire, removed most of the frieze, the best of the metopes, and nearly all of the pediment sculpture. Those treasures are now on display in the British Museum in London.

Parthenon built	Pediment statues erected	Propylaea erected		Plague in Athens
447–438 B.C.	438–432 B.C.	437–432 B.C.	431–404 B.C. Peloponnesian Wars	430 B.C.

equi

equal • equally

The Latin stem **equi** is is sometimes as seen as **equa** and **ega**. It refers to equality. Beware of confusing **equi** with **equus**, which refers to horses in words such as *equine, equestrian,* and *equites.* Here is a small selection of the interesting words that contain **equi** in its various forms:

equity:	fairness. Equity dictates that benefits for some be extended to all.
equilibrate:	to balance. She equilibrated the two currents to make a smooth waveform.
equable:	uniform. The yearly temperatures were equable and always pleasant.
equilibrium:	balance. The two forces had reached a steady state of equilibrium.
equidistant:	mid-way. We met in a small town that is equidistant from our two cities.
equivocate:	to hedge. He equivocated in order to avoid answering the question.
equivoque:	a double meaning. Her banter was filled with equivoques such as puns.
equiponderant:	of the same weight. The scale showed a balance of equiponderant masses.
equinox:	when sun crosses equator. At the equinox, day and night are of equal length.
equipotential:	of equal power. As dictator, he dreaded all equipotential political systems.
egalitarian:	for equal rights. The rebellious banner was raised for egalitarian ideals.
equalize:	to make equal. Gradually, the incomes on the island began to equalize.
equanimity:	composure. Despite the chaos and panic, she never lost her equanimity.
dis**equi**librium:	economic imbalance. Skyrocketing interest rates created real disequilibrium.
equiangular:	of equal angles. Her art consisted of designs in equiangular polygons.
equivalence:	of equal amount. There was a rough equivalence between their estimates.
equilibrist:	tightrope walker. Sometimes the theologian felt like a logical equilibrist.
equate:	to regard as equal. It would be obtuse to equate your achievement with hers.
equilateral:	having equal sides. The tiles were shaped as equilateral triangles.
equator:	sphere's mid-circle. The equator is equidistant from the poles.
equipoise:	state of balance. Three branches of government operate in a curious equipoise.

1. Why do we call an easy, lucrative job a **sinecure**? Because it is a job without (*sine*) care (*cur*). There is not much to worry about in a sinecure; you just go and pick up your check.

2. **Depose** means topple from power. The image is one of a person in a high position who is forcefully put (*pos*) down (*de*) where he belongs (we hope).

3. The **adherents** of a policy stick (*here*) to (*ad*) it. They are the stickers-on.

4. Why does **abjure** mean renounce? Well, sometimes we have to change our minds and renounce something we have previously sworn to support. We might previously have sworn it to us, but now we have to swear (*jur*) it away (*ab*).

5. An **egregious** act is a publicly outrageous one, done out (*ex*) before the group (*greg*).

6. The **intractable** person is stubborn and can not (*in*) be pulled (*tract*) from his position. He is not-pullable.

7. **Perspicuous** means brilliantly clear because what is clear can be seen (*spec*) through (*per*). A perspicuous essay is full of see-throughness.

8. A **Micropoem**: A **discursive** speech is rambling because it runs (*curs*) away (*dis*) from its topic. It is a runaway speech.

9. What is innocent or naive about the **ingenuous** person? If someone is ingenuous, that person has yet to be changed by the cruel world. The sincere and trusting ingenuous soul is still in (*in*) original (*gen*) condition.

10. **Pronunciation Tips**

    diaphanous - dye AFF an us
    egregious - ee GREE juss
    perspicuous - per SPICK yoo us
    circumlocution - sir cum lo KYOO shun
    sinecure - SIN uh cure
    somniferous - som NIF er us
    ichthyologist - ick thee AHL o jist
    soliloquy - so LILL o kwee
    analgesic - an al JEE zik

11. **Spanish Cognates**: One of the most important observations to gain from the study of the etymology of English vocabulary is that English and Spanish share thousands of words that are cognates—related words—that have common origins. Often, the English and the Spanish words share not only a stem but even more than one stem, and often in the same order. As examples, here are some English words from this lesson and their Spanish cognates:

    polyglot : políglota   oligarchy : oligarquía
    diaphanous : diáfano   intransigent : intransigente
    soliloquy : soliloquio   ingenuous : ingenuo
    egomania : egomanía   somniferous : somnífero
    analgesic : analgésico

In each case below, one of the choices was really the word used by the author in the sentence provided. All of the choices can be found in the words on the first page of this lesson. Your challenge is to decide which word the author used. This is not a test; it is more like a game because more than one word choice may work perfectly well. See if you can use your sensitivity and intuition to guess correctly which word the author used. You may need a dictionary.

1. **From Walt Whitman's *Leaves of Grass***

   The little light fades the immense and _____ shadows.
   a. caustic
   b. diaphanous
   c. intransigent
   d. gregarious

2. **From John Kennedy's *Profiles in Courage***

   He could still work himself into a rage at what he regarded as Jefferson's _____.
   a. adherence
   b. oligarchy
   c. circumlocution
   d. perfidy

3. **From Emily Brontë's *Wuthering Heights***

   The spirit which served her was growing _____.
   a. caustic
   b. somniferous
   c. intractable
   d. perspicuous

4. **From William Makepeace Thackeray's *Vanity Fair***

   He could see with a fatal _____ that there was no place there for him.
   a. perspicuity
   b. confluence
   c. egomania
   d. chiromancy

5. **From Thomas Hardy's *The Mayor of Casterbridge***

   He went on with _____ enthusiasm.
   a. egregious
   b. ingenuous
   c. gregarious
   d. discursive

Athena

synthesis

Can you think of some reasons why it might be advantageous to be governed by an **oligarchy**? What would be the disadvantages?

divergence

American culture is a result of a **confluence** of many other cultures. How many other examples of confluence can you think of?

analysis

Why does **perfidious** mean treacherous?

evaluation

Hiram provided his uncle with a **sinecure** in a family-owned company. His uncle is untrained and unmotivated. Do you regard Hiram's action as a kindness or as a wrong?

intuition

An **ingenuous** young fellow arrives in the city and is soon parted from his money by quick-talking sharks who take advantage of his lack of experience. How do they cheat him?

emotion

What would be the frequent emotions of the friends of a **gregarious** person?

aesthetics

You are given 8,000 yards of **diaphanous** blue fabric and told to make a work of art on a mountainside. What will you do?

This is part of the frieze from the Parthenon, now housed in the Museum of the Parthenon in Athens. Plaster casts take the place of the parts that are in London, Paris, and elsewhere.

egocentric	*(self-centered)*	The egocentric snob didn't notice whom he hurt.
tangible	*(touchable)*	A paycheck is one of the tangible benefits of a job.
demagogue	*(corrupt politician)*	The demagogue played on public prejudices.
preclude	*(prevent in advance)*	Don't preclude that option.
cryptologist	*(code breaker)*	British cryptologists cracked the German code.
ethnocentrism	*(racial or cultural prejudice)*	We deplore his narrow ethnocentrism.
pedagogue	*(teacher)*	A humorless pedant is a poor pedagogue.
recant	*(retract)*	Galileo was forced to recant his heliocentric statements.
revoke	*(cancel)*	Permission to travel has been revoked.
pugnacious	*(combative)*	The pugnacious bully got his comeuppance.
incisive	*(sharp)*	Her incisive questions cut deeply into the issue.
diatribe	*(abusive criticism)*	The German leader delivered a diatribe against France.
anomaly	*(abnormality)*	There is an inexplicable anomaly in the data.
enumerate	*(to list)*	Please enumerate your reasons.
circumscribed	*(limited)*	You must choose among certain circumscribed alternatives.
intercede	*(mediate)*	We are forced to intercede on behalf of the orphan.
disputatious	*(argumentative)*	The disputatious reporter irritated the official.
loquacious	*(talkative)*	The loquacious fellow wore their ears out.
abrogate	*(annul)*	We abrogate an agreement only out of dire necessity.
prescience	*(foreknowledge)*	A prescient vision came to him in a dream.
sacrosanct	*(sacred)*	He would not endanger his sacrosanct bowling night.
androgynous	*(masculine and feminine)*	The androgynous rock star performed in a mixed wardrobe.
acronym	*(initials-name)*	The acronym NATO means North Atlantic Treaty Organization.
congenital	*(at birth)*	The problem is a congenital defect.
cacophony	*(bad noise)*	The cacophonous roar of the crowd was deafening.

auto

self • for oneself • by oneself

The Greek stem **auto** is one of the most interesting prefixes in the English language, since we are interested in things that we do by, for, and to ourselves. **Auto** is sometimes shortened to **aut** in words such as *autarchy* or changed to **auth** in words such as *authentic*. Here is a small selection of the interesting words that contain **auto**:

autarchy:	absolute rule. Eventually, the dictator's rule increased to a steely autarchy.
autogamy:	self-fertilization. The autogamous fungi reproduced rapidly.
autocephalous:	self-governing. The Orthodox churches had autocephalous organizations.
autochthon:	an aborigine. Australia has a menagerie of unique autochthonous species.
autonomic:	involuntary. The autonomic nervous system automatically regulates functions.
autopsy:	a coroner's examination. The autopsy revealed no evidence of foul play.
autocracy:	dictatorship. She wouldn't allow him to act as the autocrat in their marriage.
autonomist:	an advocate of self-rule. The autonomists were furious with the compromise.
autism:	a pathological introversion. His autism made it difficult to communicate.
automaton:	robot. He seemed like an automaton, answering with automatic flatness.
authentic:	genuine. It was not a replica but an authentic artifact from the tomb.
autogenous:	self-generated. The body produces autogenous defenses against disease.
autotrophic:	self-nourishing. Plants are autotrophic through the process of photosynthesis.
autotelic:	being an end in itself. Art and astronomy are autotelic endeavors.
autodidact:	self-taught person. His discussion revealed the slight errors of the autodidact.
autograph:	one's own signature. Morrison autographed a copy of *Song of Solomon*.
autohypnosis:	self-hypnosis. She used autohypnotic states to control her fears.
autopilot:	automatic pilot. The plane flew on autopilot until the pilot was revived.
autobiography:	a self-biography. Watson's *Double Helix* is a fascinating autobiography.
autoinfection:	infection from within. The immune system no longer prevented autoinfections.
automate:	to make automatic. The factory had been automated, requiring fewer workers.

The Erechtheion was the last building erected on the Acropolis in the fifth century; its dedication closed an era. It was stunning when it was new. The frieze was black limestone with sculpture in relief in white marble. The columns were painted, gilded, highlighted in gilt bronze, and decorated with multi-colored inset glass beads. In Athenian mythology, the temple stands on the spot where Athena contended with Poseidon to be the patron god of the polis. The winner was to be the god who presented the city with the best gift. Poseidon, god of the sea, struck his trident and produced a well, but the water turned out to be salty. Athena planted an olive tree and was judged the winner because the tree gave not only fruit but also oil for lamps and wood for ships and houses. By the fifth century, Athens's prosperity would be dependent upon the sea. The Persians destroyed Athena's olive tree, but miraculously, green shoots appeared after they left. Both Poseidon's well and the tree were contained within the Erechtheion.

The sculpture on the Parthenon pediments was some of the best of all classical Greek sculpture. These three figures are from the west pediment of the Parthenon depicting the contest between Poseidon and Athena; the one on the left may be Hestia, goddess of the hearth; to the right is probably Aphrodite, who reclines on the lap of her mother Dione.

THE GREATNESS OF ATHENS
Dr. Thomas Milton Kemnitz

Ever careful to ensure against false accusations, Pericles had the accounts of payments for his building programs engraved in stone on public view on the Acropolis; some of them have survived and show that he and his successors spent massive amounts of money; in today's dollars, the Parthenon alone cost more than half a billion. That expenditure produced the prosperity and prestige that Pericles sought. It is important to remember that the cold stones we see today throbbed with color 2,500 years ago. The statues and their backdrop were all brightly painted and gilded, the friezes and metopes adorned with metal attachments and painted additions, such as spears, harnesses, swords, and jewelry. Athens not only was prosperous, it provided a draw for the talents of people throughout Hellas. Artists and craftsmen congregated around the Acropolis. All of the craftsmen and laborers were paid, and they all had money to spend. Ancillary arts blossomed; potters and vase painters flourished, creating *amphorae* and jugs and drinking cups that are still the wonder of the world for their beauty and sophistication.

Athens was more than the foremost cultural center in Greece in this period; it is legitimate to regard it as the most important cultural center in the history of the world. From Athens we get democracy; we may not practice it exactly as the Athenians did, but the concept of a free people exercising its will through a democratic state has been central to Western political thinking for the past 250 years. Athens was not only the first democracy, it was the largest and most powerful. Eventually hundreds of Greek city states would be democracies, but most had only 500 to 1,500 males who could participate. In Athens in 454 B.C., more than 30,000 men were eligible to vote in the Assembly. Athens stood not only as a democracy but also as a democracy engaged in battling autocracies, as the Peloponnesian Wars were framed in their last years.

Modern theater has its origins in this democracy; Aeschlyus, Sophocles, Euripides, and Aristophanes were all active in the fifth century B.C., bringing tragedy and comedy to the people of Athens. Playwrights today still follow many of the forms and traditions they originated. Theater requires the free expression that democracy allows, and the Athenian dramatists commented extensively upon current affairs in their plays. The prosperity of Athens meant that playwrights and performers could be supported. The first of the great fifth-century Athenian playwrights, Aeschylus, was neither born in Athens nor died there, but his epitaph commemorated his participation in the victory at Marathon, where his brother was one of the 192 who perished; Aeschylus himself was among those who fought a decade later at Salamis and perhaps at Plataea in 479. Rhetoricians were another group who flourished in the Athenian culture of free expression.

Western philosophy originated in Athens during this period. Socrates took a vigorous part in the political life of Athens, and his followers included Plato and Aristotle. Other philosophers and philosophical schools congregated in Athens.

Five hundred years after the building program on the Acropolis, Plutarch wrote that it "was all the more wonderful because it was built in a short time, and yet has lasted for ages. In beauty each of them at once appeared venerable as soon as it was built, but even at the present day the work looks as fresh as ever, for they bloom with the eternal freshness that defies time." Further, he wrote that the temples "now alone prove that the tales of the ancient power and glory of Greece are no fables."

Greek victories at Plataea, Mylcale	Delian treasury moved to Athens	Peace with Persia negotiated		Plague in Athens
479 B.C.	454 B.C.	449 B.C.	431–404 B.C. Peloponnesian Wars	430 B.C.

1. Not every corrupt politician is a **demagogue**. A demagogue is a politician who leads—if you can call it that—through corrupt means: by telling people only what they want to hear and by appealing to their prejudices. The demagogue often leads (*agog*) people (*demo*) by appealing to their basest instincts.

2. A **Micropoem**: To **preclude** an option is to prevent it in advance, to act so as not even to have a choice, to close (*clud*) that door beforehand (*pre*).

3. **Ethnocentrism** is the idea that your own group (*ethno*) is the metaphorical center (*centri*), and all other groups circle in inferior orbits around you. As human beings, we have a natural preference for the customs we know, and this sometimes gives rise to an illogical corollary: that the customs of other groups are not as good as our own. Anthropologists report that virtually all human groups exhibit some form of ethnocentrism.

4. A teacher is a leader (*agog*) of children (*ped*), a **pedagogue**.

5. When Galileo **recanted** his heliocentric views, he sang (*cant*) a different tune (*re*).

6. **Incisive** comments are sharp because they cut (*cise*) in (*in*) to the issue.

7. An **anomaly** is a special kind of abnormality. It is something so unusual that it is not (*an*) the same (*homo*). It is an an-homo-ly.

8. Why do we call a word made out of initials an **acronym**? It uses the tip (*acro*) of the name (*nym*).

N	A	T	O
North	Atlantic	Treaty	Organization

9. A **Micropoem**: Why do we refer to limited options as **circumscribed**? When choices are circumscribed, a line has been drawn (*scrib*) around (*circum*) the proper choices, and you have to stay within the line. These things inside of the line you may do; the things outside of the line you may not.

10. **Pronunciation Tips**

    loquacious - low KWAY shuss
    enumerate - ee NOO mur ate
    prescience - PRESS shence
    androgynous - an DROJ en us
    cacophony - kah KOFF fun ee

    preclude - pree KLOOD
    tangible - TANJ uh bul
    egocentric - ee go SENT rik
    disputatious - dis pyoo TAY shuss

11. **Spanish Cognates**: One of the most important observations to gain from the study of the etymology of English vocabulary is that English and Spanish share thousands of words that are cognates—related words—that have common origins. Often, the English and the Spanish words share not only a stem but even more than one stem, and often in the same order. As examples, here are some English words from this lesson and their Spanish cognates:

    egocentric : egocéntrico
    tangible : tangible
    demagogue : demagogo
    cryptologist : criptólogo
    enumerate : enumerar

    ethnocentrism : etnocentrismo
    pedagogue : pedagogo
    revoke : revocar
    incisive : incisivo
    intercede : interceder

In each case below, one of the choices was really the word used by the author in the sentence provided. All of the choices can be found in the words on the first page of this lesson. Your challenge is to decide which word the author used. This is not a test; it is more like a game because more than one word choice may work perfectly well. See if you can use your sensitivity and intuition to guess correctly which word the author used. You may need a dictionary.

1. **From Joseph Conrad's *Lord Jim***

    It made the surly taciturn Tamb'Itam almost _____.
    a. pugnacious
    b. anomalous
    c. prescient
    d. loquacious

2. **From William Shakespeare's *The Tempest***

    And by my _____ I find my zenith doth depend upon a most auspicious star.
    a. cacophony
    b. prescience
    c. acronym
    d. ethnocentrism

3. **From Eugene O'Neill's *Long Day's Journey into Night***

    For a second Jamie reacts _____ and half rises from his chair to do battle.
    a. pugnaciously
    b. egocentrically
    c. loquaciously
    d. anomalously

4. **From Arthur Conan Doyle's *The Hound of the Baskervilles***

    That cold, _____, ironical voice could belong to but one man in all the world.
    a. circumscribed
    b. tangible
    c. incisive
    d. sacrosanct

5. **From Kenneth Grahame's *The Wind in the Willows***

    My life…feels to me today somewhat narrow and _____.
    a. cacophonous
    b. circumscribed
    c. precluded
    d. egocentric

synthesis

Which words in List #23 could be used to describe a grumpy, selfish person?

divergence

Which principles of American social and political life should remain **sacrosanct**? Which principles should be reexamined?

analysis

Explain why the words **egocentric** and **androgynous** mean what they do.

evaluation

Should student behavior in public secondary schools be more or less **circumscribed** than at present? What important learning decisions should belong to the administration, and what important decisions should belong to the students? Should students be allowed to make serious mistakes in order to have a vital learning experience?

intuition

In a dream you receive a scathing **diatribe** from a stranger on the street. What breach of conduct have you committed to deserve this diatribe?

emotion

What are your emotional reactions to someone who is **egocentric**? To someone who is **pugnacious**? To someone who is **loquacious**?

aesthetics

Is all great music euphonic? Or is it possible to create a piece of great music that is partially or totally **cacophonous**? Can something that is not pleasing to hear or see still be considered art and be pleasing to the mind?

Part of the pediment statuary of the Parthenon, this horse is one of those drawing the chariot of Selene, just emerging from the sea with the rising moon.

advocate	*(speak for)*	It is time to advocate for a new policy.
ponderous	*(weighty)*	He was crushed by the ponderous burden of the decision.
retribution	*(revenge)*	Expect a brutal retribution for what you have done.
android	*(robot)*	The android's metallic eye glistened redly.
infidel	*(unbeliever)*	The crusade against the infidels was unsuccessful.
resurgence	*(rising again)*	The resurgence of patriotism began slowly.
punctilious	*(precise in conduct)*	She liked his punctilious formal conduct.
condescend	*(lower oneself)*	His condescending attitude was infuriating.
collateral	*(side by side)*	The two collateral issues could not be discussed separately.
irrevocable	*(beyond recall)*	The past is irrevocable and answers no call.
elucidate	*(explain)*	Please elucidate the matter for our less enlightened guest.
epigram	*(witty comment)*	Benjamin Franklin's epigrams amuse us still.
eccentricity	*(oddness)*	The genius's eccentric personality began to moderate.
cognizant	*(aware)*	It is wise to be cognizant of the laws regulating investments.
stringent	*(binding)*	The stringent regulations seemed excessively severe.
anthropoid	*(manlike)*	The anthropoid apes have recognizable facial expressions.
diffident	*(shy)*	Her diffident glance caught his eye.
pandemonium	*(demonic clamor)*	Sheer pandemonium erupted on the playground.
urbane	*(sophisticated)*	The diplomat's urbane manners set the tone.
tractable	*(docile)*	The tractable little boy was a pleasure to learn from.
supersede	*(replace)*	This directive supersedes all previous directives.
temporize	*(delay)*	Begin without temporizing, if you please.
somnambulist	*(sleepwalker)*	Lady Macbeth's famous somnambulism is unforgettable.
sanguinary	*(bloody)*	We still mourn the sanguinary battles of the Civil War.
inanimate	*(lifeless)*	The inanimate stones tell no tales.

mono

one • alone • single

The Greek stem **mono** is one of the most commonly found prefixes in the English language. We have defined it as meaning *one*, but it refers to various forms of singularity and lends a certain formality to most of the words containing it. Here is a small selection of the interesting words that contain **mono** or **mon**:

monoglot:	speaking one language. She was no monoglot but a six-language polyglot.
monoculture:	raising one crop. It was a monocultural society, subsisting only on cassava.
monopode:	a one-footed being. She discovered a curious myth of monopode men.
monostrophe:	poem of identical stanzas. All stanzas in the monostrophe were ballad stanzas.
monolith:	large stone block. The mysterious monolith towered over the crater.
monocle:	a single eyeglass. The baron wore a monocle instead of spectacles.
monolatry:	worshiping one god of many. The monolatrous sect worshipped only Ares.
monograph:	paper on a single subject. We read the monograph on Sapphic meter.
monologue:	a monopolizing speech. The professor's lecture was an egotistic monologue.
monophagous:	feeding on one food. The monophagous koala eats only eucalyptus leaves.
monopolize:	gain sole possession. The eldest child always monopolized the remote control.
monody:	a solo. The lyric ode in the tragedy was a monody by a single voice.
monomania:	an obsession. Ahab's monomania for the white whale finally destroyed him.
monochrome:	in one color. In Picasso's blue period he painted monochromes in blue.
monochromatism:	color blindness. In his monochromatism he saw everything in shades of gray.
monophony:	having a single melody. Bach's polyphony made monophony seem simple.
monostich:	poem of one line. He specialized in writing the haiku-like monostich.
monotonous:	lacking variety. It was a monotonous existence of factory drudgery.
monotheism:	belief in one god. Are those who believe in the devil monotheists?
monoplane:	airplane with one pair of wings. Monoplanes shot down the clumsy biplanes.
monodrama:	a drama for one actor. In the monodrama, he played Albert Einstein.

1. A person who seeks **retribution** seeks to pay (*trib*) back (*re*) someone who has wronged him. The revenge is the payback.

2. The **punctilious** person is so correct in proper conduct that he is full of (*ous*) attention to every single point (*punct*).

3. A **Micropoem**: **Elucidate** means to explain, to cast light (*luc*) out (*ex*) on the matter. Elucidation is a fine task for a luminary.

4. A person's **eccentricities** are behaviors that are way out, that are out (*ex*) from the normal center (*centri*) of things.

5. An **epigram** is a witty comment (*gram*) on (*epi*) a certain matter.

6. **Pronunciation Tips**

    elucidate - ee LOOSE ih date
    diffident - DIFF ih dent
    somnambulist - som NAM byoo list
    irrevocable - ir ree VOK uh bul
    punctilious - punk TILL ee us
    stringent - STRIN jent
    supersede - super SEED
    sanguinary - SANG win airy
    cognizant - KOG nih zent

7. **Spanish Cognates**: One of the most important observations to gain from the study of the etymology of English vocabulary is that English and Spanish share thousands of words that are cognates—related words—that have common origins. Often, the English and the Spanish words share not only a stem but even more than one stem, and often in the same order. As examples, here are some English words from this lesson and their Spanish cognates:

    retribution : retribución
    irrevocable : irrevocable
    eccentricity : ecentricidad
    pandemonium : pandemonio
    urbane : urbano
    sanguinary : sanguinario
    inanimate : inanimado
    android : androide
    advocate : advocar
    condescend : condescender
    collateral : colateral
    anthropoid : antropoide

This is part of the Parthenon frieze showing the procession.

Thucydides was held in high regard in the ancient world by the Greeks and then by the Romans after them, as the many busts of him suggest. Sometimes he is paired back to back with Herodotus—not a pairing that would have pleased Thucydides, who was critical of the previous author's reporting information that he could not himself verify. Thucydides was punctilious in maintaining a standard of veracity that included insistence of verification of all he reported.

THE PELOPONNESIAN WARS—1
Dr. Thomas Milton Kemnitz

The more Athens spent on its building program, the more prosperous it became, and the more it realized the benefit of increasing the Delian League. As Athens grew in wealth and power and as it subjugated more Greek cities, it posed a threat to the entire Greek world. Sparta remained the dominant land power, and other cities looked to it for help in resisting Athens. Moreover, Sparta realized that an increasingly vigorous Athens threatened its hegemony over the Peloponnese and in some sense over all of Greece. The tension was increased because Pericles and members of his party had portrayed themselves as opposed to Sparta to distinguish themselves from the aristocratic party as it had been led by Cimon and Thucydides the statesman. As long as Cimon was playing a leading part in Athens, relations with Sparta were cordial. Soon after Cimon was ostracized, Athens found itself at war with Sparta, and Cimon had to be recalled to arrange a peace.

We know a great deal about the conflict between the Athenians and the Spartans because Thucydides–a younger relative of the man by the same name who led the opposition to Pericles and was ostracized for his pains–wrote about the events from the origins of the war to 411. Thucydides was an Athenian general who was ostracized for the failure of a mission he led, and he spent time in the Peloponnesian polities, including Sparta. His history is particularly remarkable for his determination to record only what he could verify. His account has been sustained by archaeological evidence.

When war broke out in earnest in 431 B.C., Pericles laid out a winning strategy for the Athenians. The Spartans might have been the superior warriors on land, but they had a tremendous weakness because the Helots were more than three-quarters of their population. After the Helot revolt following the earthquake in 464 B.C., the Spartans had a perennial fear that the Helots would rebel again if the state was weakened by a prolonged absence of its warrior population. The Athenian strategy was to bring the population of the surrounding countryside within the walls of Athens and not defend the land of Attica against the land forces of the Peloponnesians. Instead the Athenians would attack their Peloponnesian foes from the sea, raiding their ports and destroying their cities in lightning strikes. The Athenians knew that the Spartans could not keep an army in the field for many weeks, but the Athenians could keep their ships at sea for long periods, and Sparta's allies would never be secure. So long as Athens controlled the Hellespont and could get grain from the Black Sea to feed its burgeoning population, Spartan destruction of the crops in Attica would not be devastating. Eventually the Athenians would win and hold onto their empire while weakening the Peloponnesian alliance.

Initially it went well for the Athenians. Their long walls from Athens to the port of Piraeus protected their access to the sea. The Spartans invaded Attica and destroyed crops and buildings, but the Athenians resupplied by sea, and the Spartans soon withdrew. However, in 430 B.C., a plague broke out and spread rapidly in Athens, which was densely packed with families from the surrounding countryside. The mortality rate was high–probably more than a third of the population. Thucydides reported that he himself contracted the plague but survived. Athens lost a significant portion of its fighting force, but no one wanted to attack a city where the plague was rampant. When the crisis passed, Athens had been doubly weakened by the plague: it had lost much of its fighting force, and it had lost the wise leadership of Pericles, who had died of the plague.

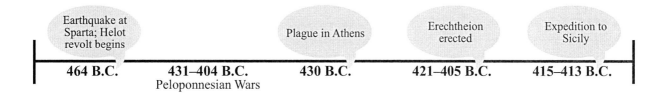

Earthquake at Sparta; Helot revolt begins		Plague in Athens	Erechtheion erected	Expedition to Sicily
464 B.C.	**431–404 B.C.** Peloponnesian Wars	**430 B.C.**	**421–405 B.C.**	**415–413 B.C.**

In each case below, one of the choices was really the word used by the author in the sentence provided. All of the choices can be found in the words on the first page of this lesson. Your challenge is to decide which word the author used. This is not a test; it is more like a game because more than one word choice may work perfectly well. See if you can use your sensitivity and intuition to guess correctly which word the author used. You may need a dictionary.

1. **From Robert Louis Stevenson's *Dr. Jekyll and Mr. Hyde***

   Professional honour and faith to his dead friend were _____ obligations.
   a. punctilious
   b. ponderous
   c. stringent
   d. diffident

2. **From Esther Forbes's *Johnny Tremain***

   A little _____ Isannah herself emerged from behind the lady's great dark skirts.
   a. diffidently
   b. irrevocably
   c. punctiliously
   d. ponderously

3. **From Virginia Woolf's *Mrs. Dalloway***

   And Lady Bruton went _____, majestically, up to her room.
   a. urbanely
   b. inanimately
   c. irrevocably
   d. ponderously

4. **From Mary Wollstonecraft's *Vindication of the Rights of Woman***

   I have always found horses…very _____ when treated with humanity and steadiness.
   a. tractable
   b. irrevocable
   c. eccentric
   d. sanguinary

5. **From William Makepeace Thackeray's *Vanity Fair***

   They cut at each other with _____ that were as sharp as razors.
   a. condescensions
   b. epigrams
   c. eccentricities
   d. resurgences

synthesis

Under what category could the words **infidel**, **android**, and **somnambulist** be grouped? Be flexible in the kinds of categories you consider.

divergence

How many instances of **pandemonium** can you think of?

analysis

Analyze the meaning of **irrevocable**, stem by stem.

evaluation

Is it a good idea or a bad idea to begin marketing personal **androids** that would perform services for their owners?

intuition

If you could talk with an **inanimate** object or material, with what would you choose to converse?

emotion

What emotions are associated with **urbane** behavior?

aesthetics

If someone gave you whatever money you would need to make some truly **eccentric** art, what eccentric object would you make?

A black-figure hydria showing Greek warriors fighting other Greeks

introspective	*(inward looking)*	The quiet boy is an introspective loner.
intervene	*(come between)*	We should not intervene in their dispute.
syndrome	*(complex of symptoms)*	Down syndrome has some well-known symptoms.
subordinate	*(lower)*	He resented his subordinate rank in the military.
dissonant	*(inharmonious)*	A dissonant clamor arose in the streets.
belligerent	*(warring)*	The belligerent nations refused to negotiate.
credible	*(believable)*	It takes money to become a credible candidate.
impending	*(overhanging)*	"The shadow of impending doom" is a trite phrase.
polyphonic	*(multi-melodic)*	Bach's polyphonic concertos are beautiful.
exculpate	*(free from blame)*	He wished to be completely exculpated.
euphemism	*(pleasant name)*	"Restroom" is a euphemism.
benefactor	*(helper)*	Who was the anonymous benefactor to little Pip?
megalomania	*(delusions of greatness)*	A Napoleon complex is a form of megalomania.
magnate	*(powerful person)*	The oil magnates in Saudi Arabia control billions of dollars.
vivacious	*(lively)*	Her vivacious personality cheered us all.
heliotropic	*(sun-following)*	The heliotropic vines clogged the window.
amour-propre	*(self-love)*	There is no lack of *amour-propre* in her!
octogenarian	*(an eighty-year-old)*	The spry octogenarian won the race.
cognoscenti	*(those who know)*	This wine is preferred by the cognoscenti.
surfeit	*(excess)*	He consumed a painful surfeit of food and drink.
primate	*(monkeys, apes, and humans)*	In what ways are the higher primates different from other species?
pellucid	*(crystal clear)*	Pellucid waters and pellucid prose are equally beautiful.
circumvent	*(get around)*	It is unwise to circumvent the rules in prison.
hemiplegia	*(paralysis on one side)*	We helped the victim of hemiplegia.
narcolepsy	*(attacks of sleep)*	She suffered uncontrollable attacks of narcolepsy.

micro

small • minute • enlarging

The Greek stem **micro** is one of the most interesting stems in the English language because it often brings us face to face with another level of reality: the work of the very small. Although **micro** usually means *small*, it also can mean *abnormally little*, and it can even have an inverse meaning of *enlarging*, as in the word *microphone*, where it refers to enlarging sounds that are small. Here is a small selection of the interesting words that contain **micro** in its various shades of meaning:

microbe:	a germ. In the end, the Martians were defeated not by war but by microbes.
micron:	one millionth of a meter. The microscope presented a vista of many microns.
microphyte:	microscopic plants. The creature was covered with parasitic microphytes.
microsome:	granules in the cytoplasm. The microsomes contribute to protein synthesis.
micrococcus:	spherical bacteria. The mass of micrococci fed on the dead protoplasm.
microeconomics:	economics of individuals. She studied consumers' microeconomic habits.
microdot:	a pinhead copy. The spy enlarged the text photographed in the microdot.
micrometeorite:	microscopic meteorite. Micrometeorites drift down to earth without burning.
micronutrient:	nutrients barely required. The micronutrient iron is needed in minute amounts.
microsecond:	one millionth of a second. The computer responded in microseconds.
microscopy:	use of a microscope. The criminal was caught through microscopy.
microtome:	instrument for cutting slices. A microtome cuts tissue for microscopic view.
microseism:	a small tremor. Microseisms too slight to feel occur almost every day.
microlith:	small flint tools. The mesolithic site contained firepits and microliths.
microprocessor:	microcomputer chip. The microprocessor's logic was printed on a silicon chip.
microcephaly:	of abnormally small cranium. The child was born microcephalic.
microevolution:	tiny hereditary changes. Microevolution created small differences in species.
microanalysis:	chemical analysis of small quantities. Microanalysis revealed the toxin.
microbus:	small motorbus. Arlo threw his guitar into the red VW microbus.
microcosm:	microscopic universe. The electron microscope found microcosms in the dust.
microbiology:	biology of microorganisms. Microbiological weapons were banned at last.

1. A **benefactor** is a person who does (*fac*) good (*bene*) to someone else. In Charles Dickens's *Great Expectations*, the young Pip is assisted in life by an anonymous benefactor who—to Pip's initial horror—turns out to be an escaped convict Pip had helped when Pip was just a young lad.

2. A **Micropoem: Introspective** means inward-looking, but especially in a metaphorical sense. A person can be introspective in the sense of being mentally inward-looking—into himself.

3. **Dissonant** sounds are inharmonious because the sounds do not go together. Sounds that harmonize go together, whereas sounds that are dissonant clash; they are away (*dis*) from each other. If the brass section plays in the key of C, the woodwinds must not play in the key of D. (Not, at least, until they attempt twentieth-century experimental compositions!) **Dissonance** is more of a clashing sound, whereas **cacophony** could refer to most any unpleasant noise.

4. In the madness (*mania*) called **megalomania**, the victim thinks of himself as larger (*mega*) than life—as more important than he really is. You sometimes hear the terms Napoleon-complex or Caesar-complex to refer to megalomania.

5. **Pronunciation Tips**

    vivacious - vie VAY shuss
    surfeit - SURR fit
    pellucid - pell LOOSE id
    amour-propre - amoor PRO pruh
    exculpate - EX kull pate
    megalomania - mega lo MAY nee uh
    heliotropic - heel ee oh TROP ik
    cognoscenti - cog no SEN tee
    euphemism - YOO fuh mism

6. **Spanish Cognates**: One of the most important observations to gain from the study of the etymology of English vocabulary is that English and Spanish share thousands of words that are cognates—related words—that have common origins. Often, the English and the Spanish words share not only a stem but even more than one stem, and often in the same order. As examples, here are some English words from this lesson and their Spanish cognates:

    introspective : introspectivo
    intervene : intervenir
    syndrome : síndrome
    subordinate : subordinar
    dissonant : disonante
    credible : creíble
    euphemism : eufemismo
    benefactor : benefactor
    magnate : magnate
    octagenarian : octagenario
    narcolepsy : narcolepsia

An archer is depicted on this cylix.

In each case below, one of the choices was really the word used by the author in the sentence provided. All of the choices can be found in the words on the first page of this lesson. Your challenge is to decide which word the author used. This is not a test; it is more like a game because more than one word choice may work perfectly well. See if you can use your sensitivity and intuition to guess correctly which word the author used. You may need a dictionary.

1. **From Stephen Crane's *The Red Badge of Courage***

   [The] girl had made _____ fun at his martial spirit.
   a. belligerent
   b. vivacious
   c. introspective
   d. pellucid

2. **From Jack London's *The Call of the Wild***

   Joe was the very opposite, sour and _____.
   a. credible
   b. subordinate
   c. vivacious
   d. introspective

3. **From Charles Dickens's *Great Expectations***

   Six days _____ between me and the date of departure.
   a. surfeited
   b. circumvented
   c. intervened
   d. exculpated

4. **From Nathaniel Hawthorne's *The House of Seven Gables***

   The Puritan _____ bade all the town to be his guests.
   a. magnate
   b. benefactor
   c. octagenarian
   d. belligerent

5. **From John Hersey's *Hiroshima***

   [There was] a curious _____ of symptoms that cropped out in the third and fourth weeks.
   a. hemiplegia
   b. narcolepsy
   c. syndrome
   d. surfeit

"[Alcibiades at Sparta] was no less popular in private life, and he deluded the people by pretending to adopt the Laconian habits. When they saw him closely shaved, bathing in cold water, eating dry bread and black broth, they wondered and began to doubt whether this man ever had kept a cook, used perfumes.... For Alcibiades, among his other extraordinary qualities, had this special art of captivating men by assimilating his own manner and habits to theirs, being able to change more quickly than the chameleon, from one mode to life to another. The chameleon, indeed, cannot turn itself white; but Alcibiades never found anything, good or bad, which he could not imitate to the life. Thus at Sparta he was fond of exercise, frugal, and severe; in Ionia, luxurious, frivolous, and lazy; in Thrace, he drank deep; in Thessaly, he proved himself a good horseman; while, when he was consorting with the satrap Tissphernes, he outdid even the Persian splendor and pomp. It was not his real character that he so often and so easily changed, but as he knew that if he appeared in his true colors, he would be universally disliked, he concealed his real self under an apparent adoption of the ways and fashions of whatever place he was in."

—Plutarch

THE PELOPONNESIAN WARS—2
Dr. Thomas Milton Kemnitz

The fortunes of war ebbed and flowed for three decades after the plague hit Athens. First one side seemed to have the upper hand, then the other. With Thucydides as a source, it is possible to trace the events with an accuracy that is astonishing. The historian gives us the accounts of councils of war and the arguments that occurred in them, including speeches that leaders made. In the Athenian democracy, the most popular citizen initiators were those who proposed the most aggressive policies. The winning strategy of Pericles had been carefully controlled aggression. Those who came after him were less restrained, and they placed Athens at risk.

No Athenian leader was more problematic than Alcibiades, who was the descendant of one of the most famous aristocratic families in Athens. His mother's family traced its lineage back to Telamonian Ajax, also known as Ajax the Great in Homer's *Iliad*. Pericles was a relative and became one of Alcibiades' guardians after his father died in battle when the boy was three years old. Alcibiades had several famous teachers, including Socrates, and he was well-trained in the art of rhetoric. At the age of eighteen he took part in a battle in which Socrates was said to have saved his life. In 421 B.C., Sparta and Athens signed the Peace of Nicias. But Alcibiades set about to undermine the truce because, according to Thucydides, he was offended that the Spartans negotiated the treaty through others, overlooking the nineteen-year-old Alcibiades because of his youth.

Alcibiades had enormous talent. He was bold, resourceful, creative—and an unscrupulous liar. He would do or say anything to get his way, and nothing or no one else mattered to him. In one Olympics, he entered several four-horse chariots in that race—the most prestigious of the games—and his teams placed first, second, and fourth. Horses were prohibitively expensive in Greece, and one team of horses was beyond the resources of any but the very wealthiest. Alicbiades's enormous wealth made possible a display such as Greece and the Olympics had never seen. He had admirers, but he made innumerable bitter enemies. Peace was probably inimical to him because it limited his scope for action. He managed to put together an alliance of Peloponnesian city states to challenge Sparta and got the war started again. However, his alliance lost badly at the Battle of Mantinea in 418.

In 415 B.C., delegates from the Sicilian city of Segesta came to Athens to plead for support in their war against Selinus. Although others argued against the expedition as costly and dangerous, Alcibiades was the key supporter and eventually led a huge expedition with the intent of conquering Sicily for Athens. His enemies in Athens sent a ship to Sicily to bring him back to stand trial on a charge of sacrilege. Alcibiades, fearing an unfavorable verdict, defected to the Spartans and betrayed the strategic objectives of the expedition. The entire expedition was wiped out, and the Athenians lost tens of thousands of men and hundreds of ships. The Athenians who were captured alive were confined in stone quarries and left to die of starvation—a process that took more than two months until the last man perished. For years Alcibiades advised the Spartans on how to do severe damage to an Athens already eviscerated by the Sicilian debacle. Eventually Alcibiades had to flee from Sparta, where he had made enemies and where his life was in imminent danger, and he went over to the Persians. There he betrayed the Spartans and induced the Persians to stop aiding them.

Plague in Athens	Erechtheion erected	Expedition to Sicily	Alcibiades defects

431–404 B.C.	430 B.C.	421–405 B.C.	415–413 B.C.	415 B.C.
Peloponnesian Wars				

synthesis

What category could include the words **introspective**, **megalomania**, **vivacious**, and **cognoscenti**?

divergence

What consumer items of different kinds are preferred by the **cognoscenti**?

analysis

Break down and explain the following words: **circumvent**, **exculpate**, and **heliotropic**.

evaluation

Should a criminal be **exculpated** if the methods used by the police to catch the criminal are themselves illegal and unconstitutional?

intuition

When you are an **octagenarian**, what will your hobby be?

emotion

What are the emotions that you associate with a **vivacious** personality?

aesthetics

Can you imagine making sculpture out of **pellucid** substances like plexiglass? How would you use plexiglass to make sculpture?

A black-figure cylix showing a slinger in action

delineate	*(to outline)*	He will quickly delineate the options.
emollient	*(softener)*	The ancient Greeks used creamy emollient for their skin.
retrograde	*(backward)*	The planet seems to move in a retrograde motion.
melancholy	*(dark sadness)*	Some people feel a black melancholy on rainy days.
intracranial	*(within the skull)*	Intracranial surgery will not exorcise her demons.
cardiovascular	*(of the heart and vessels)*	You need cardiovascular exercise.
epiphany	*(revelation)*	The epiphany was a flash, a sudden appearance of insight.
histology	*(study of living tissues)*	The classic histology textbook was out of print.
perihelion	*(orbital point nearest the sun)*	The planet reached perihelion.
inherent	*(built-in)*	Americans possess an inherent right to free speech.
plutocracy	*(government of the wealthy)*	Is the nation controlled by plutocrats?
sine qua non	*(essential element)*	Money was the *sine qua non* for acceptance.
corpulent	*(full-bodied)*	His corpulence was caused by his gluttony.
dichotomy	*(two-part division)*	The right/wrong dichotomy seemed simplistic.
pathological	*(diseased)*	The fascist dictator was a pathological liar.
cryptic	*(having hidden meaning)*	We found a cryptic inscription in the stone.
isosceles	*(having two equal sides)*	He drew an isosceles trapezoid on the board.
pathogen	*(disease-causer)*	The team's careful search did not locate the pathogen.
vociferous	*(loudly-voiced)*	His vociferous protests could be heard for blocks.
rectify	*(correct)*	Please take steps to rectify the situation and make it right.
sanctimonious	*(affectedly holy)*	His sanctimonious lectures were hypocritical.
tortuous	*(twisting)*	The tortuous mountain highway wound steeply up.
rectilinear	*(right-angled)*	Do you like the building's rectilinear architecture?
metamorphosis	*(change of shape)*	The insect's metamorphosis was miraculous.
petroglyph	*(rock carving)*	The prehistoric petroglyph was high on the cave wall.

poly

many • much • excessive

The Greek stem **poly** is one of the most useful prefixes in the English language; it lets us easily describe phenomena that are multiple. Although **poly** usually means *many*, it also can mean *much, more than usual, excessive,* or *in many parts*. Here is a small selection of the interesting words that contain **poly** in its various shades of meaning:

polymath: one of great learning. The brilliant polymath was expert in numerous fields.

polyandry: having multiple husbands. Some of the tribes had polyandrous traditions.

polyphony: harmonizing melodies. Bach is famous for his intricate polyphony.

polyglot: speaking many languages. She was a fluent, five-language polyglot.

polyphagia: excessive desire for food. His polyphagia was caused by subconscious fear.

polygraph: lie detector. The polygraph device measured pulse rate, blood pressure, etc.

polygon: many-sided figure. By *polygon*, he meant having more than three sides.

polymorphism: having different forms. The castes of polymorphic insects look very different.

polytheism: worship of many gods. The pagan polytheism endured for many centuries.

polysome: group of ribosomes. Protein synthesis occurred in the polysomes.

polychrome: of many colors. The abstract paintings were all bright polychromes.

polyrhythm: simultaneous rhythms. Polyrhythmic beats echoed through the valley.

polysemy: having many meanings. The debate degenerated into semantic polysemy.

polysyllabic: of many syllables. His polysyllabic terms revealed a sesquipedalian egotism.

polygamy: marriage to many. Variations of polygamy are traditional in different cultures.

polygyny: multiple wives. The sultan's harem was a polygynous institution.

polyphyletic: of multiple ancestry. The curious species had a polyphyletic origin.

polyptych: art panels. The five-panel polyptych made a beautiful altarpiece.

polyp: a tentacled coelenterate. Stinging cells covered the polyp's many tentacles.

polynomial: expression of multiple terms. We remember Pythagoras for his polynomials.

polysyndeton: repetition of conjunctions. His tirade sounded like a study in polysyndeton.

1. *Peri* and *apo* often are used to make opposites: **perihelion** and **aphelion**, **perigee** and **apogee**. Perihelion is the orbital point nearest (*peri*) the sun (*helio*), whereas aphelion is the orbital point away (*apo*) from the sun (*helio*). Perigee is the orbital point nearest (*peri*) the earth (*geo*).

2. A **pathogen** is a disease-causer because it originates (*gen*) disease (*patho*).

3. In ancient Greece, people referred to the appearance or manifestation of a god as an *epipháneia*. Today we might not have Apollo or Dionysus suddenly appear to us, but we might have a revelation, a revealing, a flash, a sudden appearance (*phan*) not of a god but of insight. This experience is an **epiphany**.

4. We **rectify** something wrong when we correct it, when we make (*fy*) it right (*rect*).

5. A **Micropoem**: In a **dichotomy**, things are cut (*tomy*) in two (*dicho*). Some see a dichotomized world in which everything is either/or: right or wrong, good or bad, communist or noncommunist, art or not art, American or un-American, and so forth. Others regard some dichotomies as oversimplifications.

6. The ***sine qua non*** is the thing *without-which-not*. If you have the *sine qua non*, then that is a good start. It is the essential element that must be present.

7. The **sanctimonious** person is full of (*ous*) holiness (*sanct*), but too full. Sanctimoniousness is arrogantly and pretentiously taking on airs of superior holiness that one does not merit.

8. **Pronunciation Tips**

   melancholy - MELL an koll ee
   corpulent - KORP yoo lent
   isosceles - eye SOSS uh leez
   sine qua non - SIN eh kwa nahn
   plutocracy - ploo TOCK ruh see
   perihelion - pair ih HEE lee un
   intracranial - intra KRAY nee ul
   emollient - ee MOLL yent
   sanctimonious - sank tih MO nee us

9. **Spanish Cognates**: One of the most important observations to gain from the study of the etymology of English vocabulary is that English and Spanish share thousands of words that are cognates—related words—that have common origins. Often, the English and the Spanish words share not only a stem but even more than one stem, and often in the same order. As examples, here are some English words from this lesson and their Spanish cognates:

   delineate : delinear
   retrograde : retrograda
   melancholy : melancolía
   intracranial : intracranial
   cardiovascular : cardiovascular
   epiphany : epifanía

   inherent : inherente
   corpulent : corpulento
   dichotomy : dicotomía
   rectify : rectificar
   petroglyph : petroglífico
   metamorphosis : metamorfosis

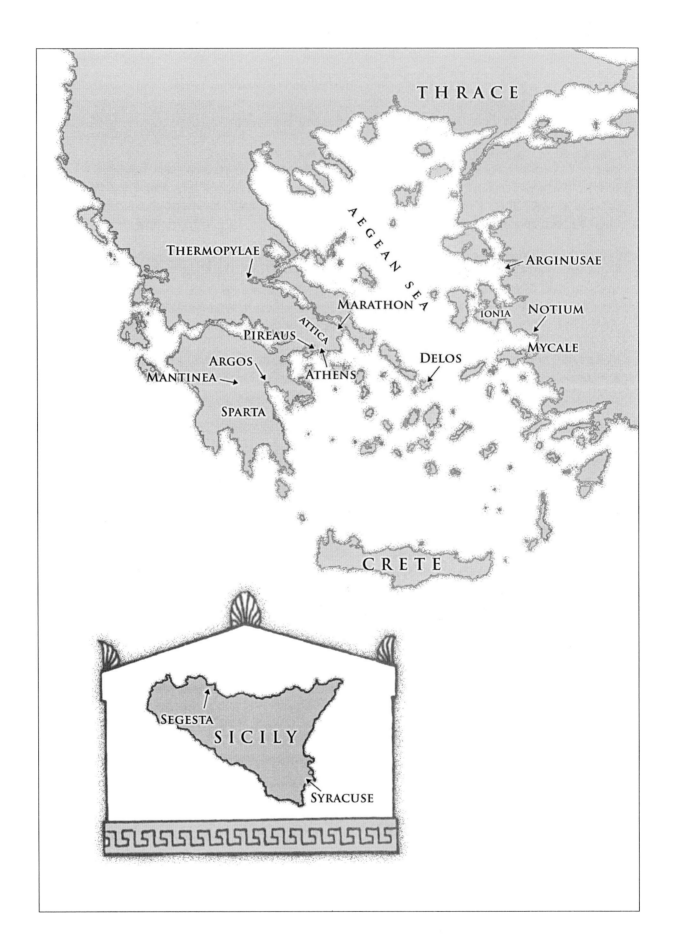

THE END OF THE PELOPONNESIAN WARS

Dr. Thomas Milton Kemnitz

Alcibiades's only hope of returning to Greece was to be forgiven in Athens, where a death sentence for treason awaited him. He devised a strategy of replacing the Athenian democracy with an oligarchy because he was convinced that was the only way he would be recalled to Athens. As a primary incentive, he claimed that he could secure for Athens from the Persians a large amount of aid in the form of money and triremes. As he hoped, an oligarchy took control of Athens, but democracy was soon restored. In the later years of the Peloponnesian Wars, the opposing sides frequently saw themselves in terms of democracy against oligarchy or as defenders of oligarchy against an extreme democracy. When one side or the other took control of a city, it installed the form of government it favored. The identification of Athens with democracy made Alcibiades's attempt to undermine Athenian democracy particularly audacious.

Alcibiades helped the Athenians win victories over the Spartans for several years before he returned to Athens to a hero's welcome in 407 B.C. By then the long years of war had depleted the Athenian treasury, and the city had few reserves to recover from misfortune. Also by then, Athens had few willing allies and a difficult time projecting its power. Moreover, the Spartans found an able admiral in Lysander, who was skilled enough as a diplomat to persuade the Persians to aid him with ships and money. The money was used to induce poorly-paid Athenian sailors to defect to the fledgling Spartan navy. Alcibiades unfortunately left his helmsman in command of the Athenian fleet at Notium, where he suffered a defeat at the hands of the Spartans. At that point Alcibiades's enemies had the ammunition they needed to have him stripped of command by the Assembly in Athens, and Alcibiades decided to escape to land he owned in Thrace.

In 405 B.C., Lysander caught the Athenian fleet beached on shore and destroyed it. He had the right hands of all the surviving Athenian sailors cut off, and he sent the survivors back to Athens with every other possible exile he could find to swell the population. Athens had no more resources to deploy and was now cut off from the Black Sea grain that was the principal source of its food supply. There was widespread famine in Athens, and people died of starvation in the streets during the winter. Finally Athens surrendered to the Spartans, who occupied Athens in 404 and replaced the democracy with an oligarchy. Alcibiades was killed in 404 or 403 B.C., probably by a party of Spartans.

Within a year the Athenians had restored democracy and began to repair the damage. They had paid a high price for the unscrupulous actions of Alcibiades, and very soon—in 399 B.C.—they would hold accountable his foremost tutor, Socrates, for clearly he had corrupted the youth of Athens, as the actions of Alcibiades showed to all. Athens was still the place for many Greeks to be, and Socrates was followed by Plato and then by Aristotle; vases were still made and painted on the north slope of the Acropolis, and trade still came in and out of Piraeus. However, much of the energy and wealth of the Greek people for half a century had been spent in the conflict; poverty became widespread in the Peloponnese, and Athens never regained the prosperity that allowed it to adorn the Acropolis with great buildings like those they had erected in the fifth century. The final wing of the Erechtheion was never completed. The Persian empire expanded to control the Ionian cities.

Alcibiades returns to Athens	Victory at Arginusae; six admirals executed	Destruction of Athenian fleet on shore	Athens surrenders	Socrates condemned
407 B.C.	**406 B.C.**	**405 B.C.**	**404 B.C.**	**399 B.C.**

In each case below, one of the choices was really the word used by the author in the sentence provided. All of the choices can be found in the words on the first page of this lesson. Your challenge is to decide which word the author used. This is not a test; it is more like a game because more than one word choice may work perfectly well. See if you can use your sensitivity and intuition to guess correctly which word the author used. You may need a dictionary.

1. **From Emily Brontë's *Wuthering Heights***

   He entered, _____ oaths dreadful to hear.
   a. delineating
   b. rectifying
   c. vociferating
   d. dichotomizing

2. **From Sir Walter Scott's *Ivanhoe***

   Our history must needs _____ for the space of a few pages.
   a. retrograde
   b. metamorphosize
   c. delineate
   d. rectify

3. **From Ralph Ellison's *Invisible Man***

   Their heavy steel plates [clicked] remote, _____ messages in the brief silence of the train's stop.
   a. cryptic
   b. corpulent
   c. tortuous
   d. inherent

4. **From Joseph Heller's *Catch-22***

   Nurse Cramer…sizzled with _____ anger like a damp firecracker.
   a. metamorphic
   b. vociferous
   c. rectilinear
   d. sanctimonious

5. **From Jane Austen's *Emma***

   It was all general approbation and smoothness; nothing _____ or distinguished.
   a. inherent
   b. melancholy
   c. delineated
   d. corpulent

synthesis

What statement can you make that is true of **petroglyphs**, **plutocracies**, and **emollients**? Obviously, making a single true statement of three such different things might cause you to consider some ingenious categories.

divergence

Imagine every physical process you can think of that would occur on or near the head of a comet as it reaches **perihelion**. Would you rather see the comet close-up at perihelion or at **aphelion**?

analysis

Explain the construction of the words **dichotomy**, **rectilinear**, **metamorphosis**, and **pathogen**.

evaluation

Is there always a clear **dichotomy** between right and wrong? Are there any behaviors that are both? Are there any behaviors that are neither?

intuition

An undiscovered **pathogen** is causing sickness in your community. What do you fear the pathogen is?

emotion

What emotions do you associate with **corpulence**? Are these emotions appropriate?

aesthetics

Do you think cities would be improved if corporations allowed local artists to carve **petroglyphs** on the stone sides of the buildings?

Socrates had two students who were particularly unpopular with the Athenian demos. *One was Alcibiades, and the other was Critias, who was a leader of the Thirty Tyrants installed by the Spartans to replace the democracy after the surrender of Athens in 404. Many who opposed the Spartan-imposed government fled the city during its short rule, but Socrates did not. He made a number of statements that were critical of democracy and democratic leaders, and that was not likely to have enhanced his reputation. Moreover in 406, he chanced to be chosen by lot to head the trial of the eight generals who had won the Battle of Arginusae only to be charged with abandoning the sailors in the water. Socrates resisted during his day in the chair the demand for a collective trial of all the generals together, and he blocked any vote until his term ended; thereafter the six generals were convicted and executed. All of these circumstances contributed to the atmosphere in which Socrates was tried in 399 for corrupting the youth of Athens and for impiety, and he was condemned to death.*

chronic	*(lasting)*	His chronic illness dragged on for years.
hyperbole	*(overstatement)*	His colorful hyperbole enlivened his conversation.
sonorous	*(full-sounding)*	Dr. King's sonorous voice echoed over the crowd.
germane	*(related)*	Her germane comments hit the mark.
convivial	*(jovial, festive)*	His convivial friends loved to celebrate.
cognomen	*(nickname)*	His cognomen is "Sterno."
anarchist	*(one against government)*	The anarchist passed out leaflets to passersby.
animadversion	*(criticism)*	Your animadversions on his behavior are superfluous.
pusillanimous	*(small-minded)*	The deliberate snub was a low, pusillanimous act.
subterfuge	*(evasive dodge)*	The mayor ducked a question with a clever subterfuge.
saturnine	*(gloomy and remote)*	Her saturnine personality won her few friends.
luminary	*(enlightening person)*	We met the amiable luminary Carl Sagan.
exorbitant	*(unreasonable)*	Their exorbitant prices are in an orbit of their own.
expatriate	*(banish)*	They were forcefully expatriated from the fatherland.
filigree	*(lacy design)*	The delicate filigree around the diamond was beautiful.
eulogy	*(words of praise)*	The reverend delivered a moving eulogy at the funeral.
sedentary	*(sitting)*	Flagpole sitting is a highly sedentary occupation.
euphoria	*(joy)*	Their love brought them a blissful euphoria.
bonhomie	*(good-naturedness)*	He was a popular fellow of appealing bonhomie.
bona fide	*(good faith)*	The company will make a bona fide offer.
bon vivant	*(indulger in luxury)*	The wealthy *bon vivant* lived the good life.
mutable	*(changeable)*	The mutable laws of high fashion can't be predicted.
impute	*(attribute discredit)*	It is unnecessary to impute evil motives to opponents.
status quo	*(the present state)*	It can be dangerous to disrupt the status quo.
paradigm	*(model)*	The incident offers an instructive paradigm for future guidance.

pre

before • in front • superior

The Latin stem **pre** is one of the most commonly found prefixes in the English language, designating things that are first in a sequence, either of time, position, or quality. **Pre** usually means *before*, but we also use it to mean *earlier*, *anterior to*, *in front of*, *surpassing*, or *superior*. Consult a good college dictionary to see the many pages of words that begin with this important prefix. Here is a small selection of the interesting words that contain **pre** in its various shades of meaning:

preamble:	an introduction. We studied the preamble to the *Constitution*.
precipice:	a sheer cliff. Carton snatched his alter ego from the precipice of disaster.
precise:	accurate. Supreme Court Justice Ginsburg was precise in her wording.
predilection:	a partiality. His early life had given him a predilection for good wine.
predominant:	superior. The predominant murder motive in the case was anger.
prehistory:	before recorded history. Archaeology pieces together the truth of prehistory.
prehensile:	grasping. Humans have prehensile hands with opposable thumbs.
prenuptial:	before marriage. The prenuptial agreement assigned all of their assets.
preliterate:	without writing. Oral history is common in preliterate cultures.
prevaricate:	to equivocate. Aunt Polly easily detected his inept prevarications.
prestige:	impressive reputation. The Nobel Prize carries with it a certain prestige.
prevail:	to triumph over. Faulkner felt that humans would not merely endure; they would prevail.
prescind:	to detach or isolate. After Finney's accident, Gene prescinded his mind.
prelude:	a preliminary part. He recognized the fugue's prelude immediately.
prefigure:	to foreshadow. The war now seems prefigured in the prior nationalism.
premeditate:	to plan. It was a premeditated crime; it involved prepense.
predestine:	to foreordain. Oedipus felt that his tragic fate was predestined for him.
précis:	a concise summary. She worked all night on a précis of the defendant's case.
preempt:	replace. A soapy sitcom was preempted by the first game of the World Series.
precipitous:	rash or impetuous. Iago manipulated Othello's precipitous emotionalism.
presage:	an omen. A lion whelped in the street as a presage of the assassination.

Athena Promachos was an enduring image, but Philip and Alexander ended completely the primacy of Athens as a military power.

When he was young, Philip had been in Thebes as a hostage during the years when Thebes was fighting Sparta, and he saw the winning tactic that allowed the Thebans to beat the Spartans. That tactic was a major thrust in the middle of the battlefield against the enemy center. Usually, battles were won—as the one at Marathon had been—by bringing overwhelming pressure on the flanks and collapsing the enemy battle line from the sides. The use of a cavalry to deliver a wedge-shaped assault on the enemy center was a tactic Philip employed and taught to his son.

PHILIP OF MACEDONIA

Dr. Thomas Milton Kemnitz

With the defeat of Athens in 404 B.C., Sparta had a brief period when it took on the Persian empire, but soon it was engaged in a series of wars with its neighbors, and it seemed that little had changed in Greece after the Peloponnesian Wars. Greek city fought Greek city; alliances were made and broken, and life carried on very much as before. Sparta had been badly weakened by its long war with Athens. In early times, there had been as many as 8,000 or 9,000 Spartan men. Already in the 520s, their numbers were so low that they had to use Helots as troops. In the fourth century, the number of Spartan men fell to fewer than 2,000. In 371 B.C. for the first time, Sparta lost a land battle when it fielded its full army. The victors freed the Helots and liberated Messina from Spartan control. The foundation of Spartan power was thereby destroyed, and Sparta was never able to reassert its hegemony.

The Greek landscape was transformed by Philip II of Macedon (386 to 336 B.C.). Philip became king of Macedonia in 359 B.C. when his elder brothers lost a battle, part of their kingdom, and their lives. Philip brought to Greek warfare an innovation of a twenty-foot-long lance called the *sarissa*. The phalanx of the Greek armies for centuries had relied on lines of men with interlocking shields and spears or short swords for use with one hand. The ancients had numerous weapons that could be fired at a distance, and arrows, javelins, and lead and stone shot were always a risk—hence the helmets and breastplates—but the cavalry and the sword were potentially the most potent weapons. The *sarissa* could be used to protect the phalanx against mounted troops and could be brought into play long before a man with a short sword could get near the Macedonian phalanx. In addition, the men in the rear of the phalanx could hold their *sarissas* vertically to hide the maneuvers behind the lines. Philip also paid his troops rather than depending upon citizen-soldiers who were only available when not engaged in agriculture. He used gold from mines in lands he conquered; this put his troops on a level for training and professionalism with the paid oarsmen of the Athenian navy and the full-time warriors of Sparta who relied on the labor of the Helots to allow the Spartan army to train continuously.

Philip conquered the Balkans, northern Greece, and the surrounding lands from the Hellespont to the Adriatic Sea, and then he brought all of southern Greece under his control with the exception of Sparta. He sent the Spartans an invitation to join his league, telling them, "If I enter Laconia, I will raze Sparta." The Spartans responded with a single word: "If." Sparta made no aggressive moves nor was strategically vital enough to necessitate a war against it, and Philip and Alexander the Great never bothered to invade it.

In their prime a century earlier, the power of Sparta and Athens rested on their cultures, organization, and way of life. Democracy and imperialism were Athens's strengths, while Sparta's was a Helot labor force and a fierce culture of honor, fitness, and warfare. Philip and the Macedonians, by contrast, had no such foundations. Rather, Philip's organizing genius, his innovative use of the *sarissa*, and his employment of full-time soldiers based on exploiting gold mines provided the sources of his power. Sparta and Athens were powerful no matter who led them; Philip was powerful only because he was the monarch.

Athens surrenders	Thebes defeats Spartan army	Philip becomes king of Macedonia	Philip founds Greek League	Philip assassinated; Alexander assumes throne
404 B.C.	371 B.C.	359 B.C.	337 B.C.	336 B.C.

1. **Convivial** people are jovial because they are like Jove—they are festive and love to celebrate with their friends. It is times of life (*viv*) together (*con*) that they relish.

2. A **Micropoem**: A trick used to evade a question, dodge a question, or duck a question is known as a **subterfuge**. We use the trick to duck: to flee (*fug*) under (*sub*) the question.

3. Why do we call a gloomy and remote personality **saturnine**? Because it is Saturn-like; Saturn is distant from us and far from the warmth of the sun.

4. A ***bon vivant*** is an indulger in luxury, an enjoyer, a person who luxuriates in the good (*bon*) life (*viv*).

5. A **paradigm** is a mental model, a pattern. It is an example that one may imitate. The idea lies in the stem *para* (beside). When one has two things side by side, both the copy and the model to copy, then it is easier to follow the pattern. We might say that someone's quick response in a time of crisis is a paradigm for future imitation, and we then pattern our behavior after that model. Physical models, such as airplane models or boat models, are not referred to as paradigms.

6. The **status quo** is the state that exists at present.

7. **Pronunciation Tips**

   chronic - KRON ik
   pusillanimous - pyoo sill ANN ih muss
   bonhomie - bohn oh MEE
   bona fide - bohn uh FIDE ee
   mutable - MYOO tuh bul
   subterfuge - SUB turr fyooj
   bon vivant - bohn vee VAHN
   paradigm - PAR uh dime
   germane - jur MANE

8. **Spanish Cognates**: One of the most important observations to gain from the study of the etymology of English vocabulary is that English and Spanish share thousands of words that are cognates—related words—that have common origins. Often, the English and the Spanish words share not only a stem but even more than one stem, and often in the same order. As examples, here are some English words from this lesson and their Spanish cognates:

   chronic : crónico
   hyperbole : hipérbole
   anarchist : anarquista
   luminary : luminaria
   exorbitant : exorbitante
   expatriate : expatriar
   eulogy : eulogía
   sedentary : sedentario
   euphoria : euforia
   bona fide : bona fide
   status quo : status quo
   paradigm : paradigma

Apollo pours a libation. On his lap is a lyre.

In each case below, one of the choices was really the word used by the author in the sentence provided. All of the choices can be found in the words on the first page of this lesson. Your challenge is to decide which word the author used. This is not a test; it is more like a game because more than one word choice may work perfectly well. See if you can use your sensitivity and intuition to guess correctly which word the author used. You may need a dictionary.

1. **From Washington Irving's *The Legend of Sleepy Hollow***

   The _____ of Crane was not inapplicable to this person.
   a. subterfuge
   b. euphoria
   c. status quo
   d. cognomen

2. **From Edith Wharton's *Ethan Frome***

   He had had no time for _____ loiterings in the village.
   a. convivial
   b. exorbitant
   c. mutable
   d. saturnine

3. **From Jane Austen's *Emma***

   It was charity to _____ some of her unbecoming indifference to the languor of ill-health.
   a. eulogize
   b. expatriate
   c. impute
   d. animadvert

4. **From James Joyce's *A Portrait of the Artist as a Young Man***

   Lynch smote himself _____ on the chest.
   a. convivially
   b. germanely
   c. chronically
   d. sonorously

5. **From Joseph Conrad's *Heart of Darkness***

   Most seamen lead, if one may so express it, a _____ life.
   a. sedentary
   b. saturnine
   c. pusillanimous
   d. mutable

synthesis

Which words in List #27 would you most like to have applied to you? Which words would you least like to have applied to you?

divergence

Who are the most famous **luminaries** in American history? Think of as many as you can.

analysis

Analyze the words **cognomen**, **sonorous**, **euphoria**, **eulogy**, **anarchist**, and **expatriate**.

evaluation

Should **pusillanimous** acts be punished, ignored, or discussed?

intuition

Everyone knows that the laws of fashion design are **mutable**. How do you imagine people will dress in 2050 A.D.?

emotion

Euphoria is an emotion. Give some examples of events that would leave you euphoric.

aesthetics

Which would be more difficult to capture in painting or sculpture: a person who is **convivial** or a person who is **saturnine**?

This is a massive bronze statue of Zeus found in the sea off Artemisium. It is from the middle of the fifth century and is in the same severe style as the metopes of the Parthenon.

schism	*(division)*	The debate created a schism in the Democratic party.
bootless	*(useless)*	His bootless effort to win acceptance was pathetic.
rubicund	*(red)*	Her rubicund cheeks matched her rosy outlook.
apotheosis	*(raising to god status)*	The media created the champ's apotheosis.
precursor	*(forerunner)*	The rumblings were the precursor of what was to come.
transpose	*(switch)*	Dyslexics sometimes transpose letters in a word.
invective	*(bitter denunciation)*	She endured her opponent's scathing invective.
prestidigitation	*(sleight of hand)*	Presto! The magician's prestidigitation was fun.
cosmology	*(study of the universe)*	The origin of atoms is a cosmological question.
effusion	*(outpouring)*	His effusion of joyful greetings made us wince.
anthology	*(literary collection)*	The anthology contains the flowers of modern poetry.
posthumous	*(after death)*	It was bittersweet to present a posthumous award.
euphony	*(beautiful sound)*	He loved the euphony of the wind in the trees.
refractory	*(stubborn)*	The refractory child broke and rebroke the rules.
platitude	*(flat, trite remark)*	We need fresh ideas, not hollow platitudes.
acrophobia	*(fear of heights)*	He began to feel acrophobia in elevators.
agoraphobia	*(fear of openness)*	Some visitors feel agoraphobia in Red Square.
veracity	*(truthfulness)*	Slowly, we began to question her veracity.
verisimilitude	*(similarity to truth)*	Notice the fable's eerie verisimilitude.
idiosyncrasy	*(peculiarity)*	We even loved his many idiosyncrasies.
alumni	*(graduates)*	The college alumni wrote to the missing alumnus.
casus belli	*(cause for war)*	The government chose to regard the act as *casus belli*.
interregnum	*(time between rulers)*	The nation enjoyed a peaceful interregnum.
infraction	*(breaking)*	It was an unintentional infraction of the rules.
condign	*(worthy)*	He will receive a condign punishment for his offense.

psych

soul • mind • mental

The Greek stem **psych** is one of the most interesting stems in English because it forms words that refer to our mental life. Depending upon what stem it attaches to, **psych** may appear as **psycho** or as **psyche**. Here is a small selection of the interesting words that contain **psych**:

psychometry:	mental testing. Only a specialist should give psychometric exams.
psyche:	the soul or mind. Derangement in his psyche explained his criminal acts.
psychomotor:	motor effects of the mind. An accident left him with psychomotor damage.
psychosocial:	social/mental development. The class trip was a good psychosocial time.
psychosomatic:	mind-caused physical disorder. Stress caused the psychosomatic condition.
psychedelic:	mind-altering. Use of psychedelic drugs had damaged his memory.
psychokinesis:	affecting objects with the mind. The Russians investigated psychokinesis.
psychogenic:	of psychic origin. The "ghosts" were found to have a psychogenic basis.
psychopath:	an amoral personality. A dangerous psychopath was stalking the street.
psychobiography:	a mental biography. The psychobiography examined Jefferson's real motives.
psychodrama:	acting-out therapy. He relived his abandonment in a poignant psychodrama.
psychology:	the science of the mind. In behavioral psychology, rats are at center stage.
psychosis:	major mental disorder. In psychosis, there is a break with reality.
psychoactive:	affecting the mind. The cancer drug had negative psychoactive effects.
psychograph:	personality chart. The psychopath's psychograph revealed no conscience.
psychoneurosis:	neurosis. The multiple personality was a psychoneurosis, not a psychosis.
psychotomimetic:	psychosis-creating. Psychotomimetic drugs produce psychosis-like states.
psychotoxic:	brain-damaging. The psychotoxic damage of alcohol was obvious.
para**psycho**logy:	study of psychic phenomena. The parapsychologist proved to be a fraud.
psychoacoustic:	subjective hearing. The ringing noise was a psychoacoustic disorder.
psycholinguistic:	the psychology of language. Reading has a psycholinguistic foundation.
psychodynamics:	mental processes behind behavior. His confidence is a psychodynamic boon.

1. **Apotheosis** is raising someone up (*apo*) to the status of a god (*theo*) or near-god. We use the word to describe what happens to, for example, American Olympic gold medal winners. We could use *apotheosis* ironically to refer to a poet whose reputation has risen to the point that it is not wise to criticize his work.

2. We use **effusion** to refer to excessive and often unpleasant demonstrations of feeling. We might refer to effusive greetings that are not reciprocal.

3. A **Micropoem**: An **anthology** is a literary collection. The word *anthology* is a metaphor that suggests that an anthology is a study (*logy*) of the flowers (*antho*) of literature or poetry. As flowers are picked selectively, so works are included in an anthology according to selective criteria that vary from anthology to anthology.

4. **Refractory** and **infraction** make an interesting pair. If an infraction is a breaking of the rule, then a refractory child is one guilty of repeated (*re*) breaking (*fract*) of the rule. *Refractory* implies a stubborn incorrigibility.

5. We find **rubicund** most often as an adjective describing the face: cheeks are rubicund.

6. The adjective **condign** is generally applied to punishments and just desserts. We do not usually apply it to worthy rewards. Villains meet their condign ends.

7. **Pronunciation Tips**

    schism - SIZZ um
    apotheosis - app uh thee OH sis
    verisimilitude - vare ih sih MILL ih tude
    interregnum - in terr REG num
    condign - kun DINE
    casus belli - kay suss BELL eye
    posthumous - POSS chu muss
    agoraphobia - uh gore uh FOE bee uh
    euphony - YOO fo nee

8. **Spanish Cognates**: One of the most important observations to gain from the study of the etymology of English vocabulary is that English and Spanish share thousands of words that are cognates—related words—that have common origins. Often, the English and the Spanish words share not only a stem but even more than one stem, and often in the same order. As examples, here are some English words from this lesson and their Spanish cognates:

    apotheosis : apoteosis
    precursor : precursor
    cosmology : cosmología
    anthology : antología
    posthumous : póstumo
    acrophobia : acrofobia
    agoraphobia : agorafobia
    veracity : veracidad
    verisimilitude : verisimilidad
    idiosyncrasy : idiosincrasia
    euphony : eufonía

"*Desiring to consult the oracle of Apollo concerning his campaign [against the Persians], Alexander now proceeded to Delphi. It chanced that he arrived there on one of the days which are called unfortunate, on which no oracular responses can be obtained. In spite of this, he at once sent for the chief priestess, and as she refused to officiate and urged that she was forbidden to do so by the law, he entered the temple by force and dragged her to the prophetic tripod. She, yielding to his persistence, said, 'You are irresistible, my son.' Alexander, at once, on hearing this declared that he did not wish for any further prophecy, but that he had obtained from her the response which he wished for.*"

–Plutarch

Before the battle of Granicus, some of the Greek generals raised a religious scruple to attacking, averring that the Macedonian kings never made war during the month Daisus. Alexander said that this could be easily remedied and ordered that the second month in the Macedonian calendar would no longer be Daisus and henceforth should be called Artemisium.

ALEXANDER THE GREAT

Dr. Thomas Milton Kemnitz

In a score of years, Philip took control of all of Greece but Sparta, something that had eluded every leader before him. Philip's achievement would have been sufficient for him to be recognized as the greatest Greek ever—if his triumphs had not been eclipsed by those of his son building upon his father's foundation. Part of that foundation was the Greek League Philip founded in 337 B.C. to attack Persia. But Philip was assassinated in 336 B.C., and his twenty-year-old son Alexander took command of the army and of the empire. Philip had sought the best tutors for Alexander, and he had chosen Aristotle to educate his son and the other youths of noble families. Alexander's fellow scholars would become known as the Companions; they would be the generals in his army. Philip also had taken Alexander to war with him, so the young man had a firm grasp of leadership, strategy, and tactics. Alexander dealt swiftly and decisively with uprisings that followed Philip's death; when faced with both Athens and Thebes defying his leadership, he attacked Thebes and razed it to the ground and then invited the Athenians to reconsider. Alexander ended the democracy in Athens; it would be reinstated on occasion before the Romans eradicated it permanently. Philip had developed his power based upon his ability; Alexander showed that he had a superior measure of that same ability and a nature impatient to exploit it on a massive scale.

In 334 B.C., Alexander had pacified all of Greece, and he led an army of about 55,000, including 6,000 cavalry and a fleet of 120 ships with about 38,000 crew, across the Hellespont. The army was drawn from much of Greece and was united by the culture that came from Athens. Central to the army were Philip's Macedonian troops, who were battled-hardened after more than twenty years of war. They were confident; by now they had followed Alexander in a series of battles in which he was always successful.

If Philip transformed Greek history utterly by conquering the city states, Alexander transformed world history. The mighty Persian empire had threatened Greece for centuries without ever conquering it; now Alexander stood history on its head and conquered the entire Persian empire—all of what is now the Middle East including Turkey and Egypt, as well as parts of what is now India, Afghanistan, and Pakistan. He destroyed the Persian empire with victories in three battles in which his outnumbered forces were invariably successful. In all three battles, he led the Greek cavalry in attacks on weak points in the Persian center, each time destroying the enemy battle line and capturing the enemy camp. In a dozen years, he conquered the world beyond the knowledge or imagination of Greeks before him. He never lost a battle. He showed great imagination and flexibility in the employment of tactics that varied with the situation and the opponent. He also showed great imagination and flexibility in his use of conquered rulers and the employment of local customs to help govern the territories he had conquered. His empire extended for some 2,000,000 square miles.

In 323 B.C. when he was only thirty-three years old, Alexander died—perhaps from drinking tainted water. He died too young and too suddenly to leave a successor. His empire had rested solely on his ability; there was no one who could match his command, and hence the empire instantly disintegrated. The empire was divided between Alexander's generals, who had armies but none of Alexander's dynamism to maintain the whole. The only other unifying element was the Greek culture Alexander had brought with him, and that proved more potent than the force of arms of the divided army.

Philip founds Greek League	Philip assassinated; Alexander assumes throne	Alexander crosses Hellespont	Alexander dies	
337 B.C.	**336 B.C.**	**334 B.C.**	**323 B.C.**	**323–146 B.C.** Hellenistic Era

In each case below, one of the choices was really the word used by the author in the sentence provided. All of the choices can be found in the words on the first page of this lesson. Your challenge is to decide which word the author used. This is not a test; it is more like a game, because more than one word choice may work perfectly well. See if you can use your sensitivity and intuition to guess correctly which word the author used. You may need a dictionary.

1. **From Joseph Heller's *Catch-22***

   Don't ever waste my time with such sentimental _____ again.
   a. effusions
   b. schisms
   c. platitudes
   d. prestidigitation

2. **From James Fenimore Cooper's *The Last of the Mohicans***

   It was known, by all present, to be the grave _____ of a weighty and important judgment.
   a. invective
   b. euphony
   c. interregnum
   d. precursor

3. **From Daniel Defoe's *Robinson Crusoe***

   Two of them...we knew to be incorrigible and _____ to the last degree.
   a. refractory
   b. condign
   c. posthumous
   d. agoraphobic

4. **From John Kennedy's *Profiles in Courage***

   He assailed his opponents and their policies with bitter _____.
   a. cosmology
   b. apotheosis
   c. invective
   d. verisimilitude

5. **From Joseph Conrad's *Lord Jim***

   He thanked me _____ and bolted out.
   a. bootlessly
   b. condignly
   c. euphonically
   d. effusively

This gold coin of Alexander the Great was minted in Macedonia with Alexander's image on the front and Nike holding a ship's mast, a symbol of naval victory, on the reverse.

synthesis

Which words in List #28 would be used often in discussions of government and politics?

divergence

What authors should an **anthology** of the best American literature include? Try not to overlook anyone important.

analysis

Break down the words **interregnum**, **cosmology**, **posthumous**, **acrophobia**, and **anthology**.

evaluation

Does an **alumnus** of a college have a moral obligation to help that college later in life? Should the **alumni** have rights to certain privileges because they have graduated from the college (use of athletic facilities, etc.)?

intuition

It is just as you feared; you are up here, and now your **acrophobia** is beginning to grip you. Where are you?

emotion

On a summer day, you go on a picnic and relax amid the **euphony** of moving leaves and running water. What are your emotions?

aesthetics

Do you think that artists who have intense visual sensitivity have more **idiosyncrasies** than most people? Why or why not?

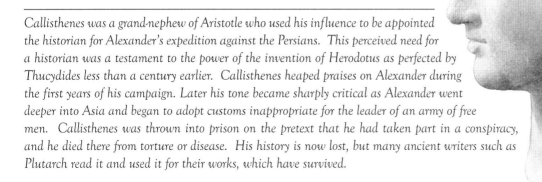

Callisthenes was a grand-nephew of Aristotle who used his influence to be appointed the historian for Alexander's expedition against the Persians. This perceived need for a historian was a testament to the power of the invention of Herodotus as perfected by Thucydides less than a century earlier. Callisthenes heaped praises on Alexander during the first years of his campaign. Later his tone became sharply critical as Alexander went deeper into Asia and began to adopt customs inappropriate for the leader of an army of free men. Callisthenes was thrown into prison on the pretext that he had taken part in a conspiracy, and he died there from torture or disease. His history is now lost, but many ancient writers such as Plutarch read it and used it for their works, which have survived.

colloquy	*(conversation)*	They had a private colloquy in the corner.
viable	*(able to live)*	Is the fetus mature enough to be viable?
synopsis	*(summary)*	Here is a brief synopsis of the course.
terra firma	*(solid ground)*	The argonauts longed to stand on *terra firma* at last.
sanction	*(authorize)*	We cannot sanction the use of our name.
Russophobe	*(one who fears Russia)*	The editor was an unapologetic Russophobe.
prognosis	*(medical forecast)*	The doctor presented a prognosis of the disease.
polychrome	*(many-colored)*	We purchased a large polychrome sculpture.
philanthropy	*(love of mankind)*	Her deeds of philanthropy were legendary.
perspicacity	*(insight)*	Everyone admired the perspicacity of her mind.
mobocracy	*(mob rule)*	The text showed the mobocracy of the revolution.
gerontocracy	*(government of the old)*	The Soviet gerontocracy is losing control.
magniloquence	*(great eloquence)*	His magniloquent oratory was impressive.
kleptomaniac	*(pathological thief)*	The police tried to arrest a kleptomaniac.
joie de vivre	*(joy of living)*	Her *joie de vivre* was inspiring.
in loco parentis	*(in place of parents)*	The school must act *in loco parentis*.
mundane	*(worldly)*	The thinker was reluctant to deal with mundane matters.
synthesis	*(combination)*	This product represents a synthesis of many ideas.
unequivocal	*(direct)*	He gave a refreshing, unequivocal answer.
nihilism	*(belief in nothing)*	The icy nihilism of his mind could be unnerving.
audiophile	*(stereo buff)*	He reads a magazine for audiophiles.
entomology	*(insect zoology)*	The oft-bitten entomologist finally caught the beetle.
omnifarious	*(of all kinds)*	His omnifarious exploits earned him fame.
invidious	*(causing envy)*	He paid one of them an invidious compliment.
deduction	*(reasoning down from principles)*	Deductive reasoning is idealistic.

1. A **synopsis** of a course is a summary, a paper that presents a look (*opia*) at the whole course together (*syn*).

2. We can land on **terra firma** with our boats, but we can also land on intellectual *terra firma*. It is tragic when erroneous opinions are quickly based on loose facts that prove not to provide intellectual solid ground.

3. When we **sanction** something, we authorize it, or approve it, or make it holy (*sanct*).

4. A **prognosis** is a medical forecast of a disease; it is the attempt to know (*gno*) in advance (*pro*) what course the disease will follow.

5. **Philanthropy** is made of stems that mean love of mankind, but actually we use *philanthropy* not to refer to someone's feelings about people but to the act of doing generous things to help mankind. Wealthy philanthropists donate libraries and art galleries to communities.

6. **Perspicacity** is similar to **perspicuous**, except that *perspicuous* refers to the product of someone's mind: a *perspicuous* essay, whereas *perspicacity* refers to the mind itself: a *perspicacious* mind.

7. **Unequivocal** reminds us of **equivocate**. To equivocate is to hedge by positioning oneself in the middle, like a hedge between two fields. To be unequivocal is therefore to take sides, to go clearly into the left field or the right field. The unequivocal politician often can gain passionate support (and opposition), whereas the equivocating politician often can gain victory.

8. A **Micropoem**: **Invidious** praise causes envy by leaving someone else unpraised—the unpraised outsider winds up on the outside looking (*vid*) in (*in*) enviously.

9. **Pronunciation Tips**

    perspicacity - purr spih KASS ih tee
    magniloquence - mag NIL oh kwence
    joie de vivre - JWAH duh vee vruh
    nihilism - NIE ill ism
    invidious - in VID ee us
    philanthropy - fill AN throw pee
    synopsis - sin OPP sis
    viable - VIE uh bul
    colloquy - KOLL oh kwee

10. **Spanish Cognates**: One of the most important observations to gain from the study of the etymology of English vocabulary is that English and Spanish share thousands of words that are cognates—related words—that have common origins. Often, the English and the Spanish words share not only a stem but even more than one stem, and often in the same order. As examples, here are some English words from this lesson and their Spanish cognates:

viable : viable	mundane : mundano
synopsis : sinopsis	synthesis : síntesis
polychrome : policromo	unequivocal : inequívoco
philanthropy : filantropía	nihilism : nihilismo
perspicacious : perspicaz	invidious : invidioso
kleptomaniac : cleptómano	deduction : deducción

This mosaic from Pompeii shows Alexander on the left riding a horse and throwing a javelin, engaged in pursuit of Darius in the center right on a chariot. The sarissas of Alexander's forces are clearly visible in this scene. The mosaic shows the hold Alexander had on the imagination of the classical world. Other battle scenes that have survived more typically are the work of a general or emperor glorifying his exploits, as in the case of Hadrian's column. Here displayed in a Roman villa we have an extensive mosaic of a battle that occurred three and half centuries earlier, and it is of a Greek battle with the Persians—in short, the glorious past being portrayed is not Rome's but rather Alexander's.

"Alexander and his troops were in the seventh month of the siege at Tyre, and the greater part of the men were resting in camp when Aristander, the soothsayer, offered sacrifice. When he saw the portents, he boldly informed all who were present that during the current month Tyre would be taken. All who heard him laughed him to scorn, as that day was the last of the month, but Alexander, seeing Aristander at his wits' end, being always eager to support the credit of prophecies, gave orders that that day should not be reckoned as the thirtieth of the month, but as the twenty-third. After this he bade the trumpets sound and assaulted the walls much more vigorously than he had originally intended. The attack succeeded, and as the rest of the army would no longer stay behind in the camp, but rushed to take their share in the assault, the Tyrians were overpowered and their city taken on that very day.

"In his dealings with Asiatics, Alexander always acted and spoke with the greatest arrogance, and seemed firmly convinced of his own divine parentage, but he was careful not to make the same boast when among Greeks."

—Plutarch

ALEXANDER'S GREATNESS

Dr. Thomas Milton Kemnitz

Nearly twenty-three and a half centuries after Alexander died, it is easy to lose sight of how great he was. Throughout history, many people have been called "The Great." As recently as the eighteenth century, Peter and Catherine of Russia and Frederick of Prussia were known as such. Sometimes the person did not turn out to be so great after all: Pompey the Great was defeated by Caesar in the civil wars. When in his thirty-third year Julius Caesar came upon a statue of Alexander, he shed tears because at the age Alexander had died, Caesar had accomplished nothing noteworthy. For the ancients, Alexander was a towering figure without equal, and so we should see him. In the intervening two and a third millennia, no one has come close to his accomplishments.

No one conquered the amount of territory that Alexander did. All of Caesar's ten years in Gaul would not equal a single year's worth of Alexander's conquests. Alexander was a man in a hurry, and he was a creative problem solver. When he was confronted with the Gordian knot—which for centuries had withstood attempts to undo it because its ends were buried within the knot—legend has it that he unsheathed his sword and simply cut it. However, ancient sources suggest a more elegant solution: he pulled out the shaft to which the knot was fastened, thus exposing its ends, which allowed him to untie it. Whatever his solution, he solved a riddle that had vexed men for ages.

The effectiveness of Alexander's solutions can sometimes be seen in what did not happen. Alexander spent two years imposing a peace on the Balkans and on Greece after his father's death, and then he marched off to conquer the rest of the world. In the more than ten years he was away, his solutions held; there was no general uprising in Greece; his regent was challenged only once by Sparta, and that led quickly to the death of the Spartan king. It is impossible to imagine the Greek cities of the fifth century B.C. being quiescent in similar circumstances. By contrast, Caesar faced almost continuous uprisings in Gaul, often from tribes he had previously subjugated; throughout his conquests, Alexander's arrangements held for the most part, and he did not have to backtrack to put down disturbances in his rear.

Alexander was ruthless when he thought it necessary. His father, Philip II, decided to take a new wife when Alexander was eighteen; Alexander and his mother fled the court for fear of their lives. Only after many months did they feel secure enough to return. Two years later, Philip was assassinated; we have Aristotle's word that Alexander was not responsible, but there is a paucity of other plausible perpetrators. A new wife and new heirs would mean other claimants to the throne and a continuous threat to Alexander's life and his future kingship. Immediately after his father's death, Alexander's friends killed the assassin before he could reveal anything. Thereafter, Alexander quickly had his step-siblings and an uncle killed, thereby nullifying any challenge they might pose to him. Alexander's mother, Olympias, did him one better and had Philip's latest queen and her young child burned to death, an act that disturbed Alexander.

The measure of Alexander's greatness is that without him the empire he built was not viable. His death meant its disintegration; his ability and command were all that had held it together. Alexander's achievements include the shape of the Hellenistic world and the civilization that emerged during the two centuries following his death.

Philip assassinated; Alexander assumes throne	Alexander crosses Hellespont	Alexander dies		Rome conquers Greece
336 B.C.	334 B.C.	323 B.C.	323–146 B.C. Hellenistic Era	146 B.C.

In each case below, one of the choices was really the word used by the author in the sentence provided. All of the choices can be found in the words on the first page of this lesson. Your challenge is to decide which word the author used. This is not a test; it is more like a game because more than one word choice may work perfectly well. See if you can use your sensitivity and intuition to guess correctly which word the author used. You may need a dictionary.

1. **From Emily Brontë's *Wuthering Heights***

   It was a marvelous effort of _____ to discover that I did not love her.
   a. mobocracy
   b. perspicacity
   c. *joie de vivre*
   d. synthesis

2. **From Kate Wiggin's *Rebecca of Sunnybrook Farm***

   The day would have been an _____ success had nothing else happened.
   a. unequivocal
   b. omnifarious
   c. invidious
   d. audiophile

3. **From William Faulkner's *As I Lay Dying***

   The _____ say it is the end; the fundamentalists, the beginning.
   a. Russophobes
   b. audiophiles
   c. kleptomaniacs
   d. nihilists

4. **From Herman Melville's *Moby Dick***

   In maritime life, far more than in that of _____, wild rumors abound.
   a. philanthropy
   b. *terra firma*
   c. entomology
   d. gerontocracy

5. **From Nathaniel Hawthorne's *The House of the Seven Gables***

   There was a(n) _____ acrimony in the zeal with which he had sought the condemnation of Matthew.
   a. invidious
   b. omnifarious
   c. viable
   d. magniloquent

synthesis

Which of the words in List #29 would be useful in a discussion of ethics?

divergence

What wonderful things would you buy for or contribute to your community if you became a wealthy **philanthropist**?

analysis

Analyze the words **philanthropy**, **prognosis**, **magniloquence**, **invidious**, and **unequivocal**.

evaluation

To what extent do you think that a school has the right to discipline children *in loco parentis* during the school day?

intuition

There is a large **polychrome** sculpture on the building across the street from your house. What does it look like?

emotion

Explain the emotional interaction that occurs when an **invidious** compliment is paid to one of two people.

aesthetics

If you were asked to paint **polychrome** patterns on a fifteen-mile stretch of highway as a county publicity stunt, what colors and patterns would you choose?

This red-figure wine jug presents a less-than-flattering portrait of the Persian enemy sitting on a mule in a most unheroic pose.

induction	*(factual reasoning)*	Science uses a process of induction.
hagiocracy	*(government of saints)*	The Iranian hagiocracy banned swimsuits.
diction	*(word choice)*	The pedant confined himself to a scholarly Latin diction.
disconsolate	*(inconsolable)*	The disconsolate widower missed his best friend.
disingenuous	*(insincere)*	His disingenuous offers of assistance fooled the ingenue.
fractious	*(unruly)*	The fractious, dissatisfied mob clamored for vengeance.
nondescript	*(of no category)*	The beggar wore a nondescript garment.
prolific	*(productive)*	The prolific writer wrote seven books in two years.
chronicle	*(a history)*	We read the chronicle of the brave knight-errant.
primeval	*(of the first ages)*	Coal is the remains of a primeval forest.
panegyric	*(elaborate eulogy)*	His speech was a panegyric on her engineering talent.
fidelity	*(faithfulness)*	He required the fierce fidelity of his lieutenants.
magnum opus	*(great work)*	Read Dante's *magnum opus*, the *Divina Comedia*.
antediluvian	*(from before the Flood!)*	He loved his grandfather's antediluvian ideas.
comport	*(behave)*	Leadership requires one to comport oneself with dignity.
insurgence	*(uprising)*	The insurgence was as soon defeated as it was begun.
expeditiously	*(rapidly)*	We need to process a customer's request expeditiously.
renovate	*(restore)*	It would be expensive to renovate the apartments.
carnage	*(butchery)*	They viewed the sickening carnage on the battlefield.
decadent	*(downfallen)*	The decadent, luxurious century saw little greatness in art.
supercilious	*(scornful)*	His arrogant, supercilious manner offended everyone.
inexorable	*(inescapable)*	Her inexorable fate followed her everywhere.
emissary	*(messenger)*	They greeted an emissary from the Queen.
improvident	*(without foresight)*	The improvident spendthrift went broke.
moribund	*(dying)*	The moribund corporation fired half its workforce.

1. **Induction** is different from **deduction**. In deduction we lead (*duct*) down (*de*) to true statements by starting from high principles, and in induction we lead (*duct*) facts into (*in*) the mind in order to form them into truths. In deduction we think downward from principle; in induction we bring facts in and think up from them.

2. An **ingenuous** person is innocent, naive, sincere. A **disingenuous** person is the opposite—experienced, deceptive, insincere. If the ingenuous person is original (*gen*) and fresh, the disingenuous person is certainly not.

3. A **nondescript** dog or a nondescript outfit is one that is indescribable because it belongs in no category. Notice that words depend upon categories. What kind of dog was it? Well, it was a…a…. What can you say about a dog that is NOT anything? It was a nondescript dog. Notice the stems: not (*non*) easily written (*script*) down (*de*).

4. A **Micropoem**: **Antediluvian** ideas are so outdated that they are from before (*ante*) the Flood (*diluvia*). THE Flood, you know. This word is deliberately humorous.

5. How does the word **comport** mean to behave? We often say that someone carries himself well. Comport is like that; the way you behave is the way you carry (*port*) yourself.

6. A **Micropoem**: **Supercilious** means scornful because it refers to the scornful, condescending raising (*super*) of the eyebrow (*cilia*) exhibited by the haughty person. When someone raises one eyebrow and looks at you down his nose, that is a supercilious gaze.

10. **Pronunciation Tips**

> panegyric - pan uh JIRR ik
> inexorable - in EX or uh bul
> supercilious - super SILL ee us
> decadent - DECK uh dent
> chronicle - KRON ik ul
> hagiocracy - haje ee OCK ruh see
> primeval - prime EE vul
> antediluvian - antee dih LOO vee un
> disingenuous - dis in JENN yoo us

11. **Spanish Cognates**: One of the most important observations to gain from the study of the etymology of English vocabulary is that English and Spanish share thousands of words that are cognates—related words—that have common origins. Often, the English and the Spanish words share not only a stem but even more than one stem, and often in the same order. As examples, here are some English words from this lesson and their Spanish cognates:

diction : dicción	insurgence : insurgencia
disconsolate : desconsolado	decadent : decadente
prolific : prolífico	inexorable : inexorable
chronicle : crónica	emissary : emisario
fidelity : fidelidad	moribund : moribundo
renovate : renovar	induction : inducción

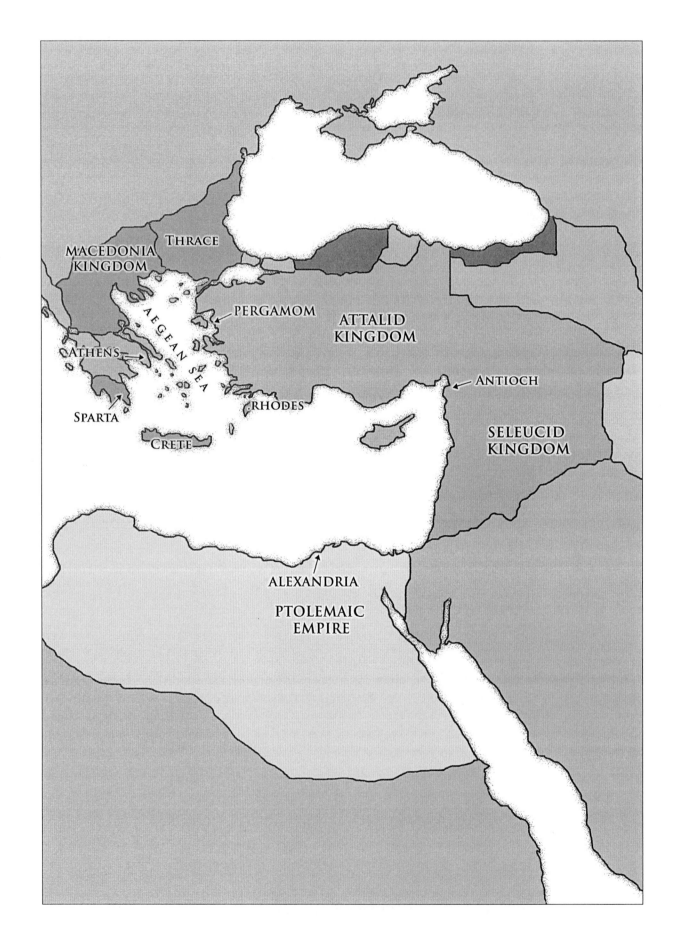

THE HELLENISTIC WORLD

Dr. Thomas Milton Kemnitz

The Hellenistic Era is a name we have given to the period of history between the death of Alexander the Great in 323 B.C. and the Roman conquest of Greece in 146 B.C. For nearly fifty years after Alexander's death, his successors—the *Diadochi*—conducted a series of wars for control over the territories he had conquered. Alexander's conquests were divided into four empires: the Ptolemaic of Egypt based in Alexandria, including the eastern part of what is now Libya, and what is now Israel; the Macedonia Kingdom, including most of Greece; the Seleucid Kingdom based in Antioch and consisting of Eastern Anatolia, northern Syria, and Mesopotamia all the way east to what is now Pakistan; and the Attalid Kingdom based at Pergamon and including western and northern Turkey along the Black Sea and parts of Bulgaria, Romania, and Macedonia.

The significant developments of this period were the spread of Greek culture and the concomitant Hellenic colonization throughout these kingdoms. Athens was the center for higher education in rhetoric and philosophy. Alexandria grew to be an important center of Greek learning, with its library of 700,000 volumes sustained by royal patronage. The city of Pergamon became a major center, with the second largest library in the world consisting of 200,000 volumes. The island of Rhodes attracted many to its school. Antioch was founded as a center of Greek learning. One new development was the royal patronage for the arts and learning in all of the centers but Athens. The Hellenistic world owed a new tolerance directly to Alexander. Before Alexander, Greeks made a sharp distinction between themselves as the people of Hellas and others they called barbarians. Alexander blurred the distinction by adopting a number of foreign customs and manners and attempting to blend them with the Greek. A continuous mix between Greek culture and a vast variety of non-Greek influences was the result.

Immediately after Alexander's death, Athens and other cities in Greece tried to break free of Macedonian control. Within a year, reinforcements from the east brought decisive defeat to Athens and its allies. Thereafter for the next two centuries, all attempts of the cities to free themselves from control of the larger kingdom ended in failure. Power lay with the larger entity, and the city states declined in significance. Athens was sometimes a democracy, sometimes an oligarchy, but by the middle of the third century, it was no longer in control of its fate, no longer a leading actor in the affairs of Greece. Sparta was defeated and occupied in 222 B.C. The next year, Philip V became the Macedonian monarch. In 215 B.C., after Hannibal had won a devastating victory and annihilated an entire Roman army, Philip formed an alliance with Carthage against Rome, with the unfortunate consequence that Greece made itself the enemy of Rome. The temporary advantage that Philip derived from this alliance was of little significance compared to engendering the enmity of Rome.

When he died a little more than a century earlier, Alexander the Great had an unfulfilled ambition to conquer the western Mediterranean. It is difficult to see any impediment to his conquest of all the territory between Greece and the Atlantic had he lived. A century later, the largest threat to Greece lay to the west in Rome and in the territory that Alexander never had time to conquer.

Philip assassinated; Alexander assumes throne	Alexander crosses Hellespont	Alexander dies		Rome conquers Greece
336 B.C.	**334 B.C.**	**323 B.C.**	**323–146 B.C.** Hellenistic Era	**146 B.C.**

In each case below, one of the choices was really the word used by the author in the sentence provided. All of the choices can be found in the words on the first page of this lesson. Your challenge is to decide which word the author used. This is not a test; it is more like a game because more than one word choice may work perfectly well. See if you can use your sensitivity and intuition to guess correctly which word the author used. You may need a dictionary.

1. **From Maya Angelou's *I Know Why the Caged Bird Sings***

   I spoke in _____ accents, and looked at the room as if I had an oil well in my own backyard.
   a. prolific
   b. disingenuous
   c. antediluvian
   d. supercilious

2. **From Jonathan Wyss's *The Swiss Family Robinson* (in translation)**

   He said there seemed to be the skeleton of an _____ monster there.
   a. insurgent
   b. antediluvian
   c. improvident
   d. inexorable

3. **From Eudora Welty's *One Writer's Beginnings***

   Time eats from the tombstones of the past the epitaphs of _____ greatness.
   a. disconsolate
   b. decadent
   c. moribund
   d. primeval

4. **From Oscar Wilde's *The Picture of Dorian Gray***

   Then had come Lord Henry with his strange _____ on youth, his terrible warning of its brevity.
   a. panegyric
   b. *magnum opus*
   c. chronicle
   d. induction

5. **From John Knowles's *A Separate Peace***

   _____ were already dropping in to confer with him.
   a. Hagiocracies
   b. Emissaries
   c. Insurgents
   d. Antediluvians

The deceased is represented sitting and saying good-bye to her loved ones; a maidservant is behind her.

synthesis

Which words in List #30 would be most useful in a discussion of social behavior?

divergence

Antediluvian ideas are ideas that are outmoded, antiquated, anachronistic. They are ideas that are so old that they date from before the Flood! What ideas can you think of that we consider antediluvian today?

analysis

Break down the following words: **nondescript**, **improvident**, **decadent**, **renovate**, and **chronicle**.

evaluation

A *magnum opus* is a masterpiece, a very great work indeed. What do you think is the *magnum opus* in American literature? In British literature? In world literature? Why do you think so?

intuition

You are entering a **primeval** forest in a strange land. What is the first living thing that you encounter? Describe your encounter with this living thing.

emotion

How would you feel if you received a **panegyric** from the boss as a result of something you had done at the office?

aesthetics

What are the criteria that distinguish good **diction** from bad **diction**? How can we apply aesthetic concepts to the use of words? Can we?

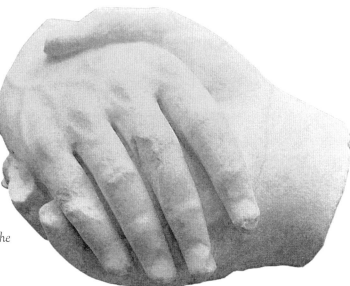

The dexiosis *was the farewell scene in which the living in leave-taking shook hands with the dead. This moment is reproduced repeatedly on gravestones and funereal plaques. The hands pictured here are a fragment of a large work in marble.*

List	Term	Definition
14	-a	plural
9	-ar	relating to
12	-be	life
11	-i	plural
9	a-	not
12	ab	away
22	abjure	renounce
23	abrogate	annul
7	acr	sharp
7	acro	high, point or tip
23	acronym	initials-name
28	acrophobia	fear of heights
11	act	to do
2	ad	to
12	aden	gland
22	adherent	supporter
24	advocate	speak for
12	aer	air
11	ag	to do
7	agog	leader
28	agoraphobia	fear of openness
12	alb	white
16	algia	pain
10	alt	high
5	alter	other
28	alumni	graduates
5	amat	love
9	ambul	walk
21	amorphous	shapeless
25	*amour-propre*	self-love
4	amphi	both
12	an-	without
22	analgesic	painkiller
27	anarchist	one against government
11	andro	man
23	androgynous	masculine and feminine
24	android	robot
16	Anglo	English
8	anim	mind
27	animadversion	criticism
11	ann	year
23	anomaly	abnormality
1	ante	before
30	antediluvian	from before the Flood!
16	antho	flower
28	anthology	literary collection
2	anthropo	man
24	anthropoid	manlike
21	anthropomorphic	man-shaped
1	anti	against
11	apo	away
28	apotheosis	raising to god status
8	apt	fit
2	aqua	water
2	archy	government
2	ard	always
15	arthro	joint
12	ase	enzyme
5	astr	star
10	ate	cause
18	atmo	vapor
20	atom	vapor or particle
2	audi	hear
29	audiophile	stereo buff
17	aur	gold
16	austro	south
2	auto	self
18	baro	pressure
11	bas	low
19	bath	deep
2	bell	war
21	bellicose	warlike
25	belligerent	warring
4	bene	good
21	benediction	blessing
25	benefactor	helper
1	bi	two
2	biblio	book
21	bilateral	two-sided
2	bio	life
15	blasto	embryo
12	bon	good
27	*bon vivant*	indulger in luxury
27	bona fide	good faith
27	bonhomie	good-naturedness
28	bootless	useless
15	brachio	arm
15	brachy	short
15	branchio	gills
7	brev	short
9	caco	bad
23	cacophony	bad noise
10	cad	fall
16	calli	beautiful
19	calor	heat
11	cant	sing
2	cap	take
10	capit	head
21	captious	fault-finding
18	cardio	heart
26	cardiovascular	of the heart and vessels
10	carn	flesh
30	carnage	butchery
28	*casus belli*	cause for war
16	cata	down
16	caust	burn
22	caustic	burning
2	cede	go
2	cent	one hundred
2	centri	center
16	cephalo	head
16	chiro	hand
22	chiromancy	palm reading
12	chlor	green
13	chrom	color
5	chron	time
27	chronic	lasting
30	chronicle	a history
2	cide	kill
1	circum	around
22	circumlocution	talking in circles
23	circumscribed	limited
21	circumspect	cautious
25	circumvent	get around
19	cirr	hair
2	cise	cut
6	clam	cry out
7	cle	small
6	clud	close
9	co	together
5	cogn	know
24	cognizant	aware
27	cognomen	nickname
25	cognoscenti	those who know
24	collateral	side by side
29	colloquy	conversation
1	com	together
21	commensurate	of like measure
30	comport	behave
1	con	together
24	condescend	lower oneself
28	condign	worthy
22	confluence	a flowing together

23	congenital	at birth		4	endo	within
5	contra	against		12	enter	intestine
27	convivial	jovial, festive		29	entomology	insect zoology
10	cor	heart		23	enumerate	to list
17	coron	crown		12	epi	on
4	corp	body		24	epigram	witty comment
26	corpulent	full-bodied		26	epiphany	revelation
18	cosmo	world or universe		1	equi	equal
28	cosmology	study of the universe		21	equivocate	to hedge
18	counter	against		14	erg	work
16	cracy	government		16	err	wander
18	cranio	skull		12	erythro	red
2	cred	believe		10	ess	female
25	credible	believable		10	ethno	race or culture
10	crypt	hidden		23	ethnocentrism	racial or cultural prejudice
26	cryptic	having hidden meaning		4	eu	good
23	cryptologist	code breaker		27	eulogy	words of praise
7	culp	blame		25	euphemism	pleasant name
19	cumu	heaped		28	euphony	beautiful sound
8	cur	care for		27	euphoria	joy
6	curr	run		3	ex	out
10	curs	run		21	excoriate	verbally flog
12	cyan	blue		25	exculpate	free from blame
18	cyclo	circle		12	exo	out
12	cyt	cell		27	exorbitant	unreasonable
15	dactylo	finger		27	expatriate	banish
1	de	down		30	expeditiously	rapidly
5	dec	ten		1	extra	beyond
30	decadent	downfallen		3	fer	carry
29	deduction	reasoning down from principles		18	ferro	iron
26	delineate	to outline		11	fic	make
23	demagogue	corrupt politician		9	fid	faith
8	demi	half		30	fidelity	faithfulness
5	demo	people		12	fil	thread
20	dendr	tree		27	filigree	lacy design
22	depose	topple from power		9	fin	end
7	derm	skin		19	fiss	split
15	dextro	right or clockwise		17	flect	bend
19	di	two		16	flu	flow
7	dia	across		20	foli	leaf
22	diaphanous	semitransparent		18	fore	front
23	diatribe	abusive criticism		13	form	shape
15	dicho	in two parts		7	fort	strong
26	dichotomy	two-part division		9	fract	break
2	dict	say		30	fractious	unruly
30	diction	word choice		14	frat	brother
24	diffident	shy		10	fug	flee
20	digit	finger		7	fus	pour
6	dign	worthy		8	fy	make
12	diplo	double		6	gamy	marriage
1	dis	away		15	gastro	stomach
30	disconsolate	inconsolable		10	gen	origin
22	discursive	rambling		5	geo	earth
30	disingenuous	insincere		6	germ	vital or related
23	disputatious	argumentative		27	germane	related
25	dissonant	inharmonious		29	gerontocracy	government of the old
14	dom	rule		8	gest	carry
4	dorm	sleep		17	glott	tongue
15	dors	back		13	glyc	sweet
4	dox	opinion		18	gno	know
3	duct	lead		15	gon	angle
5	dyna	power		20	grad	step
12	dys	bad		11	gram	writing
24	eccentricity	oddness		9	graph	write
12	eco	house		6	grat	pleasing
7	ecto	outer		19	grav	heavy
15	ef	out		6	greg	group
28	effusion	outpouring		22	gregarious	sociable
7	ego	I		13	gress	step
23	egocentric	self-centered		20	gymno	naked
22	egomania	self-obsession		11	gyn	woman
22	egregious	blatant		5	gyro	turn
24	elucidate	explain		30	hagiocracy	government of saints
12	emia	blood		15	haplo	single or simple
30	emissary	messenger		9	hedron	sided object
26	emollient	softener		5	helio	sun

251

25	heliotropic	sun-following	20	lachry	tear
3	hema	blood	9	lat	side
20	hemi	half	8	leg	read
25	hemiplegia	paralysis on one side	15	lent	full of
13	hemo	blood	18	lepsy	attack
16	here	stick	18	less	without
9	hetero	different	18	let	little
9	hexa	six	13	leuko	white
19	hibern	winter	6	liber	free
14	hippo	horse	20	lign	wood
17	hist	tissue	20	lin	line
26	histology	study of living tissues	17	lingu	tongue
15	holo	whole	15	lite	mineral or fossil
3	homo	same	17	liter	letter
12	hum	earth	9	lith	rock
3	hydro	water	4	loco	place
5	hyper	over	11	log	word or reason
27	hyperbole	overstatement	2	logy	science
3	hypo	under	10	loqu	talk
19	ichthy	fish	23	loquacious	talkative
22	ichthyologist	fish scientist	6	luc	light
2	ician	specialist	11	lum	light
10	ics	art	27	luminary	enlightening person
18	ideo	idea	5	luna	moon
12	idio	peculiar	13	lys	break down
28	idiosyncrasy	peculiarity	15	macro	large
20	ign	fire	4	magn	great
7	il	not	21	magnanimous	great-minded
12	im	not	25	magnate	powerful person
25	impending	overhanging	29	magniloquence	great eloquence
30	improvident	without foresight	30	*magnum opus*	great work
27	impute	attribute discredit	1	mal	bad
9	in	in or not	21	malediction	a curse
29	*in loco parentis*	in place of parents	21	malevolence	evil intent
24	inanimate	lifeless	8	man	hand
23	incisive	sharp	16	mania	madness
21	incredulous	not believing	6	mar	sea
30	induction	factual reasoning	4	matri	mother
9	ine	nature of	6	medi	middle
30	inexorable	inescapable	4	mega	large
24	infidel	unbeliever	25	megalomania	delusions of greatness
13	infra	beneath	12	mel	song
28	infraction	breaking	20	mela	black
22	ingenuous	innocent and naive	26	melancholy	dark sadness
26	inherent	built-in	13	mem	remember
30	insurgence	uprising	17	mens	measure
1	inter	between	13	meso	middle
23	intercede	mediate	8	meta	change
28	interregnum	time between rulers	26	metamorphosis	change of shape
25	intervene	come between	19	meteor	high
1	intra	within	5	meter	measure
26	intracranial	within the skull	3	micro	small
22	intractable	stubborn	6	migr	wander
22	intransigent	not compromising	13	milli	thousandth
1	intro	into	8	mir	wonder
25	introspective	inward-looking	1	mis	bad
28	invective	bitter denunciation	21	misanthropist	people-hater
29	invidious	causing envy	2	miss	send
24	irrevocable	beyond recall	11	mob	move
18	ish	like	29	mobocracy	mob rule
5	ism	doctrine	20	moll	soft
10	iso	equal	22	mollify	make soft
26	isosceles	having two equal sides	18	monger	seller
16	ist	one who	3	mono	one
2	itis	inflammation	21	monomania	obsession with one thing
15	ium	an element	19	mont	mountain
16	ize	make	17	mony	condition
4	ject	throw	30	moribund	dying
29	*joie de vivre*	joy of living	4	morph	shape
6	junct	join	10	mort	death
16	jur	swear	17	mot	move
11	jus	law	20	multi	many
19	kilo	thousand	16	mund	world
15	kin	motion	29	mundane	worldly
29	kleptomaniac	pathological thief	10	muta	change
13	labor	work	27	mutable	changeable

252

13	myo	muscle	17	phasia	speech
19	myria	many	17	phen	appearance
18	nano	billionth	29	philanthropy	love of mankind
20	narco	sleep	9	phile	love
25	narcolepsy	attacks of sleep	4	phobia	fear
10	nat	born	3	phon	sound
17	nav	ship	13	phor	carry
7	necro	death	15	phos	light
2	neo	new	3	photo	light
21	neologism	new word	13	phyll	leaf
21	neophyte	beginner	15	phylo	kind
18	nesia	island	13	phyte	plant
10	ness	quality	18	pico	trillionth
3	neuro	nerve	16	pithec	ape
29	nihilism	belief in nothing	20	plasm	form
9	nomy	law	7	plasto	molded
1	non	not	28	platitude	flat, trite remark
30	nondescript	of no category	9	platy	flat
11	nounce	tell	14	pleo	more
4	nov	new	6	plu	more
19	nuc	center	26	plutocracy	government of the wealthy
7	numer	number	20	pneumo	lung or air
8	nym	name	14	pod	foot
20	ob	against	7	polis	city
5	octa	eight	3	poly	many
25	octogenarian	an eighty-year-old	29	polychrome	many-colored
8	ocul	eye	22	polyglot	multi-linguist
8	oid	appearance	25	polyphonic	multi-melodic
22	oligarchy	government by a few	4	pond	weight
13	oligo	few or small	24	ponderous	weighty
19	oma	tumor	4	pop	people
3	omni	all	2	port	carry
29	omnifarious	of all kinds	16	pos	put
21	omniscient	all-knowing	1	post	after
20	oo	egg	28	posthumous	after death
19	ophthal	eye	17	pot	drink
15	opia	sight	11	potent	power
20	orb	circle	1	pre	before
7	ornith	bird	23	preclude	prevent in advance
4	ortho	straight	28	precursor	forerunner
20	oscu	mouth	21	preponderance	bulk
13	ose	sugar	23	prescience	foreknowledge
13	osis	condition	28	prestidigitation	sleight of hand
18	oss	bone	6	prim	first
7	osteo	bone	25	primate	monkeys, apes, and humans
9	ous	full of	30	primeval	of the first ages
17	ovi	egg	11	pro	forward
7	pac	peace	29	prognosis	medical forecast
10	paleo	old	30	prolific	productive
3	pan	all	19	protero	early
24	pandemonium	demonic clamor	3	proto	first
30	panegyric	elaborate eulogy	21	prototype	first model
17	par	equal	3	pseudo	false
14	para	beside or near	10	psych	soul
27	paradigm	model	17	pter	wing
11	parl	speak	7	pugn	fight
4	pater	father	23	pugnacious	combative
9	path	feeling	19	pulse	drive
13	patho	disease	4	punct	point
26	pathogen	disease-causer	24	punctilious	precise in conduct
26	pathological	diseased	27	pusillanimous	small-minded
10	ped	foot or child	4	put	think
23	pedagogue	teacher	6	pyro	fire
25	pellucid	crystal clear	16	quadr	four
3	pend	hang	18	quasi	somewhat
3	penta	five	17	quin	five
7	per	through	20	radi	ray
22	perfidious	treacherous	17	rat	think
17	peri	near or around	3	re	again
26	perihelion	orbital point nearest the sun	23	recant	retract
29	perspicacity	insight	8	rect	right
22	perspicuous	brilliantly clear	26	rectify	correct
8	petr	rock	26	rectilinear	right-angled
26	petroglyph	rock carving	28	refractory	stubborn
13	phag	eat	11	reg	rule
17	phan	appearance	30	renovate	restore

253

24	resurgence	rising again		25	surfeit	excess
24	retribution	revenge		11	surg	rise
8	retro	backward		1	sym	together
26	retrograde	backward		1	syn	together
23	revoke	cancel		25	syndrome	complex of symptoms
14	rhiz	root		29	synopsis	summary
14	rhodo	rose		29	synthesis	combination
8	rid	laugh		19	tachy	quick
11	rogat	ask		8	tact	touch
19	rub	red		6	tang	touch
28	rubicund	red		23	tangible	touchable
6	rupt	break		14	taxis	arrangement
29	Russophobe	one who fears Russia		3	tele	far
10	sacro	holy		6	tempor	time
23	sacrosanct	sacred		24	temporize	delay
8	sanct	holy		16	terr	land
26	sanctimonious	affectedly holy		29	*terra firma*	solid ground
29	sanction	authorize		5	tetra	four
4	sangui	blood		9	theo	god
24	sanguinary	bloody		5	thermo	heat
14	sapro	rotten		4	tion	act or state
19	sat	enough		3	tomy	cut
27	saturnine	gloomy and remote		9	topo	place
16	saur	lizard		8	tort	twist
28	schism	division		26	tortuous	twisting
14	schizo	divide		14	tox	poison
9	sci	know		9	tract	pull
5	scope	look		24	tractable	docile
2	scrib	write		6	trans	across
6	se	apart		28	transpose	switch
14	sect	cut		1	tri	three
8	sed	sit		6	trib	pay
27	sedentary	sitting		14	trich	hair
1	semi	half		14	troph	nourishment
11	sen	old		15	tropo	turn
8	sens	feel		13	tude	state of
18	sept	seven		13	ultima	last
13	sequ	follow		8	ultra	beyond
11	sess	sit		1	un	not
16	sine	without		17	und	wave
26	*sine qua non*	essential element		29	unequivocal	direct
22	sinecure	easy, lucrative job		10	uni	one
17	sis	condition		21	unilateral	one-sided
17	socio	society		7	urb	city
11	sol	alone		24	urbane	sophisticated
19	sol	sun		13	vac	empty
22	soliloquy	speech to oneself		14	val	worth
19	solv	loosen		18	vas	vessel
14	som	body		20	vect	carry
16	somn	sleep		19	ven	come
24	somnambulist	sleepwalker		15	ventri	belly
22	somniferous	bringing sleep		4	ver	true
5	son	sound		28	veracity	truthfulness
27	sonorous	full-sounding		28	verisimilitude	similarity to truth
6	soph	wisdom		20	vermi	worm
14	soror	sister		10	vert	turn
3	spec	look		4	vest	clothes
21	specious	false		17	via	road
7	spir	breathe		29	viable	able to live
14	spor	seed		20	vice	in place of
14	sta	stop		3	vid	look
27	status quo	the present state		5	vita	life
5	stell	star		3	viv	life
5	stereo	solid		25	vivacious	lively
19	strat	layer		8	voc	voice
6	string	bind		26	vociferous	loudly-voiced
24	stringént	binding		14	vol	will
12	struct	build		8	volv	roll
1	sub	under		15	vore	eating
25	subordinate	lower		18	xeno	stranger
27	subterfuge	evasive dodge		21	xenophobia	fear of foreigners
1	super	over		18	xylo	wood
30	supercilious	scornful		7	zo	animal
21	superfluous	unnecessary		14	zygo	yoke
24	supersede	replace		14	zym	ferment
5	sur	over				

254